GW00382229

AROMAS *of* ALEPPO

POOPA DWECK

AROMAS *of* ALEPPO

The LEGENDARY CUISINE of SYRIAN JEWS

AND MICHAEL J. COHEN

WITH PHOTOGRAPHY BY QUENTIN BACON

ecco

An Imprint of HarperCollins Publishers

AROMAS *of* ALEPPO

Copyright © 2007 by Poopa Dweck. All rights reserved.
Printed in China.

No part of this book may be used or reproduced in any manner whatsoever without written permission except in the case of brief quotations embodied in critical articles and reviews.

For information, address HarperCollins Publishers Inc., 10 East 53rd Street, New York, NY 10022.

HarperCollins books may be purchased for educational, business, or sales promotional use. For information please write: Special Markets Department, HarperCollins Publishers Inc., 10 East 53rd Street, New York, NY 10022.

Project development and styling by Michelle Ishay-Cohen
Contemporary photography by Quentin Bacon
Designed by Erica Heitman-Ford for Mucca Design

Library of Congress Cataloging-in-Publication Data

Dweck, Poopa
Aromas of Aleppo : the legendary cuisine of Syrian Jews / Poopa Dweck – 1st. ed.
p. cm.
Includes bibliographical references and index.
ISBN-13: 978-0-06-088818-3
ISBN-10: 0-06-088818-0
1. Cookery, Jewish. 2. Jews—Syria—Aleppo. I. Title.

TX724.D88 2007
641.5'676095691—dc22   2006049370
12 / 6

In memory of my beloved son

JESSE DWECK ע"ה

ישי בן שמחה

1985 – 2003

"A good heart is always celebrating"

Proverbs 15:15

לב טוב משתה תמיד

משלי טו:טו

An assortment of maza (small delights)

CONTENTS

Rabbis from Aleppo, Syria (courtesy of Joseph Segal)

PREFACE

*V*isit an Aleppian Jewish home on any given morning, and you can identify the day of the week by the richly perfumed air wafting from the busy kitchen. If you detect the nuttiness of lentils suffused with sweet onions, it is Thursday and *mujedrah* (Rice with Brown Lentils and Frizzled Caramelized Onions, page 125) is on the stove, perhaps accompanied by the homey notes of egg, cheese, and spinach that signal *spanekh b'jibn* (Spinach-Cheese Frittata, page 224). If it is Friday, the traditional Aleppian Sabbath dishes will be simmering, and you will encounter a mélange of aromas—the concentrated tang of *ou*ᶜ (tamarind concentrate) in *keftes* (Tamarind-Stewed Meatballs, page 162), the bright herbal essence of mint emanating from *kibbeh hamdah* (Lemon-Mint Broth with Mixed Vegetables and Syrian Meatballs, page 97), and the deep musk of eggplant from *s'fiha* (Stuffed Baby Eggplants with Ground Meat and Rice, page 138). While these dishes were developed long ago in Aleppo, an ancient city in the northwestern plains of Syria, Aleppian Jewish cooks around the world are still passionately preparing them today.

The kitchen is the soul of the Aleppian Jewish home, and I feel truly honored and blessed to be able to bring you *Aromas of Aleppo*, which conveys the warmth and love at the heart of our cuisine. I have been a lifelong member of the community of Aleppian Jews in New York, but my interest in our cuisine took a momentous turn during the mid-1970s when I got involved in documenting the recipes of Jewish Aleppo with a group of like-minded community cooks. Most Syrian recipes were not written down; they existed only in the minds of older cooks. My peers and I wondered whether our kids would follow our mothers' and grandmothers' approach to cooking and maintain the deep understanding of our unique customs.

America being the assimilative force it is, we were determined to ensure that the centuries-old foodways and traditions of Jewish Aleppo would continue for generations to come. Under the auspices of the Sephardic Women's Organization, in 1976 we self-published a collection of Aleppian Jewish recipes called *Deal Delights*. This humble red vinyl–bound book became an instant success in Sephardic communities around the world. It raised tens of thousands of dollars for charity. Two more volumes followed. All three can be found in the kitchen of almost every Aleppian Jewish cook.

Now the time has come to document and update our recipes more fully and add a thorough explanation of our intriguing customs, all in one book. It is with great joy that I share with sophisticated cooks everywhere the best my community has to offer. Aleppian Jewish cookery gracefully combines Mediterranean and Levantine influences with dishes that range from quotidian workman's meals fit for the midday Aleppo market siesta to the regal opulence of a traditional Passover *seder*. Our cuisine features dishes that are both disarmingly familiar, exotic, and, above all, healthful.

My community represents a link to a forgotten past. It is one of the few Jewish communities to live through the rise and fall of Moorish Spain and the Ottoman Empire and survive as a modern people in the West while maintaining its venerable traditions. Our soulful culture, with its fervid, tuneful songs and communal celebratory feasts, is at its most vibrant during the Sabbath, holidays, and life-cycle events. One of the most artful representations of Aleppian Jewish culture is our food, whose story I have yearned to tell.

I offer *Aromas of Aleppo* as a gift to my children and the community at large. I hope it will serve as another resource to teach us about our traditions and the profound values that inform our holiday practices.

Finally, with great pleasure, I say to all, *Sifrah daimeh*, "May your table always be plentiful."

Poopa Dweck

Deal, New Jersey
August 2007

ACKNOWLEDGMENTS

I will thank you G-d with all my heart; I will tell of all Your wonders.

אודה ה' בכל־לבי אספרה כל־נפלאותיך.

Psalm 9:2

Aromas of Aleppo is a tribute to all the devoted women of my community, who are the foundation of our families, not to mention some of the greatest cooks I've come to know. They pray passionately for their children when they light the Sabbath candles every week; they tirelessly prepare incomparable holiday feasts; they keep our customs alive and observe our Jewish laws with diligence; they practice *suffeh* with effortless grace and draw the Shekhinah (G-d's divine presence) into their homes. Truly, these women are the soul of our community, and I applaud each and every one of them.

I am eternally grateful to my parents, who guided me to where I am today. My mother, Sarine Kattan A"H ("May she rest in peace"), was a true woman of valor and expert cook who taught me everything I know with patience and love. My father, Mourad Kattan A"H, merits much praise for being a true Aleppian gentleman who would go to the market and assist in the kitchen after attending to his business affairs.

On an even more personal note, this book is dedicated to the memory of my beloved son Jesse A"H, may he rest in peace. When he passed on at the tender age of eighteen in 2003, I had been entrenched in *Aromas of Aleppo.* From the beginning of my dream to publish *Aromas,* Jesse was always by my side, believing in me and helping me in every way he could. When he passed on, I was unable to continue pursuing that dream for over a year. I was crushed, devastated. But I was determined to have something good come from his passing and I wanted to honor him. I immediately started the Jesse Dweck City Learning Center in New York. All of my share of the proceeds from *Aromas of Aleppo* will go to the Jesse Dweck City Learning Center. This center reflects who Jesse was: a young man who related well in this world, who cherished and touched everyone he knew, but who also had a deep, spiritual side that he always took time to nourish.

With the love and support of my husband, Sam, and the encouragement of my children—Eli, Mark, Sheri, and Sarine—my son-in-law Eddie, and daughters-in-law Nicole and Carina, and the rest of my extended family, I eventually regained the courage to continue working on *Aromas of Aleppo.* I knew that Jesse A"H would have wanted me to do so. He was my biggest fan. After his passing I saw *yad Hashem* ("the hand of G-d"), and a publisher was found. Somehow, I connect this miracle to Jesse A"H.

The rabbis of the Aleppian Jewish community are the steadfast guardians of the community's rich traditions, who continue to advance the community's great legacy of religious scholarship. With the wisdom and encouragement of our rabbis, we strive to attain the highest levels of spirituality in everything we do. I am honored and blessed to have received the contribution of the following rabbis: Rabbi Eliyahu Bakshi-Doron, Rabbi Eli Ben-Haim, Professor Rachimim Cohen, Rabbi Shlomo Diamond, Rabbi Isaac Dwek, Rabbi Yaakov Hillel, Rabbi Ezra Labaton, Rabbi Moshe Malka, Rabbi Eli Mansour, Rabbi Edmund Nahum, and Rabbi David Sutton.

A cookbook is as good as the output of its recipes. I am indebted to the many friends and family members who helped me test the recipes in this book and provided me with invaluable feedback. Heartfelt thanks to all. I am also grateful to the countless community members who graciously welcomed me into their homes and provided cultural and historical insights that are vital to our traditions and cuisine. Among this group, I extend a special thank you to our elders who were raised in Aleppo early in the twentieth century and paved the way for our successful settlement in the United States. Of our elders, I must specially acknowledge the following two, whom I had the honor and privilege to interview and are no longer with us: Joseph Beyda A"H, who dedicated himself throughout his lifetime to better the community, and Sam Catton A"H, a pillar of our community who published thousands of prayer books that have perpetuated our community's peerless liturgical traditions.

Thank you to all the grocers and specialty stores for providing the community with ingredients to enjoy our delicious cuisine and for welcoming the cameras and questions with a smile.

Sheila Schweky of the Sephardic Community Center Archives and Rabbi Ephriam Levi of Jerusalem granted me access to hundreds of precious community photographs, many of which we selected for inclusion in this book.

Marlene Ben-Dayan, Rochelle Gemal, Carol Haber, Bonnie Mansour, and Alice Shalom offered me incisive feedback on the day-to-day side, and many other women let me draw on their well-versed Torah knowledge. Thank you to Sarina Roffe for your help with the recipes and history.

On the publishing side, I'm grateful to Judith Regan, who opened her door to me and allowed my dream to begin. I'm grateful to Anna Bliss, my editor, who walked me through the process with expertise, sincerity, and grace. I must also applaud Nina Rosenstein for providing invaluable, eleventh-hour proofreading and editorial input. I cannot forget Mark Jackson, whose diligence and attention helped this project go smoothly. And I am grateful to Dan Halpern of Ecco for sharing my excitement and passion for *Aromas,* for his encouragement and fresh insight during the project's last mile.

Thanks to Erica Heitman-Ford at Mucca Design for working with the multifaceted artwork, creating an ethnic and modern design, and reflecting the community in this beautiful book. My mother-in-law, Sadie Dweck, is a true woman of valor, who I am proud to have as a shining example and as a source of invaluable wisdom. I must express gratitude for the love, warmth, and encouragement given to me by my late grandparents, Regine A"H and Shahoud Tawil A"H, and my late father-in-law, Eli Dweck A"H.

Quentin Bacon is the brilliant eye behind this book's uncompromisingly beautiful photographs. Quentin's gorgeous output lifted this project to a lofty place that I could never have dreamed of. He and his assistant, Lauren Volo, deserve the highest praise for the professionalism, punctuality, and patience over the course of the many shoots we did together.

A giant thank you goes to Michelle Ishay, my mentor, "agent," designer, and, most of all, my friend. From the beginning she believed in me and the project, exploring every resource in her arsenal; she has been with me every step of the way. She is surely one of the most uniquely talented artists and understands our remarkable community. Thanks to Michelle's extraordinary design talents, exquisite taste, and sense of style, *Aromas* is as beautiful as the story it portrays.

Another enormous thank you goes to Michael J. Cohen, who shares my love and passion for the history and food of our community. His writing has crystallized a legacy that is special and unique. Even with his busy schedule, he saw the significance of this project and took great care in documenting our legacy in the most eloquent manner. His contribution surpassed all of my expectations, and his perseverance, dedication, sincerity, devotion, and easy manner have all made this possible.

And finally, a heartfelt thank you to my extraordinary husband, Sammy. His love and faith in me, along with all his support, patience, wisdom, and guidance, have given me the courage and confidence to bring my dream to fruition.

Syrian passports of Mourad and Sarine Kattan, 1948 (courtesy of author)

Menahem and Setti Haber family,
Aleppo, Syria, circa 1890 (courtesy of
Sephardic Community Center Archives)

THE JEWISH COMMUNITY OF ALEPPO

The first Jew settled in Aleppo, Syria, around 586 BCE—and that's not counting the First Jew, Abraham, who is said to have stopped there during his sojourn to Canaan and shared the milk of his goats with the poor he found on the slopes of the hill town. That legend inspired the city's Arabic name, *Haleb*, which means "milk" or "he milked." If there ever was a town fit to carry the name of such an elemental food, it is Aleppo.

Over the centuries, Aleppian cooks have done wonders not only with milk but also with a host of spices, herbs, grains, vegetables, meats, and legumes. The most timeless recipes of the Middle East owe a debt to Aleppo, from the simple and soulful *addes* soup of red lentils dusted with cumin to the Syrian classic of fried *kibbeh nabelsieh* (Golden Ground Meat–Filled Bulgur Shells, page 53) eaten with a squeeze of lemon. The Jews of this great culinary city—the last of whom left Aleppo in 1997—have contributed to its legacy, adding their own creations as a result of their kosher diet and diverse origins. As you discover the scrumptious dishes in the pages ahead, you will find that Abraham's descendants have measurably improved upon the skins of goat's milk he left in Aleppo.

Ancient Roots

Aleppo sits on the banks of the Quweiq River amid the dry plains of northwest Syria, equidistant from the Euphrates River and the Mediterranean Sea. It is a city that has been known by many names. The Venetians adopted the name Aleppo and the French called it Alep (both are derivations of Haleb), while the Romans named it Beroa. The Jews have always referred to the city as Aram Soba, which is the name that dates back the furthest; it's mentioned in Psalm 60 and Sefer HaYashar 22:39 (an apocryphal text). The name Aram Soba derives from Aram, who was the son of Abraham's half-brother Soba. Aram was a very wealthy man and was the first to develop the land on which Aleppo sits.

Aleppo's diverse nomenclature is dwarfed by the city's long list of conquerors, which includes the Amorites, Hittites, Romans, various Arab dynasties, Mongols (twice), Mameluks, Ottomans, and the French. Aleppo vies with Damascus, its chief rival two hundred miles to the south, for the honor of the world's oldest continuously inhabited city. Aleppo has outlived most of its rulers and continues to be the home of two million inhabitants.

Jews first settled in Aleppo during the reign of King David, when legend has it that Judea's military commander, Joab ben Seruyah, captured the town. The Great Synagogue of Aleppo, a magnificent Byzantine structure dating from at least as far back as the ninth century CE, was consecrated in memory of Joab. Notwithstanding Jewish lore, Jews very likely settled in Aleppo in the sixth century BCE during the Babylonian exile that followed the destruction of the first Jewish Temple. The Jewish presence in Aleppo continued through Seleucid and Roman rule (fourth century BCE to first century CE) and certainly after the destruction of the second Jewish Temple in 69 CE. The Jews who were native to Aleppo from the time of antiquity were known as the *must'arabia,* meaning "would-be Arabs." Jewish communities also existed in Damascus and a few small Syrian towns.

During the Byzantine Empire, in the early centuries of the Common Era, regional commerce began to flourish in Aleppo. Unfortunately, the Christian overlords did not treat the Jews well, and this hampered the community's ability to prosper. However, under the rule of the Arab Abbasid dynasty (eighth to tenth centuries), the Jewish community of Aleppo began to achieve significant growth and stature, despite a relative decline in prosperity caused by incessant regional warfare. The community built the Great Synagogue during this time. Many Jews arrived from Iraq, fleeing the hostile treatment of the Persians. Leading rabbinical scholars, such as Baruch ben Isaac and Baruch ben Samuel, resided in Aleppo and corresponded with other great sages of the day who were living in Baghdad, Cairo, and Spain. In fact, Maimonides wrote his classic *A Guide for the Perplexed* in the form of a letter to his Aleppian colleague Joseph ben Judah ibn Shimon. In another of his writings, this time an epistle to the community of Lunel (located today in the French region of Languedoc-Roussillon), Maimonides praised the scholarship and spirituality of the Aleppo community, citing Aram Soba as one of the few centers of light in comparison to the lackluster standards of religious awareness that prevailed in other Diaspora (Jewish exile) communities.

The progress of Aleppian Jews continued under Ayubbid rule from 1170 to 1260, although two Mongol invasions shook the community and laid waste to the city. The Jews miraculously survived the first invasion in 1260 by hiding in the Great Synagogue as the eastern warriors indiscriminately slaughtered many other Aleppians. However, the ruthless Tamerlane, who led the second invasion in 1400, succeeded in killing many Jews. The community recovered within fifty years and continued its activities in an atmosphere of relative tolerance under the Mameluks, who ruled until 1516. But in that fateful year the future of Aleppo took yet another turn, when Selim the Excellent bloodlessly captured the city under the Ottoman flag, which would soon be flying over a vast empire spanning from Egypt to lands as far as Hungary.

From Spain to Syria

In the late centuries before the Common Era, many Jews followed their Roman colonizers, journeying beyond the Middle East to the Western Mediterranean, particularly to Spain and France. The now-vanished tombstone of young Anna Salomonula evidenced a Jewish presence in Spain as early as the third century; etched on the stone was the word *Iudea,* Latin for "Jewess." The early period of Sepharad (Hebrew for "Spain") was relatively modest for the Jews. The Romans enacted numerous regulations limiting interactions between Christians and Jews, though their rule was not oppressive. The Jews formed communities throughout every region of Spain, from Catalonia in the northeast to Andalusia in the south and Castile in the center.

In 414 the unenlightened Visigoths emerged as the new rulers of the Iberian peninsula. The fate of Spanish Jews under their rule was grim. The Jews suffered when the Visigoth king of Spain, Recared the First, promulgated a series of anti-Jewish laws, inspired by the despot's conversion to Catholicism in 586. King Sisebut ordered the forced conversion of Jews in 613. In the late seventh century, suspicion loomed in the Visigothic court that the Jews were collaborating with Islamic insurgents. By 693 the Visigoths banned the Jews from conducting any commercial activity. Relief arrived on the peninsula in 711 in the guise of the Muslim conquest that swept through the Mediterranean. Impressed with Spain's lush vegetation, the Arabs named the first town they seized Algeciras, a Latinized version of *al-jazira al-hadra,* Arabic for "the green island."

Indeed, the Iberian peninsula was a fertile land and its new conquerors immediately grasped its potential. The Arabs introduced the latest in agricultural technology and planted crops previously unknown to that region, such as rice, hard wheat, sugarcane, spinach, eggplant, artichokes, almonds, citrus fruits, bananas, and mangos, bringing about what can only be termed a revolution or a true golden age. Trade exploded throughout the Mediterranean as the Arabs took control of the great sea from east to west. In the lands under Arab rule, scholarship in philosophy, science, and medicine was unmatched by any other civilization. And the Jews played no small role. In fact, the Jews built a vast network of communities throughout Spain, Italy, and other lands under Islamic control. Armed with knowledge of many languages as a result of their wanderings, Jews served as commercial intermediaries between Arabs and Christians. This phenomenon epitomized the unparalleled era of *convivencia* ("coexistence"), in which the Muslims, Christians, and Jews of Spain prospered and lived in relative harmony.

The thriving Jews of Spain produced many leading lights in the course of their history, including the first Sephardic court noble, Hasdai ibn Shaprut; the peerless philosopher-physician Maimonides; Ramban, a great Catalan sage; Judah HaLevi, the poet, philosopher, and religious scholar who authored *The Book of the Kuzari;* and the rhapsodic poet Solomon ibn Gabirol, whose poems are still featured in the liturgy of many Sephardic communities.

The Islamic golden age ended with the conquest of southern Spain by the Almoravids in 1090 and the continued rule of the Almohads, tribal Berber groups from North Africa who ruled the Jews with a heavy hand. Most Jews fled to the northern Christian kingdoms of Castile, Aragon, Catalonia, and Navarre. The Jews, masters of the pan-Mediterranean market, now aided the Catholic kings by bringing them wealth and encouraging the royals' desire to rid the Iberian peninsula of Muslim rule and unify Spain under the Catholic flag. The marriage of Isabella of Aragon to Ferdinand of Castile in 1469 was nothing less than epochal, bringing the goal of reconquest ever closer. However, the stability of the Jewish community's standing gradually deteriorated as Catholic intolerance grew throughout Spain. Even as Don Isaac Abravanel and Don Abraham Senior helped finance the Castile-Aragon drive to chase the Nasrid kingdom—the last Moors—out of Granada, the Jews were succumbing to a similar fate.

Beginning with the unprecedented and brutal pogrom in Sevilla's *juderia* (Jewish quarter) in 1391, the prestige of Spanish Jewry began its precipitous decline. This attack was not the first expression of the ethnic cleansing of Jews in Christendom; before 1391, Jews had been systematically expelled from England, France, Holland, Germany, and Italy. However, none of these European Jewish communities compared in size and glory to the Jews of Sepharad, a rich and powerful group whose members were reduced to choosing between conversion, exile, and a fiery death.

Many prominent Jews chose conversion. These *conversos* were known as New Christians or, pejoratively, as *marranos*, archaic Spanish for "swine." *Conversos* used their vaunted skills to flourish in occupations that were previously denied them, including law, academia, government, and the military. Many rich *conversos* married into aristocratic but impecunious Old Christian families. Instantly, it seemed, these ex-Jews occupied leading positions throughout Spain. This aroused the envy of many Old Christians, who gradually lobbied for an Inquisition, which the Vatican authorized in 1480.

The Inquisition sought to prosecute New Christians who were backsliding into their old Jewish ways. A barbaric and shameful blemish on Iberian culture, the Inquisition statute remained on the books until 1834. Because the Inquisition applied only to baptized Christians, the Church had no jurisdiction over the stubborn pockets of Jews who remained in Spain despite the prevailing climate of hatred and oppression. Thus, in 1492 Ferdinand and Isabella enacted the Edict of Expulsion, which officially banned all Jews from residing in Spain. In early August of that year, some speculate around the ninth of the Jewish month of Ab, an infamously tragic date in Jewish history, the last Jew tearfully departed by ship, leaving behind the glory of a thousand-year-old civilization that brought wealth, honor, and prestige to Spain.

Spanish Jews sought refuge wherever they were welcome, including North Africa, the Netherlands, and select provinces in Italy. While many kingdoms sought out the Jews for their mercantile acumen, they periodically banished the Jews, as well. This revolving-door policy was most pronounced in Italy, particularly in Venice, Genoa, and Ancona. Only one kingdom let the Jews be—the Ottoman Empire. As the Ottoman ruler, Sultan Beyazid II, opened his lands to the refugees from Spain, he criticized Ferdinand's expulsion policy: "Can you call such a king wise and intelligent? He is impoverishing his country and enriching my kingdom."

Heichal *(ark for the Torah scrolls) at the Great Synagogue, Aleppo, Syria (courtesy of Sephardic Community Center Archives)*

The Rise and Fall of the Ottoman Empire

In the late fifteenth century, the first Jewish refugees from Spain arrived in Ottoman cities such as Istanbul, Salonika, and Smyrna. The Jews quickly made an impact. They filled high-profile positions in medicine and finance and also continued in their usual commercial roles as linguists, merchants, and artisans. One key technology that the Jews brought to their Ottoman hosts was the latest in munitions. As a result, Ottoman forces possessed more firepower, which probably contributed to the rapid expansion of the empire. The Jews also smuggled their movable type out

Joseph Sultan, circa 1900 (courtesy of Sadie Dweck)

of Spain and introduced the printing press to the Eastern Mediterranean. Salonika soon became the world center for Jewish publishing. Even as late as 1717, an English aristocrat, Lady Mary Wortley Montagu, marveled at the Jews' dominance in the Turkish city of Edirne:

> I observed most of the rich tradesmen were Jews. That people are in incredible power in this country. They have many privileges above all the natural Turks themselves, and have formed a very considerable commonwealth here, being judged by their own laws, and have drawn the whole trade of the empire into their own hands, partly by the firm union among themselves, and prevailing on the idle temper and want of industry of the Turks. Every pasha has his Jew, who is his *homme d'affaires;* he is let into all his secrets, and does all his business. No bargain is made, no bribe received, no merchandise disposed of, but what passes through their hands. They are the physicians, the stewards, and the interpreters of all the great men. . . . They have found the secret of making themselves so necessary, they are certain of the protection of the court . . . and the meanest among them is too important to be disobliged, since the whole body take care of his interests with as much vigour as they would those of the most considerable of their members.
> —*Montagu, "To the Abbé Conti"*

Spanish Jews who initially arrived in Turkey and Greece began to settle in cities farther east, such as Aleppo and Baghdad, upon the annexation of Arab lands by the Ottomans in 1516. Later in the sixteenth century, other Jews immigrated to Syria because they were fleeing the atmosphere of intolerance that was worsening in the Papal States and Italian kingdoms, capped by the auto-da-fé in Ancona in 1553, in which over two dozen Jews were killed.

At the turn of the seventeenth century, 73 of 380 Jewish households in Aleppo were of Spanish descent. Later, many prosperous Jewish traders from the lone Italian safe haven of Livorno settled in Aleppo; collectively, they were known as the Franj or Francos. Initially, the Spanish Jews, Franj, and *must'arab* (Jews native to Aleppo) communities remained separate from one other, marrying among themselves, convening their own prayer quorums, following their own rabbis, and operating within their own circles of trade. Though the *must'arab* community welcomed its brothers and sisters from the West, it did not instantly submit to the refined western lifestyle of the Spanish and Italian gentry and the learned opinions of the Spanish rabbinate on matters of Jewish law. Over time, however, the native and Sephardic communities combined and the distinctions between them disappeared.

Economically, Aleppo's star began to rise around the turn of the seventeenth century as the silk trade with Venice reached a fever pitch. For the next 150 years, Aleppo gleamed as one of the brightest gems in the Ottoman crown, bringing prosperity to its citizens and great wealth to the sultans of Istanbul. The Aleppian Jewish community contributed to this economic expansion as did other Jews throughout the Ottoman lands. Jews from distant ports and trading centers such as Baghdad, Aleppo, Salonika, Livorno, Ragusa, and Venice did business with one another, serving as brokers between East and West, sharing common languages unknown to their native hosts, and forging bonds of trust as coreligionists singed by the bitterness of exile.

The Jews' hold on Mediterranean trade was so tight that the English, who were exasperated with Aleppo's *khans* (market storehouses), *souqs* (public markets), and brokers' fees, used their unparalleled sea power and the global reach of their empire to cut out the need for the Oriental Jewish middleman and started to ship goods along the previously uncharted sea route from India and Southeast Asia around Cape Horn, all the way to the British Isles.

The period of Aleppo's ascendance, from 1600 to 1750, was not a continuous boom; when the roar of trade was intermittently silenced, Aleppo, along with many other Mediterranean cities, experienced periods of strife, disease, and disaster. Nonetheless, as market profits swelled, Aleppo blossomed into a cosmopolitan hub with an abundance of goods—Persian silk, Indian spices, Syrian cotton and wool, and a bounty of fruits, vegetables, grains, and nuts for local consumption. There were traders representing all the upstart European powers, each with its own center of operations, or "factory," as it was known.

On the raft of good times, many culinary influences converged, from Persian to Turkish to medieval Arab court cookery, and a discernible Aleppian cuisine began to develop. Recipes that once were reserved for princes, such as those documented by al Baghdadi and al Warraq a few centuries earlier, began to be enjoyed by the commoner. Food evolved from the crude, humble fare of hand-to-mouth sustenance to the multihued centerpiece of religious and life-cycle festivities and a source of regional pride.

Aleppian Jewish families, each snugly ensconced in its *haush* (multiple dwellings surrounding an inner courtyard) in the Bahsita quarter of old Aleppo, proudly adhered to their culture as they celebrated life. They would enjoy various *maza* plates on Sabbath afternoons as they reveled in poetic religious songs based on Arabic melodies. In these songs, collectively known as *pizmonim*, one could hear the faint laments of the flamenco *cantante* and the yearning of the *muezzin*. Their prayer services were also marked by this wide-ranging melodic style; the *maqamat* (the Arab system

of melodies) of the Aram Soba liturgy is still considered one of the most vibrant and moving in all of Judaism. With song came music. Once the sanctity of the Sabbath, with its prohibition against playing instruments, came to its weekly close, many Jews delighted in strumming the *'ud* (lute), tap-tapping the *dara'bukkah* (hourglass lap drum), and playing other tuneful instruments, such as the *qanun* (zither) and *nay* (flute), which define the swooning Levantine sound.

Aleppian Jews also took pride in their devotion to mysticism, sacred and profane. The Aleppian rabbinate, expert in ethics and Jewish law, participated in a regional kabbalistic brotherhood, which originated in late-medieval Safed, the famed birthplace of the Kabbalah in the heart of the Galilee. On the other hand, some of the laypeople absorbed the common superstitions of the time, taking pains to ward off the evil eye and to seek the protection of the *hamseh*, the filigreed hand still found around the necks of many Jews of Middle Eastern descent, and the *shebeh*, a cloth-enclosed stone also worn as a pendant.

As Venetian and English trade in Aleppo declined in the eighteenth century, the grip of the Ottoman court over its empire started to weaken. The world-exploring West began to triumph over the stagnating East. In this climate, Aleppo shrunk to a mere regional commercial player. Initially, this period of decline did not threaten the existence and stature of the Aleppian Jewish community. Once the nineteenth century arrived, however, the Middle East fell noticeably behind its rivals to the west, which began to reap the rewards of industrialization and modernity. The Ottoman Empire was thus dramatically diminished in this period—territorially, economically, and militarily—and the security of Jews began to unravel.

In 1869, the opening of the Suez Canal to the south relegated Aleppo to commercial irrelevance. Many Jews left Aleppo to seek their fortunes in Beirut and Cairo, while others moved to newly developed, spacious Jamaliya neighborhoods outside the old city. During the same year, the Alliance Israelite Universelle, the brainchild of liberal French Jews, established a boys' school in Aleppo. The school taught secular studies alongside a Judaic curriculum, preparing the youth for future immigration to the modernized West. However, the Aleppo rabbinate did not fully endorse this school because its curriculum and educators were not in keeping with the community's high standard of Jewish education and strict religious practices. Once the twentieth century arrived, a few intrepid Jews, mostly single men, fled to the Americas. This exodus rapidly increased as World War I approached in 1914 and the Turks began to conscript Jews for military service. Rather than fight for a crumbling empire, many Jewish families left Aleppo.

Section of the Aleppo Codex (courtesy of The Hebrew University Bible Project)

The Ottoman Aftermath

Still, many Jews remained in Aleppo during the period of the French Mandate, which followed the Ottomans' demise in 1918. In 1946 the French left the region and Syria became a sovereign nation. Virulent Arab nationalism, coupled with the announcement of the 1947 U.N. partition of Palestine, fueled a pogrom in Aleppo that has scarred the community to this day. Mobs forcibly entered the Cave of Elijah the Prophet, at the Great Synagogue, vandalized many religious objects, and left the holy place in flames.

Among the damaged items was the Aleppo Codex, known as the *Keter* ("crown" in Hebrew), one of the most—if not *the* most—sacred Jewish manuscripts extant. Until the Dead Sea Scrolls were discovered at Qumran, the Codex was the world's oldest surviving complete Old Testament text, written in the early tenth century by Shlomo ben Buya'a and later supplemented by Aaron ben Asher. In its original form, the Codex contained the full text of the twenty-four books of the Old Testament with vocalization and cantillation marks. For centuries, biblical scholars and Torah scribes from around the world traveled to Aleppo, hoping to gain the trust of the Codex's keepers and be given a chance to study the special document. In fact, scholars believe that Maimonides used the Codex as the model for his own *Sefer Torah* (parchment scroll of the Five Books of

Moses). In 1958, members of the community smuggled the considerably damaged Codex into Israel, where it resides today in the collection of the Israel Museum's Shrine of the Book in Jerusalem.

The pogrom of 1947 was one of the clearest signals that the champions of Arab nationalism did not welcome a Jewish presence in Syria. This surge in anti-Semitism led to the flight of more Jews from Aleppo. From 1946 until 1970, the remaining community suffered restrictions in human rights and faced shrinking economic opportunities under the benighted rule of a succession of Syrian dictators. In 1970, Hafez al Assad's *Ba'ath* party took control of Syria. As the new leader, Assad secularized Syrian society and attempted to modernize its economy, deflecting attention from the Jews and thus improving their living conditions. Despite the relative improvement in quality of life, the Mukhabarat (Syria's secret police) kept the Jewish community under constant surveillance. In addition, under Assad, Jews could not leave Syria without posting an onerous bond and leaving behind family members, measures cruelly designed to secure their return.

This travel ban continued until 1992, when Assad, feeling the pain of the demise of the Soviet Union, his erstwhile sponsor, finally submitted to pressure from Jewish organizations and foreign governments and lifted the travel ban. At that time, a quarter of the Jews still residing in Syria hailed from Aleppo. Most of the four thousand Syrian Jews immediately applied for tourist visas and immigrated to the United States, eventually settling in Brooklyn, though many eventually moved to Israel. The paltry few who remained in Aleppo at that time consisted mostly of the elderly and those who did not want to leave behind significant business interests. Now, for the first time in over two thousand years, there is not a single Jew living in Aleppo, but the culture of the Jewish community from Aleppo still thrives in many corners of the world.

The Contemporary Aleppian Jewish Community Endures

The exact population of Jews of Aleppian descent worldwide is not known, but it is probably over 100,000, distinguishing them as the largest Sephardic community in the Diaspora. The flagship Aleppian community in Brooklyn, New York, was founded in 1919. Smaller branches of the community exist in Latin American cities such as Mexico City, Panama City, Caracas, Buenos Aires, and São Paulo and in many places throughout Israel.

Before moving to Brooklyn early in the twentieth century, the first pioneering Aleppian immigrants settled in the cramped quarters of Manhattan's Lower East Side. These Arabic Jews, with their bizarre language and olive skin, felt like strangers among the teeming hordes on Orchard Street. In fact, many European Jewish immigrants were convinced that the Aleppians were not Jewish because they did not understand Yiddish. This sense of alienation and culture shock compelled the early community members to band together and help one another adjust to their new Western lives. The more settled immigrants lent a hand to the newcomers, providing them with a floor to sleep on, goods to peddle, and a Sabbath meal to enjoy. Instead of assimilating into the masses, Aleppian Jews strengthened their identity by following the customs and traditions that set them apart. After several years, the community jelled and, under the spiritual leadership of the peerless Rabbi Jacob Kassin, headed to the southern reaches of Brooklyn and established a permanent American home.

While the Aleppo community's environs have multiplied, very little else has. Aleppian Jews still do business with one another as they did in Aleppo, mostly as dealers in apparel and textiles, though many young men and women have acquired university degrees and joined the professional ranks. Wherever they have settled, Aleppian Jews have founded synagogues and charitable and educational institutions to maintain Jewish values and Syrian traditions and promote cohesion among all community members. The Aleppian Jews have remained a close-knit people, emigrating from Syria and forming strong communities in Israel and the Americas. Even more remarkable, the third and fourth generations born in these lands have defied assimilation. Their ties transcend national boundaries: a New York Aleppian could walk into the home of his Panamanian cousin and breathe in the same enchanting aromas that he knows well from his mother's Brooklyn kitchen. Relatives often cross national borders and fly long distances for wedding and *bar mitzvah* celebrations and to vacation together in the summer and winter. In a word, the Aleppian community is quintessentially Sephardic: proud, pious, worldly, and hardworking, maintaining a low profile despite its successes.

People of the *Souq*

Before the late nineteenth century, Aleppo was a major commercial hub, situated as it was on the major caravan routes connecting Europe and Asia. Throughout their history, Aleppian Jews, whether originally from Spain or natives of Syria, have been masters of the marketplace. According to a Syrian adage, an Aleppian can even sell a

Shaya Salem in front of his dry goods shop, Aleppo, Syria, 1918 (courtesy of Sephardic Community Archives)

dried donkey skin. Aleppian Jews are a mercantile people today, much as they were in the past. While the garment markets of Manhattan are a far cry from the serpentine *souqs* and cavernous *khans* of Aleppo, the colorful and persuasive style and the handshake agreement are still hallmarks of the Aleppian merchant.

In the same way that the identity and economic status of Aleppo's Jews has historically depended on the market, their cuisine represents the essence of the Middle Eastern *souq*. Grains such as rice, bulgur, and semolina are central ingredients in many Aleppian Jewish dishes and serve as accompaniments to an even larger number of recipes. Jews have always been fond of fruits and vegetables. As an alternative to meat, which was expensive in Aleppo and had to be ritually slaughtered and salted (see A Note about *Kashrut* on page 10), vegetables provided sustenance. Aleppian Jewish women to this day will gather and stuff any vegetable that can hold the traditional *hashu* filling. From the time of Moorish Spain, Aleppian Jews have always enjoyed fresh fruit at the close of a meal. They still insist on unblemished and flavorful fruit for dessert, which is usually accompanied by an array of dried fruit and roasted nuts and seeds. Dessert is limited to fruit and nuts because, by the end of an Aleppian Jewish meal, one is usually too full to consume any sweetmeats or pastries. Thus, Aleppians usually serve their exquisite and fragrant sweets during midafternoon coffee breaks or festive celebrations rather than at the end of typical meals.

In the Aleppian Jewish kitchen, one will find several bags filled with a veritable rainbow of spices, from the deep brown of allspice to the moody dark ochre of cumin to the bright yellow of turmeric. Most of these spices arrived in Aleppo from India and East Asia. However, not all Syrians employ them with Aleppian vigor. While the cuisine of Aleppo is greatly influenced by Turkish cookery, Aleppian cooks use spices and herbs far more liberally than the cooks of Istanbul. Aleppian Jews also depart from mainstream Syrian cuisine in their widespread use of dried fruits and fruit pastes, an homage to the flavors of Persia brought by itinerant Jewish traders and émigrés from the Jewish communities east of Aleppo.

Northern Syria is famous for the numerous olive groves that yield the deeply aromatic olive oils found in the Aleppo market. Aleppian Jewish cuisine has stood apart from the cuisines of its Syrian Arab and Christian counterparts in its use of oil as the cooking fat of choice. The traditional Syrian fats, clarified butter *(samna)* and lamb fat *(alya)*, derive from animal sources and cannot be freely mixed with many dishes because of *kashrut* restrictions. In contrast, oil can be used to cook dairy and meat dishes alike because it is a neutral vegetable product. Sephardic Jewish cuisine has been associated with olive oil since the time Jews lived in Spain. In fact Andrés Bernáldez, an Inquisition-era royal chronicler, ridiculed the Jews' trademark use of olive oil:

> They cooked their meat in olive oil, which they used instead of salt-pork or other fat, so as to avoid pork. Olive oil with meat and other fried things leaves a very unpleasant odor, and so their houses and doorways stunk with the odor of that food. The Jews too gave off the same odor, on account of those foods, and because they were not baptized.
> —*Gitliz and Davidson, A Drizzle of Honey*

Ironically, this practice is one of the few vestiges of Jewish life that have been adopted by the mainstream Ibero-Christian culture. Spanish cuisine today is unthinkable without its prodigious use of olive oil. When lighter vegetable oils became available, however, many Aleppian Jews prized their thinner body and neutral flavor and substituted them for olive oil, especially for frying.

Suffeh—the Highest Praise for the Aleppian Jewish Woman

Cooking in the Aleppian Jewish style goes beyond fine ingredients and adherence to religious laws and customs. It is a part of daily life and essential to opening one's home to family, friends, and neighbors. Women are central to the continuity and development of Aleppian Jewish cookery. Historically, the role of women in the Aleppo workplace was limited. Generally, a woman's responsibility was keeping the home in good order and gathering the ingredients needed for simple lunches and dinners. And it was no small task, especially in the days when she had to lug pots to communal ovens and deftly maneuver within the tight quarters of the *haush* in order to cook.

Aleppian Jewish women take pride in being savvy food shoppers, excellent cooks, and warm hostesses. These qualities are embodied in the concept of *suffeh* (pronounced SUH-feh), which literally means "orderliness" but is understood by Aleppian Jews to mean a high degree of poise, an appreciation of etiquette, and an ability to create a feeling of domestic warmth that even exceeds the effusive, open-armed hospitality of Middle Eastern lore. To say a woman has *suffeh* is one of the highest compliments among Aleppian Jews.

Suffeh capitalizes on a woman's sixth sense, or divine intuition, into matters of familial and communal significance. In the Jewish tradition, the woman is believed to be endowed with purity of soul and thus to

Poopa Dweck, 2007 (photo by Christine Austin)

possess the capability of entreating the *Shekhinah* (G-d's divine presence) to dwell in her home and bless her family. This concept derives from Psalm 100, which states, "Serve the Almighty with gladness, come before Him with joyous song."

This spiritual devotion informs their regular practice of reading the Book of Psalms (*Tehillim*). It also drives their preparation of food, especially for the holiday and Sabbath tables, the ultimate stages upon which the Syrian woman shines as a culinary diva. A woman with *suffeh* cooks with passion. She does not view the enormous task of preparing a holiday meal for fifteen or twenty as a chore—in fact, she feels energized by it. *Suffeh* involves looking for small shiny eggplants for pickling and stuffing, spotting firm and fresh string beans, and finding tender sweetbreads at the butcher's to prepare with mushrooms in anticipation of the favorite dishes of grandchildren, children, and guests. A woman with *suffeh* is awe-inspiring to her guests as she serenades and satiates their appetites with the bountiful delicacies before them.

The exercise of *suffeh* is not simply reserved for special occasions. An Aleppian Jewish woman must be ready at all times to greet the *zwarh bala azimeh* ("unexpected guests") with a warm *"Fadal'u!"* ("Welcome!"), whether they are new faces, friends, acquaintances, or relatives. She then repairs to the kitchen to retrieve a selection of specially prepared delicacies while the aroma of freshly

brewed *'ahweh* (Arabic Coffee, page 318) slowly fills her home. This kind of hospitality harks back to the first Jewish forefather, Abraham, who was renown for the *mitzvah* of *hakhnasat orkhim* (the greeting and receiving of guests), inviting all itinerant passersby in need of sustenance and rest into his tent.

While Aleppian women today have active lives outside the home and often are highly educated, the goal of attaining *suffeh* has not diminished. To a significant extent, it has kept the flame of Aleppian Jewish culture burning and served as the glue that has bound this unique community together. Just as Jews have handed down their *mesorah* (sacred Jewish traditions) over the centuries, Aleppian Jewish women have handed down the wisdom of *suffeh*. This process will be at work when you enter a busy Aleppian Jewish kitchen. You will more than likely encounter two, if not three or even four, generations of a family at work. They may be preparing separate dishes or laboring in unison on a single recipe. For example, if they are preparing *yebra* (Grape Leaves Stuffed with Ground Meat and Rice, with Apricot-Tamarind Sauce, page 150), you may find the eldest woman trimming the grape leaves, the youngest smoothing out the vein, her mother placing the meat filling inside and then relaying each filled leaf to *her* mother to roll and close. It is by cooking together, eating together, and remaining together that women practice the art of *suffeh* and preserve the ageless legacy of Aleppian Jewish cuisine.

A NOTE ABOUT *KASHRUT*

Aleppian Jews have always been highly traditional and strictly observant in their religious practices. The cuisine of the Aleppian Jews embodies the principles of *kashrut,* the Jewish dietary laws set out in the Torah and expanded upon over the centuries by rabbinical opinion. In addition to following the laws of *kashrut,* which is Hebrew for "fit" or "proper," Aleppian Jews recite blessings before and after eating, acknowledging G-d for the variety and quality of sustenance before them.

There is no one clear reason why the laws of *kashrut* exist. While some scholars have cited the promotion of good hygiene or the ethical treatment of animals as the primary rationales for *kashrut,* rabbinical opinions differ regarding the basis of why Jews eat kosher. Although the hygienic and ethical benefits of *kashrut* are undeniable, the fundamental belief is that the rules of *kashrut* have been prescribed by divine fiat—that is, Jews observe these rules simply because G-d commanded them to.

Kashrut restricts the kind of animals that a Jew can eat and prescribes a ritualized method of slaughtering permissible animals. All nonfowl livestock must have cloven hoofs and chew their cud (Leviticus 11:3). Cow, ox, lamb, goat, and deer are kosher, but pig, camel, and rabbit are not. The Torah sets forth the permissible and prohibited types of fowl. Permitted fowl include chicken, turkey, duck, goose, pheasant, and pigeon. Birds that are not traditionally consumed by Jews, such as many predatory birds, are designated as nonkosher.

A *shohet* (religiously ordained slaughterer) is the only person who can slaughter livestock. The procedure for kosher slaughtering is designed to inflict the least amount of pain on the animal. The *shohet* uses a flawless blade to slit the animal's trachea and esophagus quickly and precisely, limiting the duration and degree of the animal's suffering. This respect for the animal's well-being reminds each Jew to heed his ethical and humanitarian responsibilities, even in the everyday realm of gastronomy. By this logic, undertaking a mindful approach to the simple act of eating leads one to apply a greater level of conscientiousness to more serious matters.

Once an animal is slaughtered, its flesh is soaked and salted to remove all traces of blood, which Jews are forbidden to consume. They also avoid the hindquarters of nonfowl livestock, which are not kosher—a symbolic reminder of the thigh injury that Jacob sustained when he wrestled Esau's guardian angel (Genesis 32:33). However, these parts can be made kosher after the painstaking removal of certain veins and fat deposits.

The rules regarding fish are less stringent. Fish need only scales and fins to be kosher, and there is no special slaughtering procedure (Leviticus 11:9). Thus, most varieties of fish are kosher; some exceptions are swordfish, skate, sturgeon, monkfish, and catfish. Scavenging sea creatures, which include all shellfish, are not kosher because they fall into the nonkosher biblical category of "swarming organisms" (Leviticus 11:10).

All grains, fruits, and vegetables are kosher. However, Jewish cooks separate and examine grains thoroughly, wash and inspect greens, and cut open fruit to ensure that there are no unkosher insects or worms present.

Kashrut-observing Jews do not cook or eat meat and dairy foods together because of the biblical proscription against cooking a kid in its mother's milk (Deuteronomy 14:21). Thus, Aleppian Jews keep separate cookware, cutlery, and china for meat and dairy meals. They also wait six hours after consuming meat before eating dairy foods. However, the wait is negligible when eating meat after dairy because dairy foods are digested more quickly. Fish, grains, fruits, and vegetables are neutral (*pareve*) foods that can be freely eaten with meat or dairy. When Syrian Jews serve fish and meat in the same meal, however, they use a separate, clean set of cutlery and china for each.

These dietary restrictions, while very similar to the *halal* rules of the Islamic diet, have led Aleppian Jews to deviate from many Middle Eastern recipes. Thus, none of the recipes in this book call for butter or yogurt and meat together, a common Arab combination. Similarly, Aleppian Jews generally do not cook with animal fat, sheep's tail fat being the most popular variety in Syria, because it would place many neutral dishes in the meat category and thereby restrict the variety of dishes with which a cook can serve these otherwise neutral foods. Oil is used as a substitute for butter and animal fat, producing different flavor notes in these recipes than in their mainstream Arab counterparts. For instance, rice, while a neutral food, is generally cooked with oil instead of butter because it is commonly served with meat dishes. Also, many dairy desserts are served only after dairy meals or alone with coffee, which is another reason why a selection of fresh fruit and nuts is the dessert of choice after sumptuous meat meals.

Nonetheless, the recipes in this book demonstrate that the rules of *kashrut* have not hampered the development of Aleppian Jewish cuisine, but rather strengthened it by fueling culinary innovation and fostering a unique variation of Middle Eastern culture.

The Great Synagogue, Aleppo, Syria (courtesy of Elie Sutton)

Helou S'farjal
(Candied Quince, page 290)

RECIPES

Khubz 'Adi
(*Ordinary Syrian Flatbread,*
page 18)

Maza
مازا

SMALL DELIGHTS

Maza has been a Middle Eastern institution for centuries. The bright salads and ornate finger foods that begin the meal, at once exotic and accessible, have tempted many food enthusiasts to explore the divine offerings of the *maza* table. *Maza* dishes are often an outsider's first taste of Levantine food, and one can easily become so enamored of *maza* that one overlooks the rest of the cuisine. Nonetheless, *maza* is the right place to start any journey into Aleppian Jewish cookery. Just be careful not to fill up on too much Syrian flatbread along the way!

There is debate over the exact meaning of the word *maza*. Some say it's derived from *mezzo*, Italian for "half," hinting at the small size of a typical dish. Others say it's from the Arabic *t'mazza*, meaning "to savor in little bites," or from the colloquial expression *maza haza* (literally, "what's this?"). Still others cite *meze*, Greek for "porridge," as the definitive source. Etymology aside, there is no question that a festive meal can never be without several *maza* circulating among guests. *Maza* encompasses a wide variety of dishes served at the beginning of a meal and kept on the table for the duration, unlike typical Western appetizers, which are finished (or removed from the table) before the main dish arrives.

Maza dishes range from cold salads, such as *salatit banjan* (Smoky Eggplant Salad with Garlic and Parsley, page 33), and *bazargan* (Tangy Tamarind Bulgur Salad, page 44), to hors d'oeuvre–type foods, such as *kibbeh neye* (Raw Beef–Bulgur Patties, page 63), *laham b'ajeen* (Miniature Tamarind Minced Meat Pies, page 50), and

kuaisat (Pistachio-Filled Ground Meat Shells, page 60). Some of these dishes, such as *salatit batata* (Lemony Allspice-Cumin Potato Salad, page 37), are very simple to prepare, whereas others, such as *kibbeh nabelsieh* (Golden Ground Meat–Filled Bulgur Shells, page 53), require the skill of an artisan to perfect. Two or three *maza* dishes can serve as a prelude to a meal, or you can combine many of them for a complete meal. These dishes are best served family-style in a casual setting with several loaves of warm Syrian flatbread and a bottle of high-quality *arak* (Syrian anisette).

For Aleppian Jews, *maza* dishes achieve their greatest glory during the *sebbit*, the festive Sabbath luncheon (see page 334) held in the home or the synagogue to celebrate a life-cycle event with family, friends, and fellow congregants. The hungry and exuberant celebrants typically encounter ten to twenty *maza* dishes throughout the course of the *sebbit*.

Although these recipes include an approximate yield, it is difficult to quantify a yield for many *maza* recipes because there is no standard portion size for most of these dishes. A given recipe can feed anywhere from four to fourteen guests, depending on each guest's appetite and the composition of the rest of the meal. It is best to serve many dishes of *maza*, from which each person can choose his or her favorites. The most enjoyable part of preparing *maza* is deciding which dishes will best round out the meal and suit the tastes of the guests. And nothing delights a guest more than the feeling that the cook has customized the meal perfectly just for him or her.

MAZA RECIPES

Khubz 'Adi خبز عادي

ORDINARY SYRIAN FLATBREAD

"... and bread sustains a man's heart."
—Psalm 104:15

Bread, no matter how basic it is, plays a significant role in Jewish life. It is considered an essential part of any meal, requiring its own special blessings before and after it is eaten.

Historically, the Aleppian Jewish community relied on a local baker for their flatbread and other baked goods. This practice still stands today, although some women bake their own bread at home. Baking bread for one's family is one of the three special obligations that Jewish law prescribes for women.

Bread and wine consecrate the Sabbath and inspire the first blessings recited at the Friday night Sabbath dinner table. Aleppian Jews have a custom of setting the Sabbath dinner table with twelve loaves of *khubz 'adi* to correspond to the twelve loaves of shewbread (*lechem hapanim*) that were displayed in the Jewish Temple.

Khubz 'adi is traditionally baked in a clay oven called a *taboon*, which is heated to a very high temperature. A thin disk of dough is stuck against the side of the *taboon*. It bubbles and expands immediately. The loaves bake within the space of a minute or two and have a crisp exterior and a soft, pillowy interior pocket.

Syrian flatbread, like any bread, is best consumed fresh from the oven, as it tends to go stale within a few days. However, if you try this recipe or obtain fresh loaves from a Middle Eastern bakery, you can freeze them immediately for later use. A frozen loaf of *khubz 'adi* will yield a nearly fresh product after it is defrosted and reheated in an oven at 300°F or on a stove top in a dry pan or directly over a medium flame.

In Aleppo, families sent their dough to a communal oven (see page 23), and a young employee of the bakery would return the loaves. For Aleppians, a meal was incomplete without bread. Bread was a staple at every single meal and was served with everything, even chocolate. When the head of the household returned home unexpectedly for a meal, flatbread was immediately put in the oven to warm.

Nearly every savory recipe in this book would profit from the company of a few warm loaves of *khubz 'adi* on the table. What follows is a recipe for making this wonderful and simple bread a regular part of your baking repertoire.

1 teaspoon sugar

2 teaspoons active dry yeast
    dissolved in 3 cups warm water
    (add more if needed)

3 cups all-purpose white flour

1½ cups whole wheat flour

1½ cups pastry flour
    (or an additional 1½ cups
    whole wheat flour)

1½ teaspoons kosher salt

1. Add the sugar to the dissolved yeast mixture, which should be bubbly after standing for about 5 minutes.

2. Sift together the white flour, whole wheat flour, pastry flour, and salt in a large mixing bowl. Make a well in the center of the flour mixture and slowly pour in the dissolved yeast mixture. Stir to combine, and knead by hand in the bowl for about a minute, until the dough is soft and sticky. Turn out onto a flour-dusted work surface and knead gently for 3 to 5 minutes until the dough is elastic and no longer sticky to the touch. (You can also use the dough hook of a mixer to knead the dough.) Place the dough in a clean mixing bowl. Cover the dough with a damp towel. Seal the bowl with plastic wrap, and let the dough rise in a place warmer than room temperature for about 1 hour, or until it doubles in size.

3. After the dough has risen, divide it into quarters and work with one quarter at a time, keeping the rest covered. Divide the first quarter into 4 fist-size balls. On a flour-covered work surface, flatten each ball with a rolling pin or by hand until it is about 4 to 6 inches in diameter. Place the rounds of dough onto ungreased baking sheets, leaving ample space between them. Repeat with the remaining quarters. Cover each baking sheet with a towel and allow to rise for a minimum of 15 minutes.

4. Preheat the oven to 525°F.

5. Bake the rounds for 4 to 5 minutes, monitoring the process closely (loaves transition from done to burnt very rapidly). The heat must be even; otherwise, the bread does not puff properly.

6. Remove the loaves and cool on wire racks. Do not stack the loaves while cooling. Serve immediately or wrap tightly and freeze.

Yield: approximately 20 loaves

Seasoning Khubz Za'atar (Za'atar *Flatbread, page 20*)

Khubz Za'atar — Za'atar Flatbread

Za'atar is Arabic for the hyssop plant, but it also refers to a spice blend composed of hyssop or thyme, toasted sesame seeds, sumac, salt, and marjoram. This blend varies across the Middle East—there are Syrian, Jordanian, Israeli, and Egyptian versions, which are either green or dark red, depending on the proportions of the spices. Aleppians tend to favor the green varieties. *Za'atar* is widely available in Middle Eastern and gourmet markets.

    Za'atar combined with olive oil is used as a spread (*za'atar ul-zayt*) or a dip for Syrian flatbread. If the mixture is spread over the bread before it is baked, the bread is extraordinarily fragrant when fresh from the oven.

½ cup dried thyme

¼ cup dried marjoram

2 tablespoons lightly toasted sesame seeds

¼ cup ground sumac

½ teaspoon kosher salt

1 cup extra-virgin olive oil

Combine the thyme, marjoram, sesame seeds, sumac, and salt (or use 1½ cups of store-bought *za'atar*). Mix well.

    Follow the recipe for Ordinary Syrian Flatbread through step 4. Mix the *za'atar* spice blend with the olive oil in a small mixing bowl. It should be a very thin mixture. Spoon about 1 tablespoon on top of each loaf.

    Spread the mixture and press down with your fingertips all over the bread, dimpling the top. This will give the loaf a traditional shape, which will prevent a pocket from forming and the *za'atar* mixture from spilling off the loaves. Bake according to step 5.

Khubz Semsom — Sesame Flatbread

Follow the recipe for Ordinary Syrian Flatbread through step 4. Brush the loaves lightly with water and press both sides of each loaf into a dish of sesame seeds before placing the rounds on baking trays. Let rest for 15 minutes and then bake according to step 5.

ᔦ Taking *Challah* ᔧ

Taking *Challah* is one of the three special obligations that Jewish law provides for a woman (the other two are lighting the Sabbath candles and observing the laws of family purity). The act of kneading the dough and producing wonderful loaves for the Sabbath advances a woman's sacred bond with her family. It is a time of *Et Razon*, when her prayers are especially heard in heaven.

The commandment requires a woman to separate 1 ounce of dough; this separated dough is known as *challah*. The woman then recites the following blessing:

Blessed are you, G-d	ברוך אתה ה׳
our Lord, King of the Universe,	אלקינו מלך העולם
who sanctified us	אשר קדשנו
with His commandments,	במצותיו
and commanded us	וצונו
to separate	להפריש
challah which is set aside.	חלה תרומה.
Behold, this is challah.	הרי זו חלה.

This tradition recalls a practice at the Jewish Temple in Jerusalem. The separated dough symbolizes the portion of certain sacrifices that was set aside for the Temple priests. Today, in memory of the Temple, we bless the separated dough and respectfully dispose of it by burning it over the stove top. A woman can perform this ritual only if she is using at least 3 pounds and 12 ounces of flour (1.68 kilos or about 12.4 cups).

The performance of the separation ritual is a time of profound holiness for a woman. It opens a unique window of spiritual connection, allowing a woman's prayers to reach great heights with a remarkable level of purity.

Ka'ak

SAVORY ANISE-SEED RINGS

Ka'ak has the texture and crunch of a breadstick, but it is ring-shaped and has a crimped edge. A staple of the Aleppian pantry, *ka'ak* is usually offered to guests when Aleppian Jews serve coffee or tea.

Ka'ak is no boring teatime biscuit, however. It has a great deal of flavor and tang, thanks to the addition of ground sour cherry pit (*mahlab*), anise seed (*yansoon*), coriander seed (*kizebrah*), and cumin (*kamoon*). *Mahlab*, a spice native to Syria that lends a nutty, slightly flinty flavor to *ka'ak*, is not commonly available in American markets, though if you have a Middle Eastern grocer nearby, you may be in luck. Online spice merchants also tend to stock it. Once you get your hands on a supply of *mahlab*, make sure it is finely crushed before you use it for this recipe. A mortar and pestle or electric spice grinder will do the trick.

In the old country, *ka'ak* was a bakery item that most Aleppian Jews purchased from their local baker and stored in a tight-lidded tin box called a *tenekey*, which helped preserve *ka'ak*'s crispness. Today, *ka'ak* is made by commercial bakers and is available in Middle Eastern grocers. However, in the Aleppian Jewish community, many women bake *ka'ak* at home, and more and more small, independent bakers make their own. Needless to say, most discriminating *ka'ak* aficionados (meaning, virtually all Aleppian Jews) prefer the homemade product.

While *ka'ak* is a relatively straightforward baked good, it's the baker's light touch that makes or breaks a batch of *ka'ak*. If you want to try your hand at baking *ka'ak*, beware of one major pitfall: failing to introduce enough air into the dough, which will make the *ka'ak* too dense and cookielike and thus lacking a pleasing crunch. This problem is usually the result of overkneading. In any case, it takes a lot of practice to bake anything approaching perfect *ka'ak*.

3 tablespoons fresh yeast,
  or 4 packages active dry yeast

3 tablespoons plus 2 teaspoons
  kosher salt

2½ pounds (8 cups) all-purpose flour

⅓ cup and 1 tablespoon anise seed,
  washed and drained

1 teaspoon finely crushed *mahlab*
  (sour cherry pit), optional

1 heaping teaspoon ground
  coriander seed

1 heaping teaspoon ground cumin

2 teaspoons nigella seeds

2 tablespoons vegetable oil

1 teaspoon sugar

½ pound (1 cup) vegetable shortening

1 egg

¼ cup sesame seeds

The Communal Ovens of Aleppo

In Bahsita, the Jewish enclave of old Aleppo, and in the Aleppian suburb of Jamaliya, a good housewife prepared dough at home and sent her raised loaves to the communal oven for baking. The communal oven, called a *furn,* was able to achieve the high heat needed to bake bread properly.

Because houses were made of wood, most people had their dough baked in a communal oven to avoid the risk of fire. Wealthier families with enough space to maintain a detached oven in a separate building could bake at home.

The *furn* was also used to warm up the Sabbath meal. Family members brought pots of food to the *furn,* where they were cooked overnight and picked up the next day. Each family would adorn its pot with a colored thread or special ornament so that the pot could be easily identified by any family member retrieving it from the *furn.*

1. Position one rack at the top of the oven, another in the middle, and a third in the bottom. In a medium mixing bowl, sprinkle yeast and salt over 2½ cups lukewarm water. Let the mixture stand for about 5 minutes, or until the yeast has been dissolved and bubbles appear on the surface of the mixture. Stir.

2. Put the flour in a large mixing bowl and form a well in the center. Add the anise seed, *mahlab,* coriander seed, cumin, vegetable oil, sugar, and vegetable shortening. Stir until well combined. Then slowly incorporate the yeast mixture into the well, absorbing flour. Mix thoroughly.

3. Knead the dough for about 15 minutes. It should be soft, yet smooth and elastic, and it should no longer stick to the sides of the bowl. Adding a sprinkle of flour to the dough may help if the dough is too sticky.

4. Cover the mixing bowl with a dry towel. Let the dough rise for 1½ hours in a place warmer than room temperature.

5. Preheat oven to 400°F.

6. On a lightly floured work surface, punch down the dough and divide it in half. Roll half of the dough into a 2-inch-diameter log. Cut the log into ½-inch rounds and roll each of the rounds to a length of about 4 inches. If you feel like crimping the edges of the *ka'ak* to give them a fancy appearance, with a sharp knife, make ⅛-inch notches along one long edge of each dough strip at intervals of ¼ inch.

7. Shape each strip into a ring, crimped edges facing outward. Brush each ring of dough lightly with the egg beaten with 2 tablespoons water. Then dip each dough ring in sesame seeds. Place the *ka'ak* on a lightly greased or parchment-lined baking tray in even rows.

8. Bake for 10 minutes, utilizing all oven racks and rotating the trays. When all the *ka'ak* are completely baked, reduce the oven temperature to 250°F and bake for an additional 20 minutes. Then crisp by reducing oven temperature to 200°F for 20 minutes. The crisping stage is essential to produce the crunch and texture desired. The *ka'ak* should appear very light gold and crisp. Let cool and store in an airtight container.

Yield: 8 dozen

Ka'ak
*(Savory Anise-Seed Rings,
page 22)*

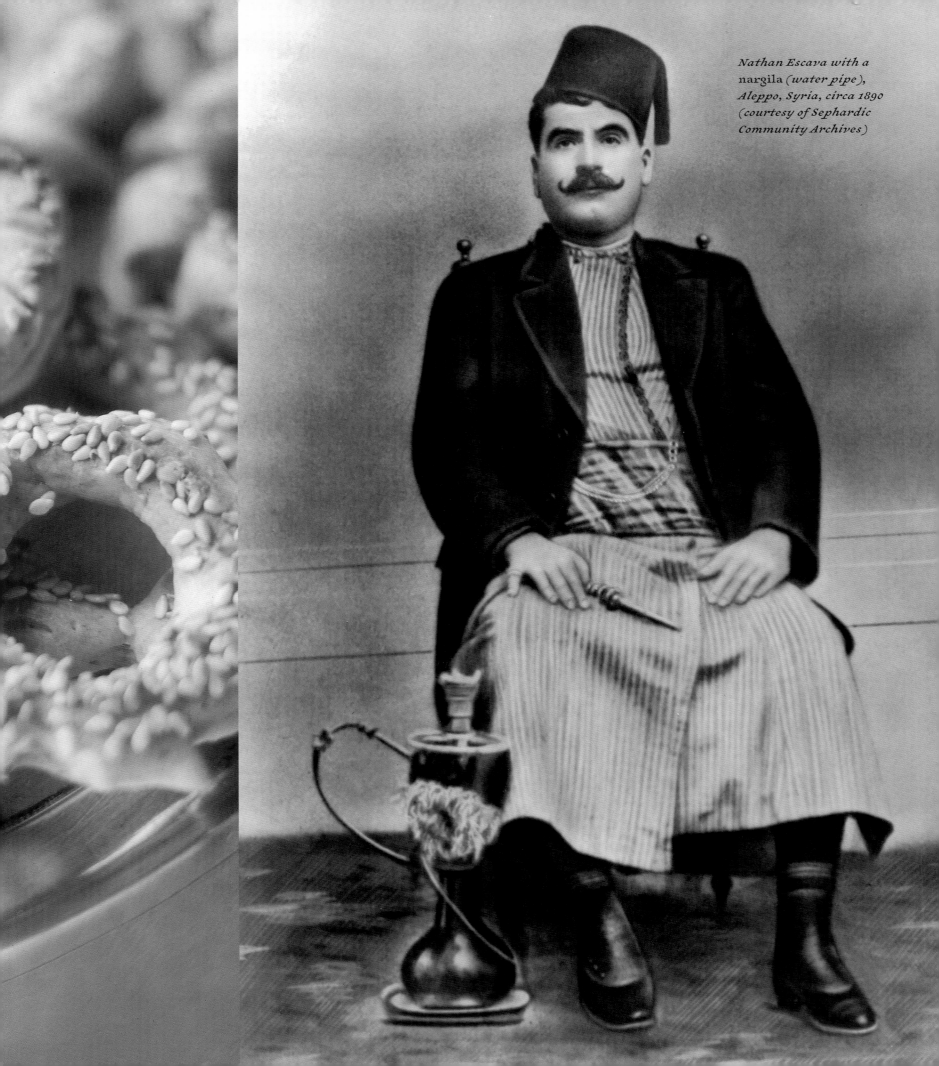

Nathan Escava with a
nargila (*water pipe*),
Aleppo, Syria, circa 1890
(*courtesy of Sephardic
Community Archives*)

Tehineh

SESAME SPREAD

Tehineh is a ubiquitous *maza* staple with all kinds of applications in Middle Eastern cuisine. It is the classic addition to *maza* and meat dishes, which Syrians use in the same manner that Americans use ketchup. Interestingly, in Aleppo, *tehineh* also made an appearance at the breakfast table. *Asal b'tehineh* (honey with *tehineh*) was the traditional breakfast of many Aleppians and is still enjoyed today. A simpler treatment of *tehineh*, without the lemon, garlic, or spices, is combined with honey and scooped up with Syrian bread. It is an inexpensive, nutritious, and delicious way to start the day.

1 to 3 garlic cloves

2 teaspoons kosher salt,
  plus additional to taste

½ cup freshly squeezed lemon juice
  (2 to 3 lemons)

½ cup *tahini* (raw ground sesame seed
  paste; see Note)

1 teaspoon ground cumin

3 tablespoons chopped fresh flat-leaf
  parsley (optional)

1 tablespoon extra-virgin olive oil

¼ teaspoon paprika

1 teaspoon pine nuts, toasted
  (see page 28) (optional)

1. Pound the garlic and salt with a mortar and pestle (or blend in a food processor) until a paste is formed. Transfer the garlic paste to a medium mixing bowl. Add 2 tablespoons of the lemon juice and the *tahini* and mix well. Add the remaining lemon juice and enough cold water to achieve a thick, smooth cream.

2. Season with the cumin and additional salt to taste. The flavor should be redolent of sesame and slightly sour. Top with the chopped parsley and drizzle with the olive oil. Garnish with paprika and pine nuts, if desired.

✎ *Note* ✎

Not all *tahini* is created equal. Make sure to get a good-quality sesame paste, because it can drastically affect the flavor of your *tehineh*. Middle Eastern shops, gourmet grocers, and health food stores carry authentic brands of *tahini* that will help you make delicious *tehineh* with the creamiest texture possible.

Yield: 4 to 6 servings

Hummus

CHICKPEA-SESAME SPREAD

Hummus entered Aleppian Jewish cuisine through the influence of the community's Arab neighbors. The spread is now a crucial component to any *maza* table and is one of the few Levantine products to have made inroads in the most remote American hamlets. Authentic *hummus* must be thick so that you can carve deep valleys over its surface and fill them with olive oil and other garnishes, such as paprika or parsley for color, or chickpeas, fava beans, or pine nuts for contrasting texture.

Wiping *hummus* clean from the dish with warm Syrian bread is a quintessentially Aleppian table custom. *Hummus* is a great thing to keep on hand. Homemade *hummus* can be stored for 5 to 7 days in the refrigerator, or it can be frozen and defrosted as needed. Many Syrian women freeze a large quantity and take out the required portions for Shabbat or unexpected guests. It keeps in the freezer for up to 2 months.

¾ cup dried chickpeas, soaked in 3 cups cold water for 6 to 8 hours or overnight, or one 15½-ounce can chickpeas

4 garlic cloves, chopped (about 2 teaspoons)

3 tablespoons *tahini* (see Note on page 26)

2 teaspoons ground cumin

1 teaspoon kosher salt

⅓ cup freshly squeezed lemon juice (a little more than 1 lemon)

3 tablespoons extra-virgin olive oil

½ teaspoon Aleppo pepper, or ¼ teaspoon crushed red pepper

Optional garnishes:

1 tablespoon extra-virgin olive oil

Paprika

Chopped fresh flat-leaf parsley

Pine nuts

⅓ cup cooked and drained fava beans (if not garnishing with chickpeas)

৯ *Snobar* — Pine Nuts ৬

There are two kinds of pine nuts: Mediterranean and Chinese. The Mediterranean variety is the best; they are from Spain and Portugal and are about three times more expensive than the Chinese ones. They have a more distinctive taste and are long and thin, whereas the ones from China are sweeter and shorter. Quality grocers sell both varieties.

These little nuts are used both in sweet dishes such as *sliha* (Sweetened Whole Wheat Grains with Mixed Nuts, page 282) and in savory dishes such as *bastel* (Ground Meat–Filled Semolina Half-Moons, page 58). Pine nuts are the product of several different species of pine trees. The hard kernels containing the nuts are found inside the scales of the cone. When the cone is dry enough for the scales to open up fully, the kernels are shaken out and cracked open to reveal the brown-skinned nuts. The nuts can be eaten raw, and even while still green. Cut the cone into quarters, extract the nuts from the soft kernels, dip them in salt, and eat.

Pine nuts are used in Aleppian Jewish cuisine raw, sautéed in a light oil, or dry roasted. To toast, toss pine nuts in a dry pan over medium-low heat for 8 to 10 minutes. They have a tendency to burn very quickly during the toasting process, so watch them carefully and remove from the stove top *before* they have reached the desired golden brown color because they will continue to cook even after you have removed them from the heat source. Another option is to bake them in a 300°F oven for 10 minutes, although the stove-top method brings out more of the nuts' flavorful oils.

1. If using dried chickpeas that have soaked overnight, drain and transfer to a saucepan. Add enough fresh water to cover the chickpeas by 2 inches and bring to a boil. Reduce the heat to low, cover, and simmer for 1½ to 2 hours. Or cook in a pressure cooker for about 20 minutes. Drain and rinse the chickpeas, reserving about ½ cup of the cooking liquid. Soak the chickpeas in cold water to cool them. When cool enough to handle, drain. Lightly rub a handful of them between your palms until the skins come off. Rinse the chickpeas, and place them in a medium bowl. Continue in this way until all the skins have been removed. This produces creamier *hummus*.

If using canned chickpeas, drain them and reserve half of the liquid. Remove the skins, just as you would for dried chickpeas. Reserve a few chickpeas for a garnish, if desired.

2. Using a blender or food processor, first puree the garlic, then add the chickpeas, *tahini*, cumin, salt, lemon juice, oil, and Aleppo pepper. Puree until a creamy paste is achieved. If necessary to reach the desired consistency, add the reserved chickpea liquid in increments of ¼ cup.

3. To serve, spread the *hummus* in a shallow serving dish. With the back of a spoon, make a deep well in the surface of the hummus. Drizzle the olive oil into the well, and, if desired, add one or more of the garnishes. Serve with warm Syrian bread.

Yield: 12 servings

Baba Ghanooj

EGGPLANT-SESAME PUREE

Although eggplants were first brought to Spain and Italy by the Arabs, Jews have been credited with introducing them to Spanish and Italian cuisine. Jews brought eggplants to the northern parts of these countries after fleeing from the Moors in southern Spain, and after the Inquisition banished them from southern Italy. Mediterranean Jews have been exceedingly fond of the vegetable and remain forever associated with it.

The key to making mouthwatering *baba ghanooj* is to ensure that the proportions are right. Most commercial producers tend to bake their eggplants, but good homemade *baba ghanooj* is infused with a smoky flavor that comes from roasting the eggplants directly over a flame, surpassing the store-bought variety. *Tehineh* (page 26)—made with sesame paste, lots of garlic, and lemon juice—makes a tangy, zesty, beautiful complement to the roasted eggplant dish. Together, they are timeless Aleppian staples.

Choose eggplants that are shiny and firm. The best eggplants have dense, sweet flesh with small seeds.

3 medium eggplants

2 to 4 garlic cloves

1 tablespoon kosher salt

½ cup *tahini* combined with 1 tablespoon water (see Note on page 26)

Juice of 3 lemons (about 9 tablespoons)

½ teaspoon ground cumin

½ teaspoon Aleppo pepper, or ¼ teaspoon crushed red pepper (optional)

2 tablespoons chopped fresh flat-leaf parsley

1. Roast the eggplants over medium-high heat on the stove top directly over the flame for 10 to 30 minutes, or until the skin blackens and looks blistered.

2. Once the eggplants are roasted, cut them in half lengthwise and discard any large seed pockets. This will reduce your yield, but the seeds are bitter and add an unpleasant texture.

3. Peel the eggplants. Press the eggplant flesh firmly against the surface of a colander to extract excess liquid.

4. Pound the garlic with the salt with a mortar and pestle, or gently blend in a mini food processor or blender.

5. Mash the eggplants with a fork in a large bowl, add the garlic mixture, and continue mashing until it begins to look creamy. Add the *tahini*, lemon juice, cumin, and pepper, if using, and blend thoroughly into the eggplant mixture. Garnish with the parsley.

Yield: 6 to 8 servings

Salata Arabi

BASIC SYRIAN SALAD
WITH LEMON-CUMIN DRESSING

When you make *salata arabi,* a relatively simple dish, it is important to use the freshest ingredients. The cucumbers and tomatoes should be firm and, ideally, locally grown. Flat-leaf parsley is also a key component. It has more flavor than curly parsley and is always preferred in Aleppian Jewish cooking. Cumin is featured in the traditional dressing for *salata.* Many people do not know that cumin is in the parsley family. It is the dried fruit of the plant, whose seeds give many Syrian dishes an earthy flavor. Fresh lemon adds a burst of acidity to the dressing. (Oil is generally not used.)

6 Kirby cucumbers, finely chopped

4 medium tomatoes, finely chopped

1 bunch fresh flat-leaf parsley, finely chopped

½ cup freshly squeezed lemon juice (2 to 3 lemons)

1 teaspoon ground cumin

1 teaspoon kosher salt

1 bunch scallions, chopped (optional)

Combine the cucumbers, tomatoes, parsley, lemon juice, cumin, salt, and scallions, if using, in a medium bowl. Toss well and serve immediately.

Yield: 6 to 8 servings

Tabbouleh

CRUNCHY TOMATO, PARSLEY, AND BULGUR SALAD WITH CUMIN

This remarkably simple dish, which you can find on tables around the world, has rather humble origins. Its principal ingredient, bulgur, or cracked wheat, has been stigmatized for ages in the lore of the Middle East as poor people's food. Despite this, Aleppian Jews adore the nutty and versatile grain. Bulgur was always inexpensive and readily available in Syria, and it has found its way into many dishes. The authentic Aleppian version of *tabbouleh* emphasizes parsley over bulgur, though some prefer more crunch and tip the balance in favor of the grain. The name *tabbouleh* is derived from *tabil* ("to spice or season" in Arabic). Supremely fresh parsley and a generous squeeze of lemon juice make this the perfect summer *maza*, though Aleppian Jews enjoy it year-round. Be sure to chop the tomatoes and herbs by hand and add them just before serving to prevent the *tabbouleh* from becoming soggy. Serve with warm Syrian flatbread to soak up the juices, or follow the custom of old Aleppo and use romaine leaves to scoop up each delicious bite.

1 cup fine bulgur (cracked wheat), soaked in hot water for 15 minutes and drained

6 tablespoons extra-virgin olive oil

¾ cup freshly squeezed lemon juice (about 4 lemons)

2 teaspoons ground cumin

1 teaspoon Aleppo pepper, or ½ teaspoon crushed red pepper

1 tablespoon kosher salt

5 tomatoes, chopped

4 bunches scallions, chopped

1 bunch fresh flat-leaf parsley, stems trimmed, and chopped

2 teaspoons dried mint leaves, or 3 tablespoons chopped fresh mint

Romaine lettuce leaves for serving (optional)

1. Combine the bulgur, olive oil, lemon juice, cumin, Aleppo pepper, and salt in a large mixing bowl. Let the mixture stand for 30 minutes, or until the bulgur softens.

2. Add the tomatoes, scallions, parsley, and mint to the bulgur mixture and mix thoroughly. Serve with leaves of romaine lettuce, if desired.

Yield: 8 to 10 servings

Salatit Banjan

SMOKY EGGPLANT SALAD
WITH GARLIC AND PARSLEY

The eggplant has been known as a suspect vegetable in some cultures. According to the food scholar Charles Perry, the Greek *melitzana* and Italian *melanzana* come from the Latin *mala insana,* meaning "mad apple." In the same vein, the Sanskrit name *vatingana,* means "belonging to the windy class," a designation associated with madness. Egyptians have a saying when someone contradicts himself: *Adi zaman al-batinjan,* or "It's eggplant time." Arabs and Jews have always embraced this curious vegetable, despite the negative associations. As early as the seventh century, Arabs ate eggplant and called it *sayyid al-khudar,* "the lord of the vegetables." The scorn historically lodged against eggplant may come from the difficulty of rendering it fit to consume; indeed, the foamlike pulp must be cooked well to be eaten.

Here, the eggplant is cooked directly over fire. The charred flavor that this method imparts is essential to this recipe. Oven roasting simply does not produce the distinctive smokiness that contrasts wonderfully with the earthy tomato and acidic lemon in this salad.

2 medium eggplants

1 medium tomato, chopped

1 green bell pepper,
  seeded and chopped (optional)

⅓ cup chopped fresh flat-leaf parsley

½ cup freshly squeezed lemon juice
  (2 to 3 lemons)

1 tablespoon extra-virgin olive oil

3 garlic cloves, chopped
  (about 1½ teaspoons)

1 teaspoon ground cumin

½ teaspoon Aleppo pepper,
  or ¼ teaspoon crushed red pepper

1 teaspoon kosher salt

1. Pierce the skins of the eggplants in a few places with a fork. Place each eggplant directly into a medium-high flame and turn occasionally. The skins of the eggplants should eventually blister and shrivel. Remove the eggplants from the heat once they are thoroughly charred and you can sense that the flesh inside has become heavy with moisture. It may take about 30 minutes to arrive at this point. Let cool.

2. Cut the eggplants in half lengthwise, scoop out their flesh, and put in a colander. Discard the peels. Press the eggplant flesh firmly against the colander to remove excess liquid. Mash the eggplants with a fork in a large bowl.

3. Combine the mashed eggplant flesh with the tomato, bell pepper (if desired), parsley, lemon juice, olive oil, garlic, cumin, Aleppo pepper, and salt. Give it a good stir.

Yield: 4 to 6 servings

Salata Banadoura

FRESH TOMATO SALAD
WITH ALLSPICE-LEMON DRESSING

This recipe celebrates the essence of the tomato—the fruity juiciness and deep earthy tones that helped this New World fruit forever transform the cuisines of the Mediterranean. The best tomatoes are seasonal, plump yet firm, and locally grown (if you have some in your garden, even better). The preparation is exceedingly simple and accentuates the beauty of the fruit. Allspice, the principal flavoring accent in the dish, is called *b'har helou* in Arabic, meaning "sweet pepper," because its subtle flavor suggests the spiciness of cloves and the sweet notes of cinnamon and nutmeg.

4 to 6 tomatoes, cored and cut into
  2-inch chunks

Dressing:

Juice of 1 lemon (about 3 tablespoons)

1 tablespoon extra-virgin olive oil

½ teaspoon ground allspice

¼ teaspoon Aleppo pepper,
  or ⅛ teaspoon crushed red pepper

1 teaspoon kosher salt

½ small red onion, sliced (optional)

1. Put the tomatoes in a medium mixing bowl.

2. To make the dressing, combine the lemon juice, olive oil, allspice, Aleppo pepper, and salt in a small mixing bowl and mix thoroughly. Pour the dressing over the tomatoes.

Add the red onions, if desired. Toss until the tomatoes are coated with the dressing.

Yield: 4 to 6 servings

Salatit Batata

LEMONY ALLSPICE-CUMIN POTATO SALAD

The Syrian version of potato salad is a welcome departure from the lumpy, creamy stuff sold in American delis. Consider this recipe for your next barbecue; the lemon and allspice flavors work particularly well with grilled meats. There is really no mystery to this dish. Once the potatoes are cooked, you simply combine with the seasonings, and add scallions for crunch, if you wish. While measurements are provided, you can adjust this dish to your taste. Experiment as you please. If you feel that the potatoes need a kick of heat, add Aleppo pepper. If the soft texture reminds you of hard-boiled eggs, crumble some egg over the top.

6 medium potatoes (about 3 pounds)

¼ cup extra-virgin olive oil

¾ cup freshly squeezed lemon juice (about 4 lemons)

1 teaspoon ground allspice

1 teaspoon ground cumin

1 teaspoon ground white pepper

1 teaspoon kosher salt

4 scallions, chopped (optional)

2 hard-boiled eggs, quartered and chopped (optional)

Fresh flat-leaf parsley for garnish

1. Boil the potatoes in a large pot of salted water over medium-high heat, uncovered, for 20 minutes, or until tender. Drain, peel the potatoes, and cut them into small chunks while still warm. Put the potatoes in a medium mixing bowl.

2. While the potatoes are still warm, add the olive oil and lemon juice to the mixing bowl. Season the potatoes with the allspice, cumin, white pepper, and salt. Add the scallions, if desired. Toss the potatoes gently. Top with the eggs, if desired, and garnish with parsley. Serve at room temperature.

Yield: 6 to 8 servings

Salatit Shawki

RAW ARTICHOKE SALAD

Artichokes are the unopened flower buds of a perennial thistle that belongs to the daisy family. While getting to the artichoke hearts involves a bit of labor, the rest of the preparation for this salad is quite simple. It is best to use fresh artichokes, since the recipe sings with the flavors of nutty artichokes and zesty lemon. Frozen or canned artichokes cannot supply the crunch that makes this salad so wonderful.

¼ cup lemon juice concentrate combined with 4 cups cold water for acidulated water

2 artichokes

¼ cup freshly squeezed lemon juice (1 to 2 lemons)

2 tablespoons extra-virgin olive oil

1 teaspoon kosher salt

1. Put the bowl of acidulated water near the work area, and begin to trim the artichokes. First cut off the top of an artichoke to flatten, then remove all the tough bracts (outer leaves). Trim the woody end of the stem and carefully peel the skin around it. Cut the artichoke in half lengthwise and remove the inner hairy choke, leaving the soft, edible bracts attached to the artichoke.

2. Cut the artichoke heart lengthwise into ¼-inch slices. Put the slices in the acidulated water to prevent the artichoke meat from discoloring. Trim and slice the second artichoke. Remove the artichoke slices from the water and transfer them to a medium bowl. Add the fresh lemon juice, olive oil, and salt. Toss gently and let stand for 30 minutes before serving. This dish will last for about 3 days in the refrigerator.

Yield: 3 to 5 servings

Shawki b'Zeit

أرضي شوكي بزيت

ARTICHOKE HEARTS
IN OLIVE OIL AND LEMON MARINADE

Freshly marinated artichokes hearts are much more flavorful than the store-bought varieties. The process is rewarding and not too difficult.

When shopping for artichokes, look for ones with bracts that are tightly closed or only slightly open. Artichokes should be firm and fresh looking, with no brown or soft spots. They should also feel heavy. If the underside of an artichoke stem has small holes, do not buy it, as it may have worm damage. Squeeze it—if it sounds squeaky, it is okay. To store, place dry artichokes in a plastic bag and refrigerate for no more than 5 days.

¼ cup lemon juice concentrate mixed with 4 cups water for acidulated water

6 fresh artichokes

2 teaspoons extra-virgin olive oil

1 cup freshly squeezed lemon juice (5 to 6 lemons)

1 teaspoon kosher salt

1. Put the acidulated water near the work area and trim the artichokes. Remove the tough bracts (outer leaves), cut the artichokes in half lengthwise, and remove the hairy inner chokes, trimming the leaves close to the hearts.

2. Cut the artichoke hearts into quarters, or into sixths if they are large. After each one is cut, place it in the acidulated water, so it will not discolor.

3. When all the artichoke hearts have been prepared, remove them from the bowl and arrange them in a large glass jar.

4. Combine the olive oil, fresh lemon juice, and salt in a small glass bowl. Mix well.

5. Pour the lemon-oil marinade over the artichoke hearts, adding more oil if necessary to cover them completely. Seal the jar tightly and leave at room temperature for 2 to 3 days, rotating the jar a few times each day. Store in the refrigerator for up to 1 week. Serve the artichokes on a tray with a small amount of the brine.

Yield: 8 to 10 servings

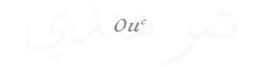

Ou^c

TAMARIND CONCENTRATE, THE SOUR SECRET TO SYRIAN COOKING

The tamarind fruit yields an intriguing flavor that appears in the cuisines of India, Southeast Asia, Persia, and Mexico. Tamarind is redolent of apricots and dates and imparts a tangy, sour flavor. It is used as a base for sauces, a condiment, a soft drink flavoring, a sweetmeat, and as a folk remedy for ailing intestines, livers, and kidneys.

Tamarind also has a connection to the Middle East. For one thing, the word "tamarind" is derived from the Arabic *tamr hindi,* meaning "Indian date." Tamarind first appeared in the *souqs* of the Levant from India via Persia around the seventh and eighth centuries. Despite its place in Persian cuisine, tamarind never gained wide acceptance in the Middle Eastern repertoire.

Aleppian Jews, however, flavor many of their dishes with tamarind concentrate, or *ou^c* (pronounced OO-r), and many still make *ou^c* from scratch, despite the widespread availability of quality concentrates in local Syrian food shops. It's important to use a good-quality tamarind; it can make or break a dish. Some *ou^c* specialists start out with 20 or 30 pounds of tamarind pulp, enough for at least several months'—if not a full year's—supply.

Ou^c is derived from the pulp found in the pods that grow from the hardy tamarind tree. Latin American, Southeast Asian, and Middle Eastern grocers sell dried tamarind pods and cakes of the pulp, intact or compressed in large sticky blocks.

To make *ou^c*, the pulp is soaked and strained to remove any seeds and plant matter, and to extract the fruit's flavor. This soaking and straining procedure is repeated up to 3 times. The tamarind liquid is reduced by half and then combined with sugar and lemon juice and boiled until viscous, nearly black, and lip-smackingly sour. It is fine to use *ou^c* sparingly, as it can last for a year in the fridge.

Ou^c is a subtler souring agent than lemon, tangier than pomegranate syrup, and has a deeper flavor than tomato. *Ou^c*, while itself rather acidic, enhances other acids, such as tomato paste, apricot, and lemon juice, rounding them out with a vibrant tang and earthiness.

For example, *bazargan* (Tangy Tamarind Bulgur Salad, page 44) combines tomato paste and *ou^c* with bulgur. In the Aleppian Jewish version of the classic Arab minced meat pie, *laham b'ajeen* (Miniature Tamarind Minced Meat Pies, page 50), the brightness of *ou^c* lifts the finger food from ordinary to heavenly. Both recipes are quite simple.

continued

Another Aleppian version of a popular dish is *yebra* (Grape Leaves Stuffed with Ground Meat and Rice, with Apricot-Tamarind Sauce, page 150), in which stuffed grape leaves are flavored with dried apricots and *ouᶜ* instead of the lemon and garlic that accent the common Eastern Mediterranean version. Aleppian Jews' penchant for tangy and fruity dishes reflects the Persian influence on their cuisine, which sets it apart from the Middle Eastern culinary mainstream. Unlike lemon-garlic stuffed grape leaves, which are almost always cooked on the stove and are often served cold, *yebra* are served hot and may be cooked slowly in the oven to allow the apricots to melt and the *ouᶜ* to absorb into the *hashu* (Aleppian Ground Meat and Rice Filling, page 136).

This recipe will yield 30 to 40 ounces of *ouᶜ*, depending on the quality of the tamarind fruit.

3 pounds tamarind pulp	1½ tablespoons freshly squeezed lemon juice (optional)	1½ ounces sour salt (citric acid) (3 tablespoons)
1½ pounds sugar (3¾ cups)		

1. In a large mixing bowl, submerge the tamarind pulp in about 6 cups water. Cover and soak for 6 to 8 hours, or overnight. After the pulp has soaked, while keeping it in the water, pull it apart to make a mashlike, pulpy, soft mixture.

2. Line the bottom portion of a colander with cheesecloth. Fit the colander over a large, nonreactive mixing bowl. Strain the tamarind pulp by pressing it firmly against the surface of the colander, squeezing to extract as much liquid as possible. Pick out any plant matter and pits from the liquid, and set it aside.

3. Place the strained pulp in a clean mixing bowl, and submerge in fresh water. Work to pull it apart again, then strain and reserve the liquid. Repeat this process a third time.

4. Combine all the reserved tamarind liquid and strain through a cheesecloth or fine-mesh strainer. Discard the pulp.

5. Pour the tamarind liquid into a large saucepan and bring to a boil over high heat. Reduce the heat to low and simmer until the liquid is reduced by half. Add the sugar, lemon juice, if desired, and sour salt to the tamarind liquid. Increase the heat to medium and boil slowly, stirring frequently with a wooden spoon, until the mixture has a silky consistency akin to a dark, thick syrup. Let the mixture cool thoroughly, then pour it into a glass jar.

❧ Note ❧
Store the sealed jar of *ou^c* in a cool, dry place for up to 1 year.

Yield: 30 to 40 ounces (4 cups)

Bazargan

TANGY TAMARIND BULGUR SALAD

The name of this dish is derived from the Persian word for "merchant," a common occupation for Jews in the Ottoman Levant. *Bazargan* may very well have been introduced to Aleppo from Persia by a returning businessman or by a Persian émigré family. Now it is a fixture on the Aleppian Sabbath lunch table, alongside the usual *hummus* and *tabbouleh*. *Bazargan* is remarkably easy to make. After the short time it takes for the bulgur to meld with the other ingredients, the dish is ready to serve.

1 cup fine bulgur (cracked wheat), soaked in hot water for 15 minutes and drained

1 small onion, finely chopped

Juice of 1 lemon (about 3 tablespoons)

2 tablespoons tomato paste

8 tablespoons *ouᶜ* (tamarind concentrate, page 41), homemade or store-bought

5 tablespoons vegetable oil

½ teaspoon Aleppo pepper, or ¼ teaspoon crushed red pepper

2 teaspoons ground cumin

Kosher salt

½ cup chopped walnuts or pine nuts (optional)

Chopped fresh flat-leaf parsley for garnish

1. Put the bulgur in a medium mixing bowl. Add the onion, lemon juice, tomato paste, *ouᶜ*, vegetable oil, Aleppo pepper, cumin, and salt to taste. Combine well. Let the mixture rest for 30 minutes, or until the bulgur is al dente, "firm to the bite."

2. If desired, add the walnuts or pine nuts shortly before serving so that they do not become soggy. Garnish with the parsley and serve.

Yield: 4 servings

﴾ Aleppo Pepper ﴿

Aleppo pepper is grown exclusively in the Levant and Turkey. The pepper is seeded, sun-dried, and pulverized. The rich red hue of Aleppo pepper stands out in the palette of Middle Eastern spices.

Aleppo pepper is a relatively mild member of the chile pepper family. The heat of Aleppo pepper comes in at 10,000 units in the Scoville index of pepper heat (compared to 20,000 for crushed red pepper and 40,000 for cayenne). Aleppo pepper is well suited to the cuisine of its region. It imparts a subtle, lingering heat that supports the soft and sour flavors in many Aleppian dishes. The spice is much prized by Aleppian cooks because, unlike fiercer chiles commonly used elsewhere, it does not overpower the core flavors of a dish or throw them off balance.

Aleppo pepper is not widely available in the West. It is worth tracking down at Middle Eastern groceries, gourmet shops, and online spice merchants. Nonetheless, a blend of 3 parts paprika to 1 part cayenne is an adequate substitute. You can also use ½ teaspoon of crushed red pepper for every teaspoon of Aleppo pepper called for in a recipe.

Salat Shwandar Maslook

TAMARIND BEET-ONION SALAD

Beets were eaten plain in Aleppo, and it is still a common sight to see freshly peeled whole cooked beets on the lunch or dinner table. The tamarind paste in this recipe is a tart contrast to the beets, making for a very interesting sweet-and-savory combination. Look for smooth, hard, round beets for this recipe. A deep red color indicates quality. Yellow or orange beets can be used as well.

6 beets (2 pounds),
    peeled and stems trimmed

1 tablespoon extra-virgin olive oil

3 tablespoons freshly squeezed
    lemon juice

2 tablespoons *ouᶜ* (tamarind concentrate,
    page 41), homemade or store-bought

1 tablespoon ground cumin

½ teaspoon Aleppo pepper,
    or ¼ teaspoon crushed red pepper

1 teaspoon kosher salt

½ cup finely chopped fresh flat-leaf parsley

½ small onion, chopped (about ¼ cup)

1. Put the beets in a large saucepan, cover with water, and bring to a boil. Reduce the heat to low, and simmer for 20 minutes, or until the beets are fork-tender. (Larger beets may be sliced in half before cooking to speed up the cooking time.)

2. Drain the beets and "shock" in a bowl of ice and cold water to stop the cooking process. Drain again. Cut into ½-inch cubes and transfer to a medium mixing bowl.

3. To make the dressing, combine the olive oil, lemon juice, *ouᶜ*, cumin, Aleppo pepper, and salt in a small mixing bowl and mix well.

4. Pour the dressing over the beets. Add the parsley and onions and give it a stir. Refrigerate until ready to serve.

Yield: 4 to 6 servings

Fūl Medammas

WARM FAVA BEANS

Fūl (pronounced "fool"), which is Arabic for fava beans, is a favorite Sunday morning dish among Aleppian Jews and a fixture of the post–Yom Kippur table (see page 354). This dish is a Middle Eastern classic that originated in Egypt. In fact, *medammas* is Coptic for "buried," which suggests the original preparation required the beans to be buried in a pot. Although there are countless ways of embellishing *fūl,* the basic recipe remains the same.

There are different kinds of fava beans, which require different cooking times depending on their size, so you must make sure you use the right kind. The only fava bean used for making this dish is the small round one called *fūl hamman* ("bath fava"). The beans should be cooked until soft; there should be no "bite" to them.

2 cups dried fava beans, soaked overnight or for 6 to 8 hours and drained, or two 16-ounce cans fava beans, drained

Dressing:

3 tablespoons extra-virgin olive oil

¼ cup freshly squeezed lemon juice (1 to 2 lemons)

1 teaspoon ground cumin

¼ teaspoon Aleppo pepper, or ⅛ teaspoon crushed red pepper

½ teaspoon kosher salt

1 bunch fresh flat-leaf parsley, chopped

2 hard-boiled eggs, sliced or chopped, or chopped scallions for garnish

1. Put the soaked beans in a medium saucepan, with enough water to cover them completely. Bring to a boil over high heat. Reduce the heat to low and simmer for 1 hour, or until the beans are soft but not mushy. Drain and transfer to a medium mixing bowl. Rinse the beans with cool water in a strainer and drain again.

2. To make the dressing, combine the olive oil, lemon juice, cumin, Aleppo pepper, salt, and parsley in a small mixing bowl and mix thoroughly. Pour over the beans and toss. Garnish the beans with the eggs or scallions.

Yield: 4 to 6 servings

Laham b'Ajeen لحم بعجين

MINIATURE TAMARIND MINCED MEAT PIES

In Aleppo, these pies were originally prepared on 10-inch rounds of bread and taken to the *furn*—the local communal oven. These large, pizzalike meat pies were prepared as a wrap and were considered a traditional fast-food snack. In Aleppo, the blessing over bread was always said on large *laham b'ajeen* because of its greater dough content.

The bite-size *laham b'ajeen* in this recipe were introduced by the Brooklyn Aleppian Jewish community and were never prepared in the old country. Nowadays, *laham b'ajeen* may be as small as 2 inches in diameter with one lone pine nut in the middle.

Laham b'ajeen freezes nicely raw or cooked and is a staple in every Syrian woman's freezer, especially Grandma's. Children from the age of one are introduced to *laham b'ajeen* and love its tangy-sour flavor, which makes it a favorite for life.

Dough:

4 cups all-purpose flour

1 teaspoon kosher salt

2½ teaspoons active dry yeast, dissolved in ¼ cup warm water

2 tablespoons vegetable oil

Meat topping:

2 pounds ground beef

3 onions, finely chopped and squeezed of excess liquid

One 6-ounce can tomato paste

Juice of 2 lemons (about 6 tablespoons)

2 cups *ouᶜ* (tamarind concentrate, page 41), homemade or store-bought

1 tablespoon ground allspice

1 tablespoon kosher salt

½ cup vegetable oil

Pine nuts for garnish (optional)

1. To make the dough, combine the flour and salt in a large mixing bowl. Add the dissolved yeast and mix well. Add the vegetable oil and mix again. Gradually add 1 cup of warm water, kneading until a soft dough is formed.

2. Cover with a clean towel and let rest in a place warmer than room temperature for 1 hour.

3. Preheat the oven to 350°F.

4. To make the topping, combine the beef, onion, tomato paste, lemon juice, *ouᶜ*, allspice, and salt. Mix well.

5. Retrieve the dough and separate into 4 pieces. On a slightly floured surface, roll each piece of dough until it is as thin as possible, without tearing it. Using a cookie cutter, or anything similar, cut dough into small rounds, 3 to 4 inches in diameter.

6. Place the rounds on greased baking sheets that have been brushed generously with vegetable oil. Spread a heaping tablespoon of meat filling on each round, pressing it in firmly.

7. Bake the pies for 15 to 20 minutes, or until the crust is golden brown. Garnish with pine nuts, if desired.

Yield: 4 dozen meat pies

Kibbeh Nabelsieh

GOLDEN GROUND MEAT–FILLED BULGUR SHELLS

Kibbeh nabelsieh is one of the great classics of Syrian cuisine: crisp, toothsome, golden torpedo-shaped bulgur shells filled with delicately spiced ground beef (*tadbileh*), or other savory fillings. The word *kibbeh* or *kubeba* means "dome" in Arabic. These rounded delights are a staple of the *maza* table. Some *sebbits*, which are festive Sabbath luncheons, do not truly begin until the tray of *kibbeh* is passed around. Do as the *sebbit* revelers do: bite off the top of the *kibbeh* and squeeze the juice of a lemon wedge into the filling, or swipe the *kibbeh* into a bowl of *tehineh* (Sesame Spread, page 26).

While eating *kibbeh* is a simple pleasure, making it from scratch is a difficult skill to master. In fact, a certain mystique is attached to the art of *kibbeh*-making. The women of Aleppo were renowned throughout the Middle East for their skill in shaping the delicate shell. In the olden days, it was said that a woman could not marry unless she could make *kibbeh,* and women with especially long, slender fingers held much promise as *kibbeh*-makers. A woman's *kibbeh*-making ability was the touchstone by which she was evaluated as a hostess and homemaker; a praiseworthy *"kibbeh* finger" represented the highest form of refinement and elegance.

Though the busy women of today are able to use food processors instead of pounding the meat and rice with a mortar and pestle, they are still devoted to making *kibbeh* in all its variations. Grandmothers, mothers, and daughters stand together by a work surface, communing with one another and sharing family news as they each play their part in the *kibbeh*-making process.

In earlier times, it was a mark of achievement to make the biggest *kibbehs* possible (some could be as long as 6 to 10 inches), but nowadays they are generally bite-size (3 to 4 inches). One *"kibbeh* line" of two to three expert women can make about 300 stuffed shells in an hour. For those looking for a simpler dish incorporating the same ingredients, consider *kibbeh bil sanieh* (Baked Bulgur–Ground Meat Pie, page 171).

Because *kibbeh* merely refers to the shape of a food, you will encounter more delicious renditions of *kibbeh* in the pages ahead, such as *kibbeh neye* (Raw Beef–Bulgur Patties page 63), *kibbeh neye w'khidrawat* (Vegetarian Bulgur Patties, page 64), *kibbeh hamdah* (Lemon-Mint Broth with Mixed Vegetables and Syrian Meatballs, page 97), *kibbeh b'fettair* (Mushrooms and Sautéed Meatballs, page 161), *bizeh b'kibbeh* (Green Peas with Allspice and Meat, page 158), *kibbeh b'garaz* (Sweet Cherry–Stuffed Beef Slices, page 166), *kibbeh kabir* (Aleppian Soup Meatballs, page 105), and *kibbeh yahniyeh* (Beef-Bulgur Dumplings, page 105). Yes, that's quite a lot of *kibbeh,* but what can we say? Syrians are crazy about their meat and want it every which way!

3 cups fine bulgur (cracked wheat), rinsed in cold water and drained	2 tablespoon ground cumin	1 tablespoon kosher salt
1 cup unsalted *matzah* meal	2 teaspoons paprika	3 tablespoons vegetable oil, plus additional for frying
1 cup all-purpose flour, plus more for dusting the work surface	1½ tablespoons Aleppo pepper, or 1½ teaspoons crushed red pepper	3 pounds *tadbileh* filling (page 55)

1. Combine the bulgur, *matzah* meal, flour, cumin, paprika, Aleppo pepper, salt, and the 3 tablespoons of vegetable oil in a large bowl. Mix by hand or with a spatula. Gradually add 2¾ to 3 cups lukewarm water in a thin stream as needed, stirring the mixture to form a moist but firm dough.

2. Shape the dough into small balls about 1 inch in diameter. Burrow your index finger into the middle of each ball, and, with your other hand, shape the dough into a long, hollow torpedolike shape, about 3 inches long. Keep a small bowl of water nearby to moisten your hands to prevent sticking. Cover dough with a towel while working. Add additional water in small increments if needed to maintain a moist firm dough.

3. Using a narrow spoon, such as an iced-tea spoon, fill the bulgur shell with the *tadbileh* filling. Pinch the rim of the filled shell closed, forming a blunt point. Make sure that no meat is attached to the outside of the shell, as it is a mark of an inelegant *kibbeh*. At this point, you can freeze the *kibbehs* in a dish or plastic container for later use (see Note).

4. In a deep fryer or a hot pan filled with 2 to 3 inches of oil, fry the *kibbehs* over medium-high heat for 3 to 4 minutes, or until golden, turning to cook evenly. If pan-frying, use a splatter guard to prevent hot oil from burning your skin.

5. If there is any leftover dough, do not throw it away. You can simply add 1 chopped onion and flatten the pieces into silver dollar–sized pancakes. These are called *urus*. Fry these in the same oil for delicious bite-size treats that kids go crazy for.

❧ *Note* ❧

Between steps 3 and 4, be sure to place the *kibbehs* on paper towels to absorb any excess water that will cause splattering when you fry the frozen *kibbehs*. The *kibbehs* will be crispier and absorb less oil.

Kibbeh shells can also be formed by using a KitchenAid grinder attachment in combination with a food shaping attachment called the Gourmet Matic, which may be found in Middle Eastern groceries and cookware stores.

Yield: 4 to 5 dozen kibbehs

Tadbileh — Spiced Ground Beef Filling

1 large onion, chopped (about 1 cup)	1 pound ground beef	¼ cup pine nuts
1 tablespoon vegetable oil	1 teaspoon ground allspice	1 teaspoon kosher salt

In a medium skillet, sauté the onion in the vegetable oil over medium-high heat until soft, about 3 minutes. Add the meat and continue sautéing, constantly breaking it up with a fork, for about 9 minutes, or until all but 1 teaspoon of the liquid has been absorbed and the meat has fully browned. Let cool. Add the allspice, pine nuts, and salt.

Yield: 1 pound (8 cups) of filling

❧ *Variation* ❧

Pomegranates are used in the *tadbileh* filling on special occasions. Substitute 1 cup pomegranate seeds for the pine nuts and add to the cooled mixture. When in season, pomegranates are seeded and stored in the refrigerator. (In the freezer they become soft and watery.) When buying pomegranates, make sure the tops are intact and the outsides are a nice bright red with no brown spots. If you buy good-quality pomegranates, they will keep in the refrigerator for up to 2 months.

A plate of Kibbeh Nabelsieh
*(Golden Ground Meat–Filled
Bulgur Shells, page 53)*

Bastel

GROUND MEAT–FILLED SEMOLINA HALF-MOONS

Aleppian Jews make savory filled pastries in both round and crescent shapes. The traditional shape for meat-filled *bastels* is round so that everyone can distinguish the pastry from the crescent-shaped *sambousak* (Buttery Cheese-Filled Sesame Pastries, page 212) and avoid eating a dairy pastry and a meat-filled one at the same sitting, which is against *kashrut* laws.

Regular semolina (*smead*) is used to make spongy cakes or fillings, whereas fine semolina (*firkha*) is used instead of flour to make *sambousaks*, *mamounieh* (Semolina Pudding with Butter, page 281), and *eras b'ajweh* (Date-Filled Crescents, page 268), to give them a light and crumbly texture.

Filling:

1 large onion, finely chopped (about 1 cup)

2 tablespoons vegetable oil

1 pound ground beef

½ teaspoon Aleppo pepper, or ¼ teaspoon crushed red pepper

½ teaspoon ground allspice

½ teaspoon ground cinnamon

½ teaspoon kosher salt

¼ cup pine nuts

Dough:

2 cups all-purpose flour

1 cup *smead* (semolina)

½ teaspoon kosher salt

2 sticks margarine (½ pound), at room temperature

1 teaspoon vegetable oil

2 tablespoons sesame seeds

1. Preheat the oven to 350°F.

2. To make the filling, sauté the onion in the vegetable oil in a medium skillet over medium heat until transparent. Add the meat and brown, breaking it up constantly with a fork. Cook until the liquid has evaporated. Cool and add the Aleppo pepper, allspice, cinnamon, salt, and pine nuts. Set aside.

3. To make the dough, combine the flour, *smead,* and salt. Fold in the margarine and add the vegetable oil. Blend well with your fingertips. Add 2 to 3 ounces of water slowly, stirring to form a smooth dough. Knead well. The dough should be soft and moist.

4. To make crescent-shaped *bastels,* first break off a small walnut-size ball of dough and flatten it into a 3-inch round with a tortilla press lined with wax paper or plastic wrap (to prevent sticking). Use a 3-inch cookie cutter to ensure that the *bastel* is perfectly round and the exact same size as the rest. Place 1 teaspoon of filling on the circle. Fold the round

in half and press to close, making sure the edges are tightly sealed. Make the remaining *bastels* the same way.

5. Alternatively, to make round *bastels,* press your finger into a walnut-size ball of dough to form a rounded shell with one open end. The thinner you can make the shell, the better; this a tricky step that requires some practice. Fill the hollowed-out shell with about 1 teaspoon of filling. Close by pinching the shell firmly and smoothing with a little water until no crease is visible. Flute the edges for a more refined appearance. Make the remaining *bastels*.

6. Brush the top of each *bastel* with water and dredge in the sesame seeds. (At this point, you may freeze the *bastels* to bake at a later date, but be sure to store in one layer in a tightly sealed container lined with waxed paper.) Bake for about 15 minutes, or for 20 minutes if frozen, until they are slightly golden.

Yield: 4 dozen, 12 to 14 servings

Kuaisat كويسات

PISTACHIO-FILLED GROUND MEAT SHELLS

Kuaiseh means "beautiful" in Arabic, and indeed, you can be sure that these lovelies will stand out on any table. Pistachios, sometimes known as *fistou halabi* ("Aleppian pistachio") in the Middle East, are a textural foil for the soft beef shells. This rich dish is first pan-fried, then stewed, recalling one of the cooking methods that al Baghdadi documents in his thirteenth-century cookery treatise. Slice the torpedo-shaped meat shells crosswise and drizzle them with their cooking juices for a nice presentation.

Outer shell:

2 pounds ground beef

1 pound ground long-grain white rice
　(see Note)

1 teaspoon kosher salt

Filling:

1 pound ground beef

1 cup pistachios, shelled, blanched,
　and peeled (see page 310)

1 teaspoon ground allspice

1 teaspoon ground cinnamon

1 teaspoon kosher salt

¼ cup vegetable oil

One 12-ounce can tomato paste

1. To make the outer shell, use a meat grinder or the grinder attachment of a food processor to grind the ground beef again with the ground rice and salt. Repeat 2 to 3 more times.

2. To make the filling, combine the ground beef, pistachio nuts, allspice, cinnamon, and salt in a medium mixing bowl. Set aside.

3. Shape the meat-and-rice mixture from step 1 into 5-inch-long hollow, tubular shells. It is best to start with a 3-inch ball of meat. Burrow into it with your index finger as you shape the outer shell with your other hand, rotating the meat on your finger while extending it downward, forming an elongated pocket approximately 5 to 6 inches long and about ¼ inch thick. Be sure to keep your hands moist so that the meat does not stick to your fingers.

4. Stuff the meat-and-pistachio filling into the outer shells, and crimp both ends closed. It should resemble a torpedo. Refrigerate for 20 minutes.

5. In a large saucepan delicately sauté the *kuaisat* in the vegetable oil, browning on all sides for 5 to 6 minutes. Using tongs, carefully remove them to a dish.

6. To the same pot, add the tomato paste and sauté in the cooking oil for 1 to 2 minutes. Place the *kuaisat* back into the pot and add enough water to cover (approximately 2 quarts). Bring the mixture to a boil, then reduce heat to medium-low. Cook for 30 minutes, uncovered, then cover and simmer for an additional 30 minutes, or until the liquid is reduced by half. Remove from the heat and let cool.

7. When the shells are cool, cut them into ¼-inch-wide slices and pour the cooking liquid over the shells.

❧ Variations ❧

EGG-STUFFED KUAISATS
Instead of preparing the filling in step 2, prepare 10 hard-boiled eggs and remove their shells. In step 4, stuff each shell with a whole hard-boiled egg instead of meat.

GARLIC-MINT KUAISATS
In step 2, substitute ¼ cup chopped garlic and ¼ cup chopped fresh mint for the pistachio nuts, and omit the allspice and cinnamon. Skip steps 5 and 6. Instead, poach the stuffed shells in a medium saucepan filled with a mixture of 2 cups white vinegar, ½ cup sweet red wine, and 2 cups water. Simmer for 45 minutes. Continue with step 7.

❧ Note ❧
Ground rice is available at Middle Eastern groceries.

Yield: 10 kuaisats

Imwarah b'Lahmeh

GROUND MEAT–FILLED *FILLA* TRIANGLES

This delicate *maza* is a pleasant departure from its more assertively prepared meat counterparts, such as *laham b'ajeen* (Miniature Tamarind Minced Meat Pies, page 50) and *kibbeh nabelsieh* (Golden Ground Meat–Filled Bulgur Shells, page 53). The harmony of texture and flavor that comes with one's first bite of an *imwarah b'lahmeh*—the crispy, paper-thin *filla* pastry, followed by the moist filling, punctuated by allspice and pine nuts—may be one of the more unforgettable moments at a *maza* table.

Filla, which is also known as phyllo dough, is an extremely delicate puff pastry dough, which originated in Istanbul during the Ottoman Empire. Almost no one still makes *filla* at home. Fresh *filla* can be purchased from Greek or Middle Eastern bakeries and is a superior product to the frozen variety. If fresh *filla* is not available where you live, you can buy the frozen variety and keep some on hand. It is sold in sheets of varying widths, with the number of sheets per pound ranging from 20 to 24. Frozen *filla* should be defrosted in the refrigerator and opened just before using. When working with *filla,* the untended sheets should be kept stacked, covered with wax paper and a damp towel, and refrigerated so the pastry does not dry out.

---

24 sheets *filla* (about 1 pound)

2 tablespoons vegetable oil for working with *filla*

1 cup (2 sticks) margarine, melted, or additional vegetable oil for brushing the triangles

1 pound *tadbileh* (page 55)

¾ cup sesame seeds

---

1. Preheat the oven to 375°F.

2. To make the pastry, cut all the *filla* sheets with a sharp knife crosswise into 3 rectangular sections about 3 inches wide. Work with only one strip of *filla* at a time. Cover the remaining *filla* with wax paper and a damp towel.

3. Brush the strip with vegetable oil, and fold it in half lengthwise. Spoon a teaspoon of the *tadbileh* about 1 inch from a short edge. Fold one corner diagonally over the filling, forming a triangle. Continue to fold over the *filla,* making a triangle each time, until the whole strip is used.

Tuck the loose ends neatly into the space between the folds of the triangle. Repeat with the remaining strips and *tadbileh.*

4. Lay the pastries close together on baking sheets and brush with margarine or oil. Sprinkle the glazed triangles with the sesame seeds.

5. Bake for about 30 minutes, or until crisp and golden.

Yield: 72 triangles, about 30 servings

Kibbeh Neye

RAW BEEF–BULGUR PATTIES

Kibbeh neye is a Middle Eastern version of steak tartare that's traditionally eaten on Friday or for Sunday lunch—never on Saturday. These days, *kibbeh* is enjoyed year-round, but in old Aleppo, before people had refrigerators, it was eaten only in winter. The old tradition involved placing the raw meat in a big brass bowl called a *hon* or *jorn,* and pounding it with a 30-inch-long brass pestle. Today, a mortar and pestle will still work, but you may simply ask your local butcher to grind the meat 3 times (or use your own meat grinder or the grinder attachment of a food processor).

Fresh and flavorful scallions and parsley play an important part in the success of this dish. Be sure to look for scallions with bright green, moist tops, and parsley with shiny, dark green leaves and firm stems.

1 cup fine bulgur (cracked wheat), rinsed in cold water and drained

2 bunches fresh flat-leaf parsley, chopped

2 bunches scallions, minced

1 tablespoon ground cumin

1 teaspoon Aleppo pepper, or ½ teaspoon crushed red pepper

1 tablespoon kosher salt

1 tablespoon extra-virgin olive oil

One 6-ounce can tomato paste

One 28-ounce can peeled tomatoes, drained

1 pound raw lamb or lean beef, ground 3 times

1. In a large bowl, combine the bulgur, parsley, scallions, cumin, Aleppo pepper, salt, olive oil, tomato paste, and tomatoes. Blend with your hands. Fold in the ground meat and blend again.

2. Form the mixture into small torpedo shapes, about 3 inches long. Serve immediately.

❧ *Note* ❧

Because the meat is eaten raw, it is very important that it be very fresh and kept chilled while you are preparing and serving. To ensure the proper temperature during preparation, nestle the mixing bowl in a larger bowl filled with ice. Keep the bowl of meat on ice until serving time, which should be immediately after preparation.

Yield: 25 patties, about 10 to 12 servings

Kibbeh Neye w'Khidrawat

VEGETARIAN BULGUR PATTIES

Kibbeh neye w'khidrawat are a perennial favorite among Aleppian Jews because their neutral, or *pareve,* kosher designation makes them compatible with both meat and dairy dishes.

½ bunch fresh flat-leaf parsley, chopped

4 to 5 scallions, chopped

1 large red bell pepper, chopped

2 small green bell peppers, chopped

3 tomatoes, chopped

6 onions, chopped (about 3 cups)

1½ cups red lentils, washed

2 cups extra-virgin olive oil

3 cups fine bulgur (cracked wheat), rinsed in cold water and drained

One 6-ounce can tomato paste

1 tablespoon ground cumin

1 teaspoon Aleppo pepper, or ½ teaspoon crushed red pepper

1 tablespoon kosher salt

½ cup *ouᶜ* (tamarind concentrate, page 41), homemade or store-bought (optional)

1. Combine the parsley, scallions, red and green bell peppers, and tomatoes in a large bowl. Mix together with half the onions and set aside.

2. In a medium saucepan over medium-high heat, sweat the lentils in 1 cup water with the remaining onions until the lentils and onions are soft, about 10 minutes.

3. While the lentils and onions are hot, add them to the minced vegetable mixture in the bowl; add the olive oil, and stir. Add the bulgur, tomato paste, cumin, Aleppo pepper, and salt. Blend the mixture thoroughly by hand and adjust the seasoning, if necessary. Cover with foil, and refrigerate for about 30 minutes to let the mixture solidify.

4. Form the mixture into torpedo shapes, about 3 inches long. Serve the *kibbeh* at room temperature with *ouᶜ*, if desired.

Yield: 25 patties, about 10 to 12 servings

Yebra war Einab يبرق ورق عنب

ZESTY COLD STUFFED
GRAPE LEAVES

This dish is another Mediterranean staple whose reputation has suffered because of the poor quality of many of the canned versions commonly found on the shelves of Western supermarkets. Make this dish fresh, and you'll wince the next time you stroll past the stuffed grape leaves offered at luncheon and supermarket salad bars. Use fresh herbs, high-quality spices, and freshly dry-roasted pine nuts. This substantial, all-purpose item may become a regular accompaniment to your dinner salad.

In Aleppo, grape leaves were picked fresh from vines grown in the family courtyard. Today, many Aleppian Jews still grow their own vines, assuring a steady supply of grape leaves—fresh or home preserved—all year-round. If you are fortunate enough to grow your own, choose young, tender leaves.

4 onions, chopped (about 2 cups)

3 tablespoons extra-virgin olive oil

½ cup dry-roasted pine nuts
  (see page 28)

2 bunches fresh flat-leaf parsley,
  chopped

¼ teaspoon Aleppo pepper,
  or ⅛ teaspoon crushed red pepper

¼ teaspoon ground cinnamon

¼ teaspoon ground allspice

3 garlic cloves, peeled and chopped,
  plus 9 garlic cloves, peeled and whole

3 tomatoes, finely chopped
  (about 3 cups) (optional)

1 cup long-grain white rice, parboiled
  (see Note)

36 drained and rinsed preserved
  grape leaves (about one 8-ounce jar),
  or 36 fresh leaves, blanched

2 tomatoes, sliced
  (optional)

½ cup freshly squeezed lemon juice
  (2 to 3 lemons)

1 tablespoon dried mint,
  or ½ cup chopped fresh mint

½ teaspoon kosher salt

2 teaspoons sugar
  (optional)

1. To make the filling, sauté the onions in 1 tablespoon of the olive oil in a medium saucepan over low heat for 5 to 6 minutes, or until they turn translucent. Add the pine nuts, parsley, Aleppo pepper, cinnamon, allspice, the 3 chopped garlic cloves, and the chopped tomatoes, if using. Transfer the mixture to a medium bowl, add the rice, and stir to combine.

2. To stuff the leaves, pat them dry. Flatten one leaf on a cutting board, vein side up. Cut off the stem. Spread 1 heaping teaspoon of filling across 2 inches of the center of the leaf, near the stem. Fold the stem end over the filling. Fold the sides in, and roll up tightly. Squeeze gently with the palm of your hand to ensure that the filling is compacted well. Repeat with the remaining leaves. (At this point, the stuffed leaves may be frozen to be served later. They will keep for 2 weeks.)

3. To cook the stuffed grape leaves, drizzle the remaining 2 tablespoons of olive oil on the bottom of a large saucepan. Line with the sliced tomatoes, if using, and add 3 whole garlic cloves. Pack the stuffed leaves tightly in the pan.

Wedge the remaining 6 whole garlic cloves between the stuffed leaves.

4. In a small dish, combine the lemon juice, mint, salt, and sugar, if desired. Pour over the grape leaves. Add enough water to fill the pan three-quarters full.

5. Place a heat-proof plate on top of the stuffed leaves to weigh them down. Bring the liquid to a boil over medium-high heat, and then reduce the heat to low. Cover the pot and simmer for at least 45 minutes, or until most of the liquid is absorbed. Let the leaves cool in the pan. The leaves can be served at room temperature or chilled.

❧ *Note* ❧

To parboil rice, use ½ the amount of water than would ordinarily be needed to fully cook the rice. For 1 cup of rice you would use ¾ cup water to parboil.

Yield: 36 stuffed grape leaves, 12 to 14 servings

Mehalallat

ASSORTED VEGETABLES
PICKLED IN BRINE

A rainbow selection of pickles is a fixture on the *maza* table. The Aleppian Jewish tradition of stuffing any vegetable that can be stuffed also applies to pickling. The practice of pickling harks back to the premodern practice of preserving harvested vegetables in salty brine so that they would last as long as possible. Today, pickles satisfy the desire of all Aleppian Jews to have something to munch on while waiting for the "real" food to reach the table. Pickles are a typical lunchtime *maza* dish as well as an accompaniment to the Syrian breakfast of bread, cheese, olives, and vegetables. These pickle recipes are common in the Levant, where cooks are fond of using beets to color cauliflowers and turnips pink. The methods described here are not for long-term storage. If properly made, these pickles should keep for about a month under refrigeration.

Pickling is a relatively simple process, but before starting, follow these simple hints:

· Use firm vegetables, free of blemishes.
· Use white vinegar with 4 to 5 percent acidity, or apple cider vinegar, which is less pungent in flavor and has added health benefits (it's a powerful detoxifying and purifying agent).
· Use kosher salt, not the iodized kind.
· Measure the brine ingredients with care. Insufficient salt results in cloudy pickles, while too much salt or vinegar produces tough or shriveled vegetables.

Brine:

3 cups spring or filtered water

1 cup white or apple cider vinegar

¼ cup kosher salt

½ teaspoon Aleppo pepper
or ¼ teaspoon crushed red pepper

For pink pickles (use 1 gallon glass jar):

1 large head green cabbage, cut into eight chunks, or 1 cauliflower, cut into small florets, or 2 pounds turnips, trimmed and sliced in thirds, ¼-inch width (about 6 turnips; use one 2-quart container)

2 to 3 beet slices for color

For green pickles (use 1 gallon glass jar):

2 pounds green bell peppers, seeded and cut into 1-inch vertical strips (about 6 peppers), or 2 pounds whole Kirby cucumbers (about 6 Kirby cucumbers; use one 2-quart container)

6 garlic cloves, halved

1 carrot, chopped in ¼-inch diagonals

1 rib celery, chopped in ½-inch diagonals

1. Combine all brine ingredients in a lidded glass jar. Brine recipe is for a 1-quart container. Double the recipe for a 2-quart container. Triple brine recipe if using a gallon container.

2. Fill wide-mouthed glass jars with ingredients for green or pink pickles. Pour the brine in, completely covering the vegetables. Close the jar tightly. Glass-topped jars with rubber seals are excellent. For other jars, place a square of aluminum foil over wax paper on the mouth of the jar and secure with a rubber band. Then top it with the lid. Leave the pickles in a dark place for at least 24 hours, then refrigerate. For a crisper batch of pickles, leave them out only 1 day before refrigerating. They should be ready to eat after 4 to 6 days. The pickles will keep for 2 to 3 weeks in the refrigerator.

❧ Note ☙

To enrich the flavor of green pickles, top off a jar with 1 tablespoon vegetable oil or olive oil.

Yield: 1½ gallons of pickles

Mehalal Banjan

BABY EGGPLANTS PICKLED IN ALEPPIAN BRINE

The intriguing beauty of the eggplant—from its curvy, pear shape to its shiny, smooth skin—is indisputable. Eggplants come in a variety of sizes (from tiny to large), shapes (from oval to spherical), and colors (deep purple, pale violet, white, or green). They are grown in many places, including the United States, Italy, China, Japan, India, and Thailand. The daintier varieties, such as Japanese eggplants, tend to have a mild flavor and fewer seeds than the typical large variety. For this recipe, it is essential to start off with tiny, firm, farm-fresh eggplants; their calyxes (the leafy crowns) should be bright green. When the pickled eggplants are cut open, they are usually slightly pink at their core.

1 dozen baby eggplants, stems trimmed, leaving leafy crowns intact

Brine:

2 ribs celery, chopped into 2-inch pieces

4 unpeeled garlic cloves, halved

½ cup white vinegar

½ teaspoon Aleppo pepper, or ¼ teaspoon crushed red pepper

½ cup kosher salt

1. Pierce each eggplant with a fork in two places. In a large pot, bring 3 cups water to a boil over high heat. Carefully put the eggplants in the boiling water and cook, uncovered, for 5 minutes or until tender. Drain and rinse with cold water to cool.

2. To make the brine, combine 3 cups water, celery, garlic, vinegar, Aleppo pepper, and salt in a large bowl.

3. Put the eggplants into several jars. Pour the brine over the eggplants, filling each jar to the brim. Cover tightly (see step 2, page 69). The pickles will be ready in 3 to 4 days and will last 2 months in the refrigerator.

Yield: 12 to 15 pickles (1 ½ gallons)

Mehalal Lemouneh

PICKLED LEMONS

Pickled lemons are used as a condiment to add a tantalizing flavor to Syrian dishes. Today, these softened lemons are sold in jars, but in the old days, they were sold in bulk by the spice merchants in the grand *souqs* of Aleppo. You can make them at home; they'll be ready to serve in a few weeks and will last a year. The lemons should be firm and plump with shiny skins.

8 lemons

5 tablespoons kosher salt

1 teaspoon paprika (optional)

1 cup freshly squeezed lemon juice (approximately 5 lemons; optional)

½ cup extra-virgin olive oil

1. Cut the lemons lengthwise three-quarters of the way down the fruit. Alternatively, cut the lemons lengthwise into ¼-inch segments. Transfer to a medium bowl.

2. Sprinkle 2 tablespoons of the salt liberally over the lemons and toss. Nestle a plate underneath a colander. Put the lemons in the colander. Let stand overnight or for 8 hours.

3. Pack the lemons tightly in layers in a glass jar, sprinkling the remaining 3 tablespoons of salt and the paprika, if desired, between each layer.

4. Add the lemon juice, if using, and enough water to nearly fill the jar. Top with the olive oil.

5. Leave at room temperature, shaking the jar daily. See step 2, page 69, for pickling process. After 2 to 3 weeks, the lemons should be ready to eat. Stored in the refrigerator, they will last up to 1 year and will continue to pickle. Rinse before using, if desired.

Yield: 24 pickles (1 quart)

Zeitoon زيتون

ASSORTED SYRIAN OLIVES

In the Levant, olives have always been a fundamental element of the landscape and the table. Syria is the original home of the olive tree, where it has been cultivated for thousands of years as an important food source. The trees grow to be quite old—more than a thousand years, in some cases—and continue bearing fruit into old age. The olive fruit is harvested in early autumn and processed for storage.

Olives appear on the Aleppian Jewish table at almost every meal, including breakfast. In Aleppo, families would cure between 30 and 40 pounds for their annual household use. Whole families would work for a few nights after the harvest to crack the green olives with the bottom of a heavy *halwan* pot. The olives were then cured in glass jars.

Today, the fresh olives required for this recipe may be available at farmers' markets or gourmet shops.

1 pound fresh green or black olives

1 tablespoon kosher salt

½ cup extra-virgin olive oil
(if using green olives)

1 lemon, cut lengthwise into quarters
(if using green olives)

½ cup freshly squeezed lemon juice
(about 3 lemons; if using green olives)

2 ribs celery, cut into 2-inch pieces
(if using green olives)

1 long hot green chile pepper
(if using green olives)

1. To prepare and preserve green olives (*zeitoon akhdar*), first crack the olives with the flat side of a chef's knife or the bottom of a small heavy pot. Soak the olives in a *tishet* (large metal bowl) filled with water, covered, for 3 to 4 days, changing the water daily. Drain the olives and toss with the salt, ¼ cup of the oil, and 1 lemon wedge. Let the olives cure for 3 to 4 days, or until softened. Then place the olives in jars with the lemon juice, celery, chile pepper, remaining ¼ cup oil, and the remaining lemon wedges.

2. To prepare and preserve black olives (*zeitoon aswan*), soak in a *tishet* filled with water and a generous amount of coarse salt for 7 to 10 days to extract the bitterness. This process will cause the olives to release their water. The olives will keep in the refrigerator for 2 to 3 weeks. When serving, marinate the olives lightly in extra-virgin olive oil.

❧ Variation ☙

Another alternative is to cure the olives in olive oil. First, soak the olives in salt water for 3 to 4 days, then cover with extra-virgin olive oil. This method will take no more than 2 weeks.

❧ Note ☙

Garlic, Aleppo pepper, thyme, lemon slices, vinegar, or bitter orange juice may be added during the curing process.

Kibbeh Hamdah
(Lemon-Mint Broth with Mixed
Vegetables and Syrian Meatballs,
page 97)

Khidrawat wa Shurba
خضروات وشوربة

LEGUMES, VEGETABLES, AND SOUPS

As a result of Aleppo's geographical location in the heart of the Middle East and its status as a major center of trade for centuries, it benefited from the wealth of produce native to the surrounding regions. At the height of the harvest season, Aleppo's markets were awash in an assortment of vegetables. As a result, many Syrian dishes involve the simple preparation of fresh vegetables. Favoring a hearty approach, Aleppians often stew their vegetables, adding herbs and spices to enhance their unique flavors.

The soups you will find in this section are generally light. Many of them are summertime fare, such as *rai'yeb b'labaniyeh* (Chilled Yogurt and Cucumber Soup, page 110) and *lebneh w'spanekh* (Spinach-Yogurt Soup, page 111).

The reason for this is that many Syrian meat and poultry dishes already have a stewlike quality to them.

In Aleppo, it was imperative to arrive at the market early in the morning, not only to get the pick of the best vegetables, but also to get back home in time to make a delicious soup for supper. Farmers from Aleppo's fertile hinterland would crowd Aleppo's huge market with their wicker baskets full of turnips, okra, gourds, and artichokes. Long before the age of organic agriculture, it was common to have chemical-free vegetables that had been nestled in the ground only hours before coming to market. Today, many Aleppian cooks prefer to use organic produce for its health benefits and superior taste.

الوجبات

LEGUME, VEGETABLE, AND SOUP RECIPES

Fassoulieh فاصوليا

GREAT NORTHERN BEANS
STEWED IN TOMATO SAUCE

This dish is a fixture on the Aleppian Sabbath dinner table. The beans used in this dish are small white ones. Like all dried beans, they need to be covered with cold water and soaked overnight before draining and cooking.

2 garlic cloves, chopped
   (about 1 teaspoon)

1 onion, chopped (about ½ cup)

2 tablespoons vegetable oil

1 pound flanken or beef chuck in 2-inch
   cubes, or 3 beef marrow bones

1 cup dried Great Northern beans,
   soaked overnight or for 6 to 8 hours
   and drained, or 2½ cups canned
   Great Northern beans, drained

2 tablespoons tomato paste

½ teaspoon ground cinnamon

¾ teaspoon kosher salt

½ teaspoon white pepper
   (optional)

1. In a medium saucepan, sauté the garlic and onion in the vegetable oil over medium heat for 4 to 6 minutes, or until the onions are translucent. Add the meat to the saucepan and brown for about 2 minutes.

2. Add 2 quarts water to the saucepan. Reduce the heat to low and simmer, uncovered, for 1 hour, or until the meat is tender. Skim off any foam that rises to the top.

3. Add the beans, tomato paste, cinnamon, salt, and white pepper, if using. Raise the heat to medium-high and bring to a boil. Reduce the heat to low and simmer, covered, for 2 hours. Cook longer if a thicker consistency is desired. You can also finish this dish in a preheated 350°F oven for the final 30 minutes.

Yield: 8 to 10 servings

Fawleh

BRAISED STRING BEANS
WITH ALLSPICE AND GARLIC

This dish is traditionally cooked on a stove top—as are most hot dishes in the Syrian repertoire—which reminds us that Aleppian Jewish home cooking as we know it evolved without the benefit of ovens. Even after generations in the modernized Western kitchen, many Syrian women refuse to cook in ovens, preferring instead the more familiar gas-burning stove tops, so they can maintain more control over the heat, especially for dishes such as *riz halabieh* (Classic Aleppian Rice, page 116), with its *a'hata* (crispy golden rice crust), and the many varieties of *mehshi* (stuffed vegetable dishes), which simmer for a long time.

6 garlic cloves, chopped
   (about 1 tablespoon)

2 tablespoons vegetable oil

3 pounds string beans, ends trimmed

1 teaspoon ground allspice

1 teaspoon kosher salt

¼ teaspoon ground cinnamon (optional)

½ teaspoon white pepper (optional)

One 6-ounce can tomato paste

In a medium saucepan, sauté the garlic in the vegetable oil over medium heat for 2 minutes, or until soft. Add the string beans, allspice, salt, 2 cups water, and, if desired, cinnamon and white pepper. Dollop the tomato paste by the heaping tablespoon over the surface of the cooking liquid. Do not stir. By letting the tomato paste remain undistributed, its thick consistency allows for maximum adherence to the string beans as the cooking liquid reduces.

Bring to a boil. Reduce the heat to low and simmer, covered, for 30 minutes.

❧ *Note* ❧
Some people braise the beans in a 350°F oven for 2 hours after simmering so that the beans are exquisitely tender.

Yield: 10 servings

Lubieh b'Lahmeh

BLACK-EYED PEAS WITH VEAL

According to Aleppian Jewish custom, *lubieh* (black-eyed peas) are eaten during the New Year festival of Rosh Hashanah. Black-eyed peas are a symbol of wealth and plenitude, so they are served (and heartily eaten) during the holiday dinner.

3 garlic cloves, chopped
(about 1½ teaspoons)

2 tablespoons vegetable oil

1 pound boneless veal, 1-inch cubes

1 teaspoon kosher salt

1 tablespoon tomato paste

2 cups fresh or frozen black-eyed peas, or
8 ounces dried black-eyed peas, soaked
overnight or for 6 to 8 hours and drained

1. In a medium saucepan, sauté the garlic in the vegetable oil over medium heat for 2 minutes, or until soft. Do not allow the garlic to change color. Add the meat to the saucepan and brown for 4 to 5 minutes, or until the meat is no longer pink. Add salt and tomato paste and stir.

2. Add peas, coating both meat and peas with tomato paste and pan drippings. If using frozen peas, add 3 cups water. With fresh peas, add 4 cups water. Increase the heat to medium-high. Bring to slight boil. Cover and reduce heat to medium-low and simmer for 1 hour, or until the meat is tender.

❧ *Note* ❧

Some people braise the beans in a 350°F oven for 2 hours after simmering so that the beans are exquisitely tender.

Yield: 8 to 10 servings

Fūl b'Zeit فول بزيت

FAVA BEANS IN OLIVE OIL

Fava beans have a much greater nutritional value than most other kinds of legumes. They are rich in protein and carbohydrates and have long been a substitute for meat. Vegetarians who discover the substantiality of this bean look for ways to incorporate it into their diets. This dish is a delicious example of how to do so with ease.

2 pounds fresh, small fava beans, ends trimmed and pods slit open (see Note)

3 tablespoons extra-virgin olive oil

1 teaspoon ground allspice

1 teaspoon ground cinnamon

½ teaspoon kosher salt

4 garlic cloves, chopped (about 2 teaspoons, optional)

1. In a medium saucepan, sauté the fava beans in the olive oil over medium heat for 2 minutes, or until crisp-tender. Add the allspice, cinnamon, salt, water to cover, and garlic, if using. Bring to a boil.

2. Reduce the heat to low, cover, and simmer for 1 hour, or until the beans are tender.

❧ *Note* ❧

If the pod of the fava bean is fibrous, remove the bean and discard the pod.

Yield: 12 servings

Fūl b'Lahmeh

FAVA BEANS WITH MEAT

This dish is a long-simmering vegetable stew, common in the repertoire of Aleppian cuisine. The meat adds a savory flavor to the fava beans. In the past, lamb was the popular choice of meat, but today, veal and flanken are more commonly used.

1 pound boneless veal, cut in 1-inch cubes, or flanken, cut in 2-inch cubes

1½ tablespoons vegetable oil

1 teaspoon ground coriander seed

1 teaspoon kosher salt

½ teaspoon Aleppo pepper, or ¼ teaspoon crushed red pepper

2 pounds fresh fava beans, ends trimmed and shelled (see Note, page 84), or frozen fava beans

4 garlic cloves, chopped (about 2 teaspoons)

1. In a medium saucepan, brown the meat in vegetable oil over medium heat for about 5 minutes. Add coriander, salt, and Aleppo pepper.

2. Add the beans, garlic, and approximately 4 cups water to cover. Bring to a boil over medium-high heat. Reduce heat to low and simmer, covered, for 1½ hours.

Yield: 6 to 8 servings

Bamia b'Mishmosh

OKRA WITH PRUNES AND APRICOTS IN TAMARIND SAUCE

In the Middle East, okra is also known as ladies' fingers because of its dainty shape. Okra is extremely popular in the Eastern Mediterranean and Middle East, where it is much smaller and more flavorful than okra grown in the West. It has a lot of small seeds and a very glutinous texture, which can be lessened considerably by soaking it in a saltwater–lemon juice solution before cooking. Small okras have small seeds and are not as tough and stringy as the larger variety. Therefore, try to buy the smallest fresh okra you can find, or buy frozen Egyptian baby okra from a Middle Eastern grocery. Before sautéing, rinse the okra quickly, so that it does not absorb too much water.

1 pound fresh small okra, stems trimmed, or frozen Egyptian baby okra (about 2 cups)

2 tablespoons vegetable oil

4 garlic cloves, chopped (about 2 teaspoons)

1 tablespoon tomato paste

3 tablespoons *ou^c* (tamarind concentrate, page 41), homemade or store-bought

Juice of 1 lemon (about 3 tablespoons)

1 teaspoon kosher salt

½ cup dried apricots

½ cup pitted prunes

1. In a medium saucepan, gently sauté the okra in the vegetable oil over medium heat for 2 to 3 minutes.

2. Add the garlic and sauté until the okra is lightly browned, 1 to 2 minutes. To prevent the okra from emitting its characteristic starchy, mucilaginous liquid, do not stir with a spoon; rather, shake the pot occasionally as it cooks.

3. Dollop the tomato paste and *ou^c* over the okra. Add 1 cup water, the lemon juice, and salt. Cover and simmer over low heat for 30 minutes, then add the apricots and prunes. Cook for 30 minutes more until okra is crisp-tender, not mushy.

Yield: 8 to 10 servings

Bamia b'Franji بامیا فرنجي

OKRA IN TOMATO SAUCE WITH MEAT

Okra is a vegetable native to Africa and was introduced to the Middle East by slave traders. When sliced and cooked slowly, its texture becomes gooey, which makes it perfect for thickening and adding body to stews. Okra has become a common ingredient in many Middle Eastern dishes, melding deliciously with tomatoes, garlic, onions, and spices. The gooey texture is less prominent when the okra is left whole and cooked simply and quickly, as in this dish.

6 garlic cloves, chopped
   (about 1 tablespoon)

2 tablespoons vegetable oil

1 pound flanken, boneless veal,
   or lamb, cut in 1¼-inch cubes

1 teaspoon kosher salt

2 pounds fresh small okra,
   stems trimmed, or frozen
   Egyptian baby okra
   (28-ounce bag; about 2 cups)

4 tomatoes, chopped, or two
   16-ounce cans diced tomatoes
   (about 4 cups)

Juice of 1 lemon (about 3 tablespoons)

1 teaspoon sugar (optional)

1. In a medium saucepan over medium heat, sauté the garlic in the vegetable oil for 2 minutes, or until soft. Add the meat and stir for 4 to 5 minutes until browned. Add the salt.

2. Add the okra, tomatoes, lemon juice, sugar (if using), and 1½ cups water. Bring to a boil. Reduce heat to simmer. Cook, covered, for 1 hour.

Yield: 8 to 10 servings

Silleq b'Lahmeh

SWISS CHARD STEWED WITH MEAT

Swiss chard, also known as silverbeet, is closely related to the beet. The vegetable has large, crinkled green leaves and thick stems, both of which are edible. The wilted leaves are used in salads or are combined with other ingredients, such as cheese, to fill savory pastries. Braised, boiled, or steamed, the stems are also delicious dressed with olive oil and lemon juice. Choose the youngest bunches with firm, inflexible stems and the smallest leaves.

This dish is commonly prepared as one of the symbolic dishes for Rosh Hashanah (the New Year festival).

1 large onion, diced (about ½ cup)

2 garlic cloves, chopped
(about 1 teaspoon)

2 ribs celery, finely chopped
(about 1 cup)

2 tablespoon vegetable oil

4 beef marrow bones (optional)

1 pound flanken, cut in 2-inch cubes

1 large bunch Swiss chard, rinsed and
coarsely chopped

One 15½-ounce can chickpeas, drained,
or ¾ cups dried chickpeas, soaked
overnight or for 6 to 8 hours
and drained

2 teaspoons ground allspice

½ teaspoon ground cinnamon

1 teaspoon kosher salt

1. Preheat the oven to 300°F.

2. In a large ovenproof saucepan, sauté the onion, garlic, and celery in the vegetable oil over medium heat for 4 to 6 minutes, or until the mixture softens.

3. Add and sauté the bones and meat. Add 2 cups water to the saucepan and cook for 5 to 6 minutes, or until lightly browned. Reduce the heat to low and simmer, covered, for 40 minutes, or until the meat is tender.

4. Add the Swiss chard, 1 cup water, chickpeas, allspice, cinnamon, and salt to the saucepan. Continue simmering for 5 minutes.

5. Transfer the saucepan to the oven and braise the Swiss chard mixture, covered, for 1½ hours. Remove the bones. Cook for an additional ½ hour.

Yield: 8 to 10 servings

Kerrateh b'Lahmeh

STEWED TRUMPET GOURD WITH MEAT

The trumpet gourd in this recipe adds a great deal of substance to the dish. A bowl of *kerrateh b'lahmeh,* eaten with Syrian flatbread, is more than enough for a meal.

1 onion, diced (about ½ cup)

2 garlic cloves, chopped
(about 1 teaspoon)

2 ribs celery, finely chopped
(about 1 cup)

2 tablespoons extra-virgin olive oil

4 beef marrow bones

1 pound flanken, cut in 2-inch cubes

1 trumpet gourd
(approximately 3 pounds),
peeled and cut into 1-inch dice

One 15½-ounce can chickpeas,
drained, or ¾ cup dried chickpeas,
soaked overnight or for 6 to 8 hours
and drained

2 teaspoons ground allspice

½ teaspoon ground cinnamon

1 teaspoon kosher salt

1. Preheat the oven to 300°F.

2. In a medium ovenproof saucepan, sauté the onion, garlic, and celery in the olive oil over medium heat for 4 to 6 minutes, or until the mixture softens.

3. Add the marrow bones, meat, and 2 cups water to the saucepan. Bring to a boil, reduce the heat to low, and simmer, uncovered, for 40 minutes, or until the meat is tender.

4. Add the gourd, chickpeas, allspice, cinnamon, and salt to the saucepan. Continue simmering for 5 minutes.

5. Transfer the saucepan to the oven, covered, and braise the gourd mixture for 1½ hours. Remove the bones before serving.

Yield: 8 to 10 servings

Banjan Meqli

FRIED EGGPLANT SLICES

It is a very old Jewish tradition in many countries to serve fried eggplant slices cold or at room temperature at the Sabbath lunch. This dish is very good as it is, but you might like to add a squeeze of fresh lemon juice or a sprinkle of chopped flat-leaf parsley after the eggplant is fried.

3 eggplants (about 3¾ pounds), cut crosswise into ⅓-inch-thick slices

3 tablespoons kosher salt

Vegetable oil for frying

1. Lay the eggplant slices on paper towels and sprinkle the salt over them. Let stand for about 30 minutes, then pat the eggplant slices dry. As a result of this process, the eggplants will be crispier when fried.

2. Place a 10-inch skillet over medium-high heat. Pour enough oil into the skillet to fill it halfway. The oil will be ready for frying when it sizzles upon contact with a drop of water. Be careful, however—if the oil is too hot, the outer surface of the eggplant slices will brown before the interior flesh is fully cooked.

3. Place a single layer of eggplant slices in the oil. Fry for about 1 minute, then turn them over and fry for 1 minute more. They should be slightly brown. Remove the slices with a slotted spoon and drain on paper towels. Repeat with the remaining slices, adding more oil if necessary. Drain on paper towels.

Yield: 8 to 10 servings

Banjan Meqli
(*Fried Eggplant Slices, page 91*)

Lift Meqli

FRIED TURNIP SLICES

The unique taste of fried turnip slices brings to mind the combined taste and texture of roasted potatoes and carrots. These turnips are absolutely delicious when eaten hot from the skillet with fresh Syrian flatbread.

¾ cup vegetable oil

6 turnips, ends trimmed, and cut into
¼-inch slices

1. Place a 10-inch skillet over medium-high heat. Pour enough vegetable oil in the skillet to fill it halfway.

2. The oil will be ready for frying when it sizzles upon contact with a drop of water. When the oil is hot, add a batch of turnip slices in a single layer. Fry the turnips until they are slightly brown, about 1 minute on each side. Remove with a slotted spoon and drain on paper towels. Serve soon after frying.

Yield: 8 to 10 servings

'Arnabeet Meqli

FRIED CAULIFLOWER FLORETS

Cauliflower is a popular vegetable in the Aleppian kitchen. It is enjoyed in many forms—fried, pickled, or breaded—as an addition to the traditional Thursday night dairy meal. This dish is sometimes called *semak bela adam* ("fish without bones") because the cauliflower's tender white flesh tastes wonderful when fried.

1 cup all-purpose flour

1 teaspoon kosher salt

1 medium cauliflower, trimmed and cut into florets (2½ to 3 cups)

2 eggs beaten with 2 tablespoons water for an egg wash

1 cup vegetable oil

1. Combine the flour and salt in a shallow bowl.

2. In a medium saucepan, parboil the cauliflower in 3 cups salted water over high heat until almost tender (about 3 minutes). Drain on paper towels until completely dry.

3. Dip each floret in the egg wash and then dredge in the flour mixture.

4. Add the vegetable oil to an 8-inch skillet over medium-high heat. The oil will be ready for frying when you see thin ribbons of smoke rising from the pan.

5. Place about ½ cup cauliflower in the oil and fry until golden. Drain and continue frying the remaining cauliflower in batches, adding more oil if necessary. Serve hot.

❧ *Note* ❧

For a more health-conscious version of this dish, toss the cauliflower in a small amount of oil to coat and bake at 350°F for 20 minutes instead of frying.

Yield: 8 to 10 servings

Kibbeh Hamdah كبة حامضة

LEMON-MINT BROTH
WITH MIXED VEGETABLES
AND SYRIAN MEATBALLS

Kibbeh hamdah, also known by the shortened name *hamud,* is a regular on the Sabbath dinner table; its unmistakable aroma wafts throughout Syrian homes every Friday afternoon. *Kibbeh hamdah* is a sour, palate-cleansing broth, perfect for balancing out the richer Sabbath meat dishes. While it is typically served over rice, some Aleppian Jews start off their Sabbath dinner with *kibbeh hamdah* served in small cups.

Garlic is a key flavor in the broth. In Talmudic lore, garlic was thought to have many beneficial properties: "On Friday night one should eat plenty of garlic (*toom*), for five reasons: it warms the body, makes the face shine, kills germs, increases fertility, and fills you up." One of the more sagacious Talmudic commentators, Baba Kama, added a sixth reason: "It gives you more love!" Thus, young Aleppian brides were traditionally encouraged to cook *kibbeh hamdah* every Sabbath, liberally spiking the broth with a handful of garlic cloves. While it is still debatable whether *kibbeh hamdah* is an effective aphrodisiac, it certainly can be said that many generations of Aleppian Jews have fallen in love with its minty-garlicky tang.

6 to 8 garlic cloves, peeled

1 medium potato, peeled and cut
   into 1-inch dice (about ¾ cup)

2 inner ribs celery, chopped
   (about 1 cup)

2 carrots, peeled and cut into 1-inch
   dice (about 1 cup)

Juice of 3 lemons (about 9 tablespoons)

1 tablespoon dried mint leaves

1 teaspoon kosher salt

1 teaspoon sugar (optional)

10 to 15 *kibbeh* (Stuffed Syrian Meatballs
   with Ground Rice, page 156)

1. Smash the garlic cloves with the flat side of a chef's knife.

2. In a medium saucepan, combine the garlic, potato, celery, carrots, lemon juice, mint, salt, sugar, if using, and 5 cups water. Bring to a boil over medium heat. Reduce the heat to low, and simmer for 15 minutes, or until the vegetables are fork-tender.

3. Add the *kibbeh* to the saucepan and simmer, uncovered, for another 30 minutes. Be sure the broth reduces and is not too watery.

Yield: 8 to 10 servings

Haloob حلوب

ARTICHOKES IN TAMARIND BROTH
WITH SAUTÉED MEATBALLS

Haloob is a nice alternative to *kibbeh hamdah* (Lemon-Mint Broth with Mixed Vegetables and Syrian Meatballs, page 97), especially when fresh artichokes are available. In this particular recipe, frozen artichoke hearts work fine. Just be careful to add them at the end so that they do not overcook. For a lighter broth and a quicker recipe, omit step 1 and substitute water for the meat stock.

1 pound flanken (or beef chuck) or boneless veal, cut into 2-inch cubes; or 4 beef marrow bones

2 artichokes, quartered (see page 38, step 1), or one 10-ounce box frozen artichoke hearts

7 to 8 garlic cloves, chopped (about 4 teaspoons)

3 tablespoons *ou^c* (tamarind concentrate, page 41), homemade or store-bought

Juice of 1 lemon (about 3 tablespoons)

1 teaspoon kosher salt

1 teaspoon sugar (optional)

1 dozen *kibbeh* (Stuffed Syrian Meatballs with Ground Rice, page 156)

1. In a large saucepan, boil the flanken in 1 quart water over medium-high heat until the beef stock is reduced by half to about 2 cups of stock, about 30 minutes.

2. Add the artichokes, garlic, *ou^c*, lemon juice, salt, and, if desired, sugar. Bring to a boil. Add the *kibbeh* and continue

boiling for 1 minute. Reduce the heat to low and simmer, covered, for 30 minutes. (If using frozen artichokes, reduce simmer time to 10 minutes.)

Yield: 10 servings

Kibbeh bi'Kizabrath

CILANTRO-TOMATO BROTH
WITH SYRIAN MEATBALLS

This is a refreshing broth, great to serve during the summertime. Cilantro resembles parsley but is thinner and lighter in color and has a more distinctive flavor. Heat will dull the flavor of cilantro, so it should be added just before serving.

6 garlic cloves, chopped
(about 1 tablespoon)

1 tablespoon extra-virgin olive oil

6 tomatoes, chopped, or two 8-ounce
cans diced tomatoes

One 8-ounce can tomato sauce

1 tablespoon tomato paste

1 teaspoon kosher salt

12 to 16 *kibbeh* (Stuffed Syrian Meatballs
with Ground Rice, page 156)

1 cup chopped fresh cilantro

1. In a large saucepan, sauté the garlic in the olive oil over medium heat for 1 minute, or until soft. Add the tomatoes, tomato sauce, tomato paste, and salt to the saucepan. Raise the heat to medium-high and bring the mixture to a boil. Reduce the heat to low, and simmer for 10 minutes.

2. Add ½ cup water to the saucepan. Let the mixture return to a boil. Reduce the heat to low, add the *kibbeh*, cover, and simmer for 30 minutes. Add the cilantro to the broth before serving.

Yield: 10 servings

Yebra wa Shawki

STUFFED GRAPE LEAVES
WITH ARTICHOKES AND GARLIC

In Syria, people had free access to fresh grape leaves, which grew throughout the region. Today, in Brooklyn, Aleppian Jews still have vines growing among their trees as they did in Syria. If you do not have your own vines, you can easily purchase preserved grape leaves year-round from Middle Eastern or Greek groceries and some supermarkets.

Once this dish is cooked, it is quite versatile. You can serve it hot, cold, or any temperature in between.

¼ cup extra-virgin olive oil

10 garlic cloves, chopped (2½ to 3 tablespoons)

Two 10-ounce packages frozen artichoke hearts, thawed, or 4 fresh artichokes, trimmed and quartered (see page 38, step 1)

36 _yebra war einab_ (Zesty Cold Stuffed Grape Leaves, page 66), uncooked (omit the sauce) or _yebra_ (Grape Leaves Stuffed with Ground Meat and Rice, with Apricot-Tamarind Sauce, page 150), uncooked (omit the sauce)

Juice from 6 lemons (about 1 cup plus 1 tablespoon)

1 teaspoon dried mint leaves

1 teaspoon kosher salt

1. Drizzle 2 tablespoons of the olive oil into a large saucepan. Lay the garlic cloves along the bottom of the saucepan, then layer the artichokes over the garlic. Arrange the _yebra_ over the artichokes. Drizzle the remaining 2 tablespoons olive oil over the contents of the saucepan. Place a heat-proof plate over the mixture to weigh it down.

2. Cook the _yebra_ over medium-low heat for about 5 minutes, or until the _yebra_ begin to moisten and yield their juices.

3. Remove the plate, add the lemon juice, mint, salt, and enough water to cover the _yebra_. Re-cover with the plate, and bring to a boil over medium-high heat. Reduce the heat to low, cover, and simmer for about 40 minutes, or until one-quarter of the liquid remains.

4. Remove from the heat and let stand for 3 minutes to allow the _yebra_ to tighten. Remove the plate. When ready to serve, lay a serving platter on top of the saucepan. Hold the platter tightly and carefully invert the saucepan. In this manner, the _yebra_ will not unravel and the artichokes will settle on top.

Yield: 10 to 12 servings

Kolkeh

BULGUR AND LENTIL SOUP

Adding to the classic lentil soup model, Aleppians like to use bulgur, a longtime favorite in a variety of dishes. As a result, the dish is quite substantial and filling, often serving as a main dish rather than an appetizer.

1 cup red lentils

1 cup fine bulgur (cracked wheat), rinsed in cold water and drained

2 whole onions

1 green bell pepper, chopped (about 1 cup)

1 teaspoon kosher salt

1 teaspoon Aleppo pepper, or ½ teaspoon crushed red pepper

1 onion, chopped (about ½ cup)

1 tablespoon extra-virgin olive oil

1. Combine the lentils, bulgur, the 2 whole onions, and the green bell pepper in a large saucepan with water to cover. Bring to a boil over high heat. Reduce the heat to low and simmer, uncovered, for 45 minutes, or until the soup is slightly thick but can still flow easily from a spoon. Season with salt and Aleppo pepper.

2. While the lentil-bulgur mixture is simmering, fry the chopped onion in the olive oil in a small skillet for 8 to 10 minutes, or until caramelized. To serve the soup, top individual servings with the fried onions.

Yield: 10 servings

Shurba w'Kibbeh

SMOOTH TOMATO-RICE SOUP
WITH MEATBALLS

If there were ever a perfect tomato soup for a cold winter's night, this would be it. The furthest thing from the canned American product, this sweet and savory mixture of cinnamon and meat makes for a delicious twist on the childhood classic. The meatballs are a hearty addition, but the soup can be made without them.

½ pound flanken, beef chuck, or boneless veal, cut into 2-inch cubes; or 3 beef marrow bones; or ½ chicken, quartered

½ cup short-grain white rice

3 tablespoons tomato paste

12 *kibbeh kabir* (Aleppian Soup Meatballs), or *kibbeh yahniyeh* (Beef-Bulgur Dumplings)

1 tablespoon kosher salt

Lemon wedges for serving

1. Put the meat in a large saucepan, add 2 quarts water, and boil, uncovered, for 30 minutes, skimming the foam off the surface periodically.

2. Add the rice and continue boiling, uncovered, for about 30 minutes. When the rice begins to appear creamy, add the tomato paste, *kibbeh kabir*, and salt. Lower heat and simmer, covered, for 30 more minutes. Serve with the lemon wedges.

Yield: 8 to 10 servings

Kibbeh Kabir—Aleppian Soup Meatballs

½ pound ground beef

2 tablespoons short-grain white rice

1 teaspoon ground allspice

1 teaspoon ground cinnamon

1 teaspoon kosher salt

Combine the beef, rice, allspice, cinnamon, and salt in a medium mixing bowl. Mix thoroughly. Shape into balls 2 inches in diameter. Add to the soup and cook as directed.

Kibbeh Yahniyeh—Beef-Bulgur Dumplings

These dumplings can be used in any hearty soup served during the winter; they are a favorite of kids and adults alike. Because these *kibbeh* are large, the accompanying dinner should be light, such as a vegetable or lightly dressed chicken pieces. These dumplings are particularly delicious in *shurba w'kibbeh* (Smooth Tomato-Rice Soup with Meatballs).

Filling:

1 pound ground beef

2 tablespoons chopped fresh flat-leaf parsley

1 teaspoon ground allspice

1 teaspoon ground cinnamon

1 teaspoon kosher salt

Shell:

1 pound ground beef

1 cup fine bulgur (cracked wheat), rinsed in cold water and drained

1 teaspoon ground cinnamon

1 teaspoon kosher salt

1. To make the filling, combine the beef, parsley, allspice, cinnamon, and salt in a medium mixing bowl. Set aside.

2. To make the shell, combine the beef, bulgur, cinnamon, and salt. Using a meat grinder or food processor, grind or blend this mixture 2 times.

3. Shape the shell mixture into balls 1 inch in diameter. To shape, moisten your hands with water, then use your index finger and the palm and finger of your other hand to burrow into the meat, creating a hollow with a small round opening.

4. Spoon a small amount of meat filling into the center of each meatball. Pinch the meatball closed. The meatball should resemble a large teardrop.

5. To cook, add the dumplings to a simmering soup and simmer, covered, for 45 minutes.

Yield: 10 to 12 servings

Shurbat Addes شوربة عدس

THICK AND HEARTY RED LENTIL SOUP WITH GARLIC AND CORIANDER

This satisfying and healthful dish harks back to one of the oldest "cookbooks"—the Five Books of Moses. There we learn that Esau, the son of Isaac and twin brother of Jacob, regularly enjoyed his favorite dish, a "pottage of lentils." This meal—chock-full of beneficial nutrients and hardly any fat—was perfect for restoring Esau's strength after long days spent hunting. It was also decisive in bringing about one of the greatest coups in ancient Middle Eastern history: Jacob tried his hand at this recipe and persuaded Esau to exchange his right to inherit the land of Canaan for a kettle full of the soup (it was that good!). Though *shurbat addes* is probably not exactly true to Jacob's original recipe, there is a good chance that it is very close—northern Syria grows many fruits and vegetables that were cultivated in the ancient land of Canaan.

The tricky part of this otherwise simple recipe is achieving the correct consistency. This soup should be smooth and thick but not lumpy. If the soup is too thick, add water in small measures.

2 cups red lentils

6 garlic cloves, peeled

1 teaspoon coriander seed

1 tablespoon kosher salt

2 tablespoons vegetable oil

Chopped fresh cilantro
  for garnish

Ground cumin for garnish

¼ teaspoon Aleppo pepper or ⅛ teaspoon
  crushed red pepper (optional)

Fresh lemon wedges for serving

1. In a medium stockpot or large saucepan, combine the lentils with 2 quarts of water. Bring to a simmer over low heat and cook until the lentils begin to disintegrate into a puree, about 40 minutes.

2. Meanwhile, with a mortar and pestle, pound the garlic, coriander seed, and salt into a paste. (Alternatively, you can gently smash the garlic, grind the coriander seed in a pepper mill or crack it, then combine the garlic and coriander seed with the salt.) In a medium saucepan, sauté the garlic-coriander paste in the vegetable oil over medium-high heat for 1 to 2 minutes, or until soft.

3. Add the garlic-coriander paste to the lentil mixture, and simmer for 20 minutes. Before serving, garnish the soup with a few sprigs of cilantro and a sprinkling of cumin and Aleppo pepper, if desired. Serve with the lemon wedges on the side. This soup is ideal with toasted Syrian bread broken into small pieces for dipping.

Yield: 8 to 10 servings

Addes b'Spanekh

LENTIL AND SPINACH SOUP

Winters are colder in Aleppo than in Damascus and Beirut, to the south, so it's not surprising that soup plays an important role in Aleppo's culinary tradition. Old-time moms from Aleppo would call their daughters early in the morning to make sure they were preparing this soup for their kids; it was—and still is—a versatile, tasty, and healthful centerpiece to a weekday supper. There are many recipes for lentil soup in Syrian cookery, but this one is a favorite staple.

2 cups red lentils

1 onion, chopped (about ½ cup)

3 tablespoons extra-virgin olive oil

2 garlic cloves, chopped
  (about 1 teaspoon)

1 teaspoon ground coriander seed

One 10-ounce package frozen spinach,
  thawed and chopped, or 1 pound
  fresh spinach, trimmed and chopped
  (about 1¼ cups)

1 teaspoon kosher salt

½ teaspoon Aleppo pepper,
  ¼ teaspoon crushed red pepper,
  or ¼ teaspoon ground cinnamon

Lemon wedges for serving

1. In a large saucepan, combine the lentils and 6 cups water and cook over medium-low heat for 15 minutes, or until the lentils have softened.

2. In a large saucepan over medium heat, sauté the onion in the olive oil for 4 to 6 minutes, or until translucent. Stir in the garlic and coriander and mix well. Add the spinach and cook for 1 minute, or until wilted.

3. Add the spinach-and-garlic mixture and the salt to the lentils. Simmer for about 10 minutes, or until the soup has a thick consistency. Sprinkle some Aleppo pepper or cinnamon over the surface of each bowl and serve with a lemon wedge on the side.

Yield: 8 to 10 servings

Rishta b'Addes

NOODLES AND LENTIL SOUP

This is another popular version of lentil soup. Add the noodles minutes before serving to ensure that they do not become mushy, and, if you like, sprinkle the finished soup with dried mint.

1 cup red lentils

1 cup dried egg noodles

1 teaspoon kosher salt

1 medium onion, chopped (about 1 cup)

2 tablespoons vegetable oil

1 tablespoon dried mint (optional)

1. Combine the lentils and 2 cups water in a large saucepan. Bring to a boil, reduce the heat to low, and simmer, covered, for 15 minutes.

2. Add 4 more cups water and bring to a boil. Add the egg noodles and salt. Stir to separate. Return to a boil, reduce the heat to low, and simmer for about 10 minutes.

3. Meanwhile, sauté the onions in the vegetable oil in a small skillet over medium heat for 6 to 8 minutes, or until the onions are translucent. Add the onions to the noodles and lentils and simmer for 2 more minutes. Right before serving, add dried mint, if desired.

Yield: 8 to 10 servings

Rai'yeb b'Labaniyeh

رايب بلبنية

CHILLED YOGURT AND CUCUMBER SOUP

This refreshing summer favorite tastes similar to *cacik*, Turkish cucumber and yogurt salad. Because of the silky texture of *rai'yeb b'labaniyeh* and its delightfully cool sensation on the gums, many elderly men and women in the Middle East subsist on this dish and flatbread. The soup is also a common food for teething babies. It is an immutable part of our culture; old Aleppian Jewish women can be seen doting over their newborn great-grandchildren and sharing the same meal.

1 cup plain yogurt

1 garlic clove, chopped
(about ½ teaspoon)

1 teaspoon kosher salt

1 cup ice-cold milk or water

1 large cucumber, or 3 Kirby cucumbers, peeled and chopped

1 tablespoon dried mint

2 tablespoons finely chopped scallions (optional)

2 tablespoons finely chopped fresh dill (optional)

1. Combine the yogurt, garlic, and salt in a medium mixing bowl. Gradually add the cold milk. Stir well. Add the cucumbers. Stir again and refrigerate.

2. Before serving, garnish with mint, and, if desired, scallions, dill, or both.

Yield: 8 servings

Lebneh w'Spanekh

SPINACH-YOGURT SOUP

Lebneh w'spanekh is a refreshing summertime soup. Traditionally made with spinach, this Egyptian soup can be made with *silleq* (Swiss chard) as well. In the Middle East, yogurt is thought to have cooling properties—and not simply because it is eaten chilled. Many believe that yogurt helps to combat fevers.

1 onion, chopped (about ½ cup)

2 tablespoons extra-virgin olive oil

One 10-ounce package frozen spinach, thawed and chopped, or 1 pound fresh spinach, trimmed and chopped (about 1¼ cups)

1 cup short-grain white rice

1 tablespoon kosher salt

1 pint whole-milk yogurt

2 Kirby cucumbers, peeled and chopped (about 1½ cups)

1 garlic clove, finely chopped (about ½ teaspoon)

2 teaspoons dried mint leaves

1. In a large saucepan, sauté the onion in the olive oil over medium heat for 4 to 6 minutes, or until translucent. Add the spinach and sauté for 2 minutes, or until wilted.

2. Add the rice, salt, and 1 cup water. Bring to a boil over medium-high heat, then reduce the heat to low and simmer, covered, for about 15 minutes, or until the rice is fluffy. Refrigerate the spinach-rice mixture.

3. Combine the yogurt, cucumbers, garlic, and mint in a medium mixing bowl. Mix thoroughly.

4. Fold the yogurt mixture into the spinach-rice mixture until they are well blended. Serve cold.

Yield: 6 to 8 servings

Riz wa Loz
*(Ring of Rice with Nuts,
page 122)*

Riz, Hinta w'Rishta رز وحطة وريشتا

RICE, GRAINS, AND PASTA

In Aleppo and the rest of the Middle East it is unheard of to have a meal without rice, pasta, bulgur, or some other type of grain. A great many of the savory dishes in this book are spooned onto a plate of rice. Sabbath dinner is never served without a huge steaming platter of rice at the center of the table.

Rice or grains are traditionally prepared as close to mealtime as possible. Aleppian Jewish cooks take great pride in their rice; they want it as fresh and fluffy as it can be. On a Friday afternoon, you will often hear a woman say, "I have to go home and make the rice." The Aleppian way of making rice is to fry the grains briefly in a little oil before cooking them in water.

When planning your meals, choose the grain you plan to use with care. If a main dish is light and fruity, perhaps it would contrast well with the dense, nutty flavor of bulgur. If the dish is heavier, with large cuts of meat, perhaps it will sit best on a bed of rice. No matter what you choose, consider the rice, grains, and pastas in this section the backbone of a Syrian meal.

Calsonnes w'Rishta
(Buttery Noodles with
Cheese Ravioli, page 127)

الوجبات

RICE, GRAINS, AND PASTA RECIPES

Riz Halabieh

CLASSIC ALEPPIAN RICE

Rice is one of the most highly prized grains in Middle Eastern cuisine. In late medieval times, it was relatively costly and used sparingly by families of modest means. Instead, most cooks used bulgur to add heft to ground beef and to accompany vegetable dishes.

To enhance the flavor of rice, most Arab recipes call for butter. Because Jewish law prohibits mixing dairy and meat ingredients, Aleppian Jews use vegetable oil instead, lightly sautéing the rice before adding the water. In addition to enriching the flavor of the rice, the oil produces *a'hata*, the crispy golden rice crust that sticks to the bottom of the pot, which is much fought over when it reaches the table. *A'hata* can be enjoyed alone or eaten mixed with the fluffy rice, adding a terrific textural contrast.

¼ cup vegetable oil	2 cups long-grain white rice
1 teaspoon kosher salt	

1. In a medium saucepan over medium heat, heat the vegetable oil for about 30 seconds, then add the rice. Stir for 30 seconds. Add the salt and 3 cups water. Bring to a boil over high heat. Reduce the heat to low, and simmer, covered, for 30 minutes, or until the rice is fluffy.

2. To make *a'hata* (crispy rice), if desired, reduce the heat to the lowest possible setting and let the rice cook until the rice at the bottom of the saucepan begins to transform into a toasted crust, about 1 hour. Monitor the *a'hata* closely so that the rice doesn't burn.

Yield: 6 to 8 servings

Riz wa Sha'riyya

RICE WITH VERMICELLI

The addition of *sha'riyya,* or vermicelli, is common in Levantine cookery. *Sha'riyya* is Arabic for "hair," which aptly describes the thin strands of vermicelli.

½ cup vermicelli

3 tablespoons vegetable oil

2 cups long-grain white rice

1 teaspoon kosher salt

1. In a medium saucepan, toast the vermicelli in the vegetable oil over medium-low heat until it begins to brown. Watch the vermicelli carefully as it tends to burn quickly.

2. Add the rice to the vermicelli immediately and mix well. Add the salt and 3 cups water. Bring to a boil over high heat, then reduce the heat to low, cover, and simmer for 30 minutes, or until the rice is fluffy.

3. To make *a'hata* (crispy rice), if desired, reduce the heat to the lowest possible setting and let the rice cook until the rice at the bottom of the saucepan begins to transform into a toasted crust, about 1 hour. Monitor the *a'hata* closely so that the rice does not burn.

Yield: 6 to 8 servings

Bizeh b'Jurah

GREEN PEAS AND RICE
WITH CORIANDER AND MEAT

Bizeh b'jurah is a delicious example of how various beans, legumes, and cuts of meat are added to rice dishes to create a hearty and nutritious meal. This dish is often eaten with a basic *salata arabi* (Basic Syrian Salad with Lemon-Cumin Dressing, page 30).

4 garlic cloves, chopped
(about 2 teaspoons)

2 tablespoons plus 1 teaspoon
vegetable oil

1 pound flanken, cut in 2-inch cubes,
or veal, cut in 1-inch cubes

1 teaspoon coriander seed

¾ teaspoon kosher salt

1 cup long-grain white rice

One 10-ounce package frozen peas
or 1¼ cups fresh shelled peas

1 heaping teaspoon ground allspice

1 teaspoon ground cinnamon
(optional)

1. In a medium saucepan, sauté half the garlic in 2 tablespoons of the vegetable oil over medium heat for 2 minutes, or until soft.

2. Add the meat to the saucepan and brown for 5 to 6 minutes. Add 3 cups water to the meat, bring to a boil on medium-high heat, and cook, covered, for 1 hour and 15 minutes, or until the meat is tender.

3. Pound the remaining garlic, coriander seed, and salt in a mortar and pestle until it forms a paste (alternatively, use a mini food processor).

4. In a small saucepan, sauté the garlic-coriander paste in the 1 teaspoon of oil over medium heat for about 30 seconds.

5. Pour the broth from the simmering meat into a measuring cup and add enough water to equal a total of 2 cups of liquid. Add liquid to saucepan with meat. Cook over medium-high heat until the liquid boils.

6. Add the rice and peas to the meat mixture. Return the mixture to a boil, then add the garlic-coriander paste, allspice, and cinnamon (if desired). Reduce the heat to low, cover, and simmer for 20 minutes, or until the rice is fluffy.

Yield: 6 to 8 servings

Ríz b'Spanekh

رز بالسبانخ

RICE WITH SPINACH

Spinach is used in this recipe to add a wonderful color and flavor to the rice. This practice harks back to the days of the Arab and Ottoman courts. The cooks in those noble kitchens would beautify dishes by imbuing them with a vibrant color, a culinary process known as endoring.

9 garlic cloves

4 teaspoons coriander seed

1 teaspoon kosher salt

2 to 3 tablespoons vegetable oil

Three 10-ounce packages frozen spinach, thawed and chopped, or 1 pound fresh spinach, trimmed and chopped

2 cups long-grain white rice

½ teaspoon ground allspice

¼ teaspoon white pepper (optional)

1. Pound the garlic, coriander seed, and salt with a mortar and pestle until it forms a paste. (Alternatively, use a mini food processor.)

2. In a large saucepan, sauté the garlic-coriander paste in vegetable oil for 30 seconds. Add the spinach to the saucepan and sauté for 2 to 3 minutes, or until wilted.

Add the rice, allspice, white pepper (if desired), and 4 cups water; stir well. Bring to a boil over high heat, then reduce the heat to low, cover, and simmer for 30 minutes, or until the rice is fluffy.

Yield: 10 to 12 servings

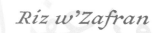

Ríz w'Zafran

SAFFRON RICE

In Aleppo, turmeric was often substituted for the pricey saffron, although it could never match the flavor of the profoundly aromatic exquisite red threads. This rice dish would often be prepared for a happy occasion or for a *hefle,* which is the Arabic word for party.

1 onion, chopped (about ½ cup)	1 cinnamon stick	1 cup long-grain white rice
2 tablespoons vegetable oil	½ teaspoon ground cardamom	½ cup toasted pine nuts (page 28) or pistachios, shelled and toasted (optional) (see page 310)
1 tablespoon kosher salt	3 saffron threads	

1. In a large saucepan, sauté the onion in the vegetable oil over medium heat for 6 to 8 minutes, or until translucent. Add 1½ cups water, the salt, cinnamon stick, cardamom, and saffron. Give the mixture a stir, raise the heat to high, and bring to a boil.

2. Add the rice and return to a boil. Reduce the heat to low, cover, and simmer for about 30 minutes, or until the rice is fluffy. Garnish with nuts, if desired.

Yield: 6 to 8 servings

Ríz wa Loz

RING OF RICE WITH NUTS

This dish is especially well received on special occasions because of the elegant and decorative array of nuts as well as its rich flavor and crunch.

¼ cup almonds, blanched, peeled, and chopped (see page 310)

¼ cup vegetable oil

¼ cup pistachios, shelled, blanched, peeled, and chopped (see page 310)

¼ cup pine nuts

2 cups long-grain white rice

1. Preheat the oven to 300°F.

2. Toast the almonds with 1 tablespoon of the vegetable oil in a medium skillet over medium-low heat for 3 minutes. Transfer the almonds to a small mixing bowl. Add the pistachios and 1 tablespoon of the vegetable oil to the skillet and toast for 2 minutes. Transfer the pistachios to the bowl. Add the pine nuts and 1 tablespoon of the vegetable oil to the skillet and toast for 1 minute, tossing often. Transfer to the bowl.

3. In a large saucepan, sauté the rice in the remaining 1 tablespoon of oil over medium heat for 2 minutes. Add 3 cups water and bring to a boil. Reduce the heat to low, cover, and simmer for 30 minutes, or until the rice is fluffy.

4. Spread out the nuts evenly over the bottom of a 4-cup ring mold. Pack the rice into the mold. Cover the mold with aluminum foil.

5. Place the mold in the oven. Be sure to position the nuts away from the heat source. Bake for 30 minutes. Remove the mold from the oven and place a serving platter over the opening of the mold. Invert the mold, turn out the rice onto the platter, and serve.

Yield: 6 to 8 servings

Ríz w'Fūl Akhdar

RICE AND FAVA BEANS WITH GARLIC

This is a popular dish in the springtime, when the beans are young and tender. Just as North Africans adore couscous, Aleppian Jews love rice every which way and try to serve it at nearly every meal. The fava beans add a hearty note to this dish, so it is usually served with *laban* (Yogurt, page 241) and *salata arabi* (Basic Syrian Salad with Lemon-Cumin Dressing, page 30).

1 onion, chopped (about ½ cup)

¼ cup vegetable oil

1 pound fresh fava beans, shelled,
   or frozen fava beans, or one
   15½-ounce can fava beans, drained

4 garlic cloves, chopped
   (about 2 teaspoons)

1 tablespoon coriander seed

1 teaspoon kosher salt

2 cups long-grain white rice

¼ teaspoon white pepper (optional)

1 bunch fresh flat-leaf parsley,
   finely chopped

1. In a medium saucepan, sauté the onion in 2 tablespoons of the vegetable oil over medium heat for 4 to 6 minutes, or until translucent.

2. If using fresh or frozen fava beans, add them to the saucepan, along with ½ cup water, and cook for 10 minutes. If using canned fava beans, add them to the onions and set aside.

3. Pound the garlic, coriander seed, and salt in a mortar and pestle until it forms a paste. (Alternatively, use a mini food processor.)

4. In a small skillet, sauté the garlic-coriander paste in the remaining 2 tablespoons of the vegetable oil for 30 seconds. Transfer to the fava-onion mixture and add the rice, white pepper (if desired), and 3 cups water. Give the mixture a stir and raise the heat to high. Bring to a boil. Reduce the heat to low, and simmer, covered, for 30 minutes, or until the rice is fluffy. Garnish with parsley before serving.

Yield: 8 to 10 servings

Mujedrah

RICE WITH BROWN LENTILS
AND FRIZZLED CARAMELIZED ONIONS

Mujedrah is still a Thursday night staple for Aleppian Jewish families, just as it was back in Aleppo. The nutty flavor of lentils and the silky caramelized onions give this dish amazing depth and richness, especially when eaten with a refreshing bowl of *laban* (Yogurt, page 241), mint, and chopped cucumber.

¾ cup brown lentils

2 cups thinly sliced onions
   (3 to 4 onions)

½ cup vegetable oil

1 cup long-grain white rice

1 teaspoon kosher salt

3 tablespoons butter

1. Combine the lentils with 1 cup water in a large saucepan over medium heat. Bring to a boil. Reduce the heat and simmer, uncovered, for 10 to 15 minutes, or until the lentils are al dente, or slightly firm.

2. Meanwhile, in a large skillet, sauté the onions in the vegetable oil over medium heat for 30 minutes, or until thoroughly caramelized.

3. When the lentils are al dente, drain the liquid into a measuring cup and add enough water to bring the total amount of liquid to 1½ cups. Return to the saucepan and add the rice, salt, and a third of the onions. Bring to a boil over high heat, then reduce the heat to low, cover, and simmer for 30 minutes.

4. Add the butter to the rice and continue simmering for 10 more minutes. Before serving, top the *mujedrah* with the remaining fried onions and their cooking oil.

Yield: 6 to 8 servings

Riz w'Hummus

RICE WITH CHICKPEAS
AND ONIONS

Chickpeas look like pale, golden hazelnuts and are the most popular of the Mediterranean legumes. Along with other peas and beans, they are widely used in cold, garlicky dressed salads and are the basis for many types of soup. This is a humble dish that can be made quickly at any time. It is traditionally served with *bamia b'mishmosh* (Okra with Prunes and Apricots in Tamarind Sauce, page 87).

1 large onion, chopped (about ¾ cup)

¼ cup vegetable oil

1 tablespoon kosher salt

1 cup long-grain white rice

¾ cup dried chickpeas, soaked overnight or for 6 to 8 hours and drained, or one 15½-ounce can chickpeas, drained

¼ cup butter (½ stick)

In a medium saucepan, sauté the onion in the vegetable oil over medium heat for 4 to 6 minutes, or until translucent. Add 1½ cups of water and the salt. Bring to a boil. Add the rice and chickpeas to the onion. Give it a stir. Raise the heat to high and return to a boil. Reduce the heat to low and simmer, covered, for about 20 minutes. Add the butter to the rice, stir well, and cook, covered, for 10 more minutes.

Yield: 6 to 8 servings

Calsonnes w'Rishta

BUTTERY NOODLES
WITH CHEESE RAVIOLI

Calsonnes is one of the most well-received dairy dishes in the Aleppian Jewish repertoire. It has a linguistic connection to the Italian *calzone,* which makes sense when you consider that both are types of stuffed dough. The principal components of this dish are cheese ravioli, which are baked to a crisp with butter and noodles, although some prefer their *calsonnes* on the tender side.

The dish is prepared for weekday dairy meals. It is also served with other dairy foods during the holiday of Shavuot—the festival of the first fruits and the giving of the Torah at Mount Sinai. This custom of eating dairy foods commemorates the Israelites' avoidance of meat on the momentous days before they received the Torah. The Israelites' cooking utensils, which they had used to cook meat and dairy ingredients together, were rendered unkosher by the brand-new dietary laws (known as *kashrut*) that Moses brought down from Mount Sinai. Thus, the Israelites ate simple dairy dishes to stay within the dictates of their newly acquired dietary laws.

Dough:

5 cups all-purpose flour

2 eggs, beaten

1 teaspoon kosher salt

Filling:

2 pounds Muenster cheese, grated

2 eggs

Pinch of kosher salt

1 teaspoon baking powder

1 cup (2 sticks) unsalted butter

One 16-ounce package wide egg noodles

1. To make the dough, combine the flour, eggs, and salt in a large mixing bowl. Then slowly add 2 cups water. Mix until the dough is soft and elastic. Cover with a dry towel until ready to use.

2. To make the filling, combine the cheese, eggs, salt, and baking powder. Mix well. The mixture should be thick. Set aside.

3. With a rolling pin, roll out half the dough on a large floured surface to ⅛-inch thickness.

4. Divide the rolled-out dough in half, keeping one half in front of you and setting the other aside, covering it with a towel to prevent dryness. Every 3 inches, place a teaspoon of the filling onto the rolled-out dough.

continued

5. Cover the filling and dough with the remaining sheet of rolled-out dough. Cut around the mounds with a 2-inch circular ravioli cutter to make circles. Repeat steps 3 to 5 with the remaining dough and filling. Refrigerate ravioli until ready to prepare *calsonnes*. Use 24 ravioli for this dish. (You can freeze the rest in a single layer on a wax paper–lined baking sheet . After they are fully frozen, the ravioli can be placed in a plastic bag.)

6. Preheat the oven to 300°F.

7. Bring 6 quarts salted water to a boil in a large saucepan. Gently drop the ravioli into the boiling water and cook until they are almost tender, 5 to 6 minutes. Drain and place into two 3-quart baking dishes. Add ½ stick butter to each dish of ravioli while they are still hot.

8. Meanwhile, add the egg noodles to another pot of salted boiling water and cook until al dente, 4 to 6 minutes.

9. Drain the noodles and combine with the ravioli in the baking dishes. Dot the noodles and ravioli with dollops of the remaining stick of butter. Cover the dishes and bake for 30 minutes. For extra crispy *calsonnes*, uncover and bake for another 10 minutes.

Yield: 8 to 10 servings, 5 dozen calsonnes

Burghol w'Hummus

BULGUR WITH CHICKPEAS

Simple and healthful, bulgur and chickpeas were readily available in Aleppo's markets. This inexpensive, satisfying, yet relatively light dish is eaten by the average Aleppian Jewish family on Thursday night. Dairy meals such as this one (*burghol w'hummus* is prepared with butter) are typically eaten on Thursdays so families save room and build a large appetite for the many meat dishes of the Friday night Sabbath feast. Delicious when served with *laban* (Yogurt, page 241), *burghol w'hummus* is often garnished with dried mint and chopped cucumber.

1 onion, chopped (about ½ cup)

6 garlic cloves, chopped
(about 1 tablespoon)

2 tablespoons vegetable oil

1½ cups coarse bulgur (cracked wheat),
rinsed in cold water and drained

¾ cup dried chickpeas, soaked
overnight or for 6 to 8 hours
and drained, or one 15½-ounce
can chickpeas, drained

1 teaspoon kosher salt

3 tablespoons butter
(or an additional 2 tablespoons
vegetable oil to accompany
meat dishes)

1. In a medium saucepan, sauté the onion and garlic in the vegetable oil over medium-high heat for 4 to 6 minutes, or until soft. Add the bulgur to the onion-garlic mixture and toss over low heat until the bulgur is coated. Add 2 cups water, the chickpeas, and salt. Bring to a boil over high heat, reduce the heat to very low, cover, and simmer for 30 minutes.

2. Before the bulgur fully absorbs the cooking liquid, add the butter. When the water is absorbed, remove from the heat. Stir and serve.

Yield: 6 to 8 servings

Burghol b'Jibn

BULGUR WITH CHEESE

Nowadays, bulgur (which Arabs call *burghol,* and Turks call *bulgar*) is marketed as a gourmet food product, but in the Middle East it has always been an inexpensive staple food. Its nutty flavor sets it apart, and it is the principal ingredient in this particular dish. Rather than pay high prices at gourmet shops, try buying bulgur at a Middle Eastern market for one-half to one-third the price. Also, there is no need to limit yourself to the cheese listed below. Feel free to use your favorite melting cheese.

1 onion, chopped (about ½ cup)

2 tablespoons vegetable oil

1½ cups coarse bulgur (cracked wheat), rinsed in cold water and drained

¾ cup dried chickpeas, soaked overnight or for 6 to 8 hours and drained, or one 15½-ounce can chickpeas, drained

1 teaspoon kosher salt

6 tablespoons butter (¾ stick)

½ pound Muenster cheese or farmer cheese, grated

1. Preheat the oven to 375°F.

2. In a medium saucepan over medium-high heat, sauté the onion in the vegetable oil for 6 to 8 minutes, or until it begins to brown. Reduce the heat to low and add the bulgur. Toss for 1 minute, or until the bulgur is coated. Add 2 cups water, the chickpeas, and salt. Raise the heat to high and bring the bulgur-onion mixture to a boil. Reduce to very low heat, cover, and simmer for 20 minutes.

3. Before the bulgur fully absorbs the cooking liquid, add the butter to the saucepan. When the bulgur fully absorbs the cooking liquid, after about 10 minutes, remove the saucepan from the heat. Transfer the onion-bulgur mixture to a 3-quart baking dish. Stir in the grated cheese.

4. Transfer to baking dish and bake, covered, for 5 minutes, or until the cheese is melted. Uncover the dish and continue baking for 5 more minutes, or until the cheese begins to turn brown.

Yield: 6 to 8 servings

Cascasoon

ACINI DE PEPE
WITH BUTTER AND CHICKPEAS

The name of this dish shares the same etymology as North Africa's couscous. The Arabic word *cuscusu* means "minced into small pieces," which perfectly describes the tiny pasta used in this dish. The Israeli variety of couscous is an ample substitute for acini de pepe (the texture of Moroccan couscous is too fine, however, and is not right for this dish). *Cascasoon* is a longtime favorite for evening dairy meals. Make enough so that your kids can have some the next day—they will be the envy of the school lunch table.

1 onion, chopped (about ½ cup)

¼ cup vegetable oil

One 16-ounce package acini de pepe
(tiny peppercorn-size pasta)
or Israeli couscous

¾ cup dried chickpeas, soaked
overnight or for 6 to 8 hours
and drained, or one 15½-ounce
can chickpeas, drained

1½ tablespoon kosher salt

¼ cup butter (½ stick), cut into pats

½ pound Muenster cheese, grated
(optional)

1. In a medium saucepan, sauté the onion in the vegetable oil over medium heat for 6 to 8 minutes, or until translucent. Add the acini de pepe and continue sautéing until the pasta turns brown, 4 to 5 minutes.

2. Add the chickpeas, salt, and 3½ cups water. Bring to a boil. Reduce the heat to low and simmer, covered, for about 25 minutes.

3. When the water is absorbed, add the pats of butter and toss gently. If you like, you can pour the *cascasoon* into a baking dish and top with cheese. Then bake, uncovered, in an oven preheated to 350°F for 10 minutes, or until the cheese melts.

Yield: 6 to 8 servings

Keftes
(*Tamarind-Stewed
Meatballs, page 162*)

Laham

لحم

MEAT

This chapter delves into the central role that meat plays in Aleppian Jewish cuisine. Because meat was a luxury food in the old country, these dishes are elaborate and most often appear on the Sabbath and holiday tables. This chapter begins with *hashu,* the ground meat filling that is a principal ingredient in many Aleppian Jewish meat dishes. Then it works its way into complex preparations, such as *s'fiha* (Stuffed Baby Eggplants with Ground Meat and Rice, page 138), *yebra* (Grape Leaves Stuffed with Ground Meat and Rice, with Apricot-Tamarind Sauce, page 150), and *rubuh'* (Succulent Roast Veal Stuffed with Spiced Ground Meat and Rice, page 168). Included among these recipes are the many varieties of *mehshi* (stuffed vegetables), such as *mehshi kusa* (Zucchini or Yellow Squash Stuffed with Ground Meat and Rice, page 143) and *mehshi basal* (Caramelized Onions Stuffed with Ground Meat and Rice, page 147). So skilled were the native cooks with these stuffed dishes that Aleppo was known as the "Queen of the *Mehshis.*" Therefore, the following recipes represent refined versions of the stuffed vegetable dishes found elsewhere in the region.

Due to the lack of refrigeration in the old days of Aleppo, meat had to be used shortly after an animal was slaughtered.

Many Aleppian Jewish women would make sausages and other dried meats in order to preserve as much as possible. Sausages called *salchicha* (Spicy Sausage, page 175) were hung in the cellars of Aleppian Jewish homes. The cellars were also devoted to the storage of jars of pickled vegetables and other preserved foods.

Here in the United States, we have incorporated meat into a daily diet. Though we rarely have dried meats hanging in our cellars (thanks to freezers), we still make *salchicha,* which are a perennial favorite. Many of these dishes are made in large quantities so that extra portions can be frozen for later use. If you freeze meals at the right stage, very little of the original flavor is lost.

In addition to the usual cuts of meat, Aleppian Jews also enjoy various kinds of offal, such as tongue, brain, and sweetbreads. Ask a local butcher to help you get the best cuts available and try each at least once. Though they can be harder to prepare than the average meat dish, your effort will be doubly rewarded with succulent tenderness, divine flavor, and an excitingly original experience.

MEAT RECIPES

Hashu

ALEPPIAN GROUND MEAT AND RICE FILLING

In Aleppo, any *hashu* that was left over after stuffing vegetables was often cooked immediately over the stove, lightly sautéed in oil, along with a chopped onion. Today, the leftover *hashu* is formed into torpedo shapes and added to the roasting pan with any of the stuffed vegetable (*mehshi*) dishes.

When the Jewish community still lived in Aleppo, *hashu* consisted mostly of rice because meat was expensive. When cooking any of the *mehshi* dishes, it was necessary to place a plate on top of the stuffed vegetables and a small bottle filled with water on top of that to weigh down the dish, in order to prevent the rice in the *hashu* mixture from growing too large and escaping the vegetable cavity. Today, because many cooks can afford to use a greater proportion of meat in *hashu,* less weight is needed and they use only the plate. When there is a fancy occasion, *snobar* (pine nuts) are added to the *hashu.*

1 pound ground beef	2 tablespoons vegetable oil	¼ teaspoon white pepper
⅓ cup short-grain white rice	1 teaspoon ground cinnamon	1 onion, chopped (½ cup, optional)
1 teaspoon ground allspice	1 teaspoon kosher salt	1 cup pine nuts (optional)

1. Soak rice in water, enough to cover, for 30 minutes. Drain.

2. Combine the meat, rice, allspice, vegetable oil, cinnamon, salt, white pepper, and, if desired, onion and pine nuts in a large mixing bowl. Mix well. Use as required by other recipes.

❧ *Note* ❧

Extra *hashu* can be shaped into walnut-size balls or torpedo shapes and added to the roaster when preparing a recipe using *hashu.*

Meatless *Hashu*

1 cup short-grain white rice

1 tablespoon plus ½ teaspoon
   kosher salt

3 tomatoes, chopped (about 3 cups)

1 onion, chopped (about ½ cup)

1 bunch fresh flat-leaf parsley, chopped
   (about 1 cup)

2 tablespoons dried mint leaves

½ teaspoon ground allspice

½ teaspoon ground cinnamon

6 garlic cloves, chopped
   (about 1 tablespoon)

½ cup extra-virgin olive oil

1 teaspoon sugar

Juice of 1 lemon (about 3 tablespoons)

1. In a small saucepan, bring ¾ cup water to a boil. Add the rice and ½ teaspoon of the salt, cover, and simmer for 10 minutes.

2. Combine the cooked rice, tomatoes, onion, parsley, mint, allspice, cinnamon, and the remaining 1 tablespoon salt in a medium mixing bowl and mix thoroughly.

3. Fill a large saucepan halfway with water. Add the rice mixture, garlic, olive oil, and sugar to the saucepan. Cook over low heat, covered, until the mixture is tender and well blended. Stir in the lemon juice.

Yield: 8 to 10 servings

S'fiha صفيحة

STUFFED BABY EGGPLANTS WITH GROUND MEAT AND RICE

It is important not to overstuff the baby eggplants in this dish. Let the meat of the eggplant have as much prominence as the stuffing in order to balance every bite. Because the seasoning in this dish is unusually sparse, its flavor really depends on the delicious, natural essence of the eggplant and meat stuffing to produce a mouthwatering result.

¾ cup dried chickpeas, soaked overnight or for 6 to 8 hours, or one 15½-ounce can chickpeas, drained

1 onion, chopped (about ½ cup)

1 bunch flat-leaf parsley, chopped

1 pound *hashu* (page 136)

24 small fresh eggplants, cored, or 24 dried eggplant skins (see Note)

1 cup vegetable oil

½ recipe fried eggplant slices *(banjan meqli, page 91)*

1 tablespoon ground allspice

1 tablespoon kosher salt

1. If using dried chickpeas that have soaked overnight, drain and add enough fresh water to cover the chickpeas by 2 inches in a pan, and bring to a boil. Reduce the heat to low and simmer for 1½ to 2 hours in a covered saucepan, or for about 20 minutes in a pressure cooker. Drain and rinse the chickpeas, reserving some of the cooking liquid.

Soak the chickpeas in cold water. When they are cool enough to handle, lightly rub a handful of them between your palms until the skins separate. Keep rubbing off the skins and rinsing the chickpeas, placing them in a medium bowl, until all the skins have been removed.

2. Fold the chickpeas, onion, and parsley into the *hashu* filling.

3. Stuff each eggplant with *hashu.*

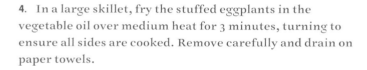
Core the eggplants with the long vegetable corer known as a ma'vdeh (see page 143).

4. In a large skillet, fry the stuffed eggplants in the vegetable oil over medium heat for 3 minutes, turning to ensure all sides are cooked. Remove carefully and drain on paper towels.

5. Cover the bottom of a large ovenproof saucepan with fried eggplant slices. Lay the stuffed eggplants over the slices. Intersperse the remaining fried eggplant slices among the stuffed eggplants. Place a heat-proof plate over the stuffed eggplant as a weight.

6. Over medium-low heat, cook for about 10 minutes, or until the eggplants release moisture. Remove the saucepan from heat and remove the plate. Sprinkle the allspice and salt over the eggplants. Add enough water to cover the eggplants three-quarters of the way. Top with the heat-proof plate for weight. Bring to a boil over medium-high heat, then reduce the heat to low, cover, and simmer for 30 minutes, or until ¼ of the liquid remains.

7. Preheat the oven to 300°F.

8. Transfer the saucepan to the oven and braise the eggplants for 45 minutes. Uncover and braise for 30 more minutes.

✎ *Note* ✎

When eggplants are in season, as a preparation for winter, eggplants and peppers are dried. The flesh inside the eggplant is scooped out, and the skins are dried on strings. They may be available in Middle Eastern markets.

If using dried eggplant skins, in a large saucepan bring 1 quart of water to a boil. Reduce heat to medium and place dried eggplants in water for 3 to 4 minutes or until plump.

Yield: 6 to 8 servings

Mehshi Banjan wa S'farjal

STUFFED EGGPLANT WITH QUINCE

Although quince and eggplant may seem like an unlikely pair, they are actually quite exquisite together. The tart, fruity taste of the cooked quince mingles with the earthy eggplant for an almost bitter, yet brilliant result. The two are reminiscent of green olives and lemons; each adds its essential flavor to the other, while still maintaining its own distinctness.

2 dozen very small eggplants, cored
   (see page 139)

2 pounds *hashu* (Aleppian Ground Meat
   and Rice Filling, page 136)

3 quinces, cored, peeled,
   and cut into 6 pieces each

Sauce:

3 tablespoons *ouͨ* (tamarind concentrate,
   page 41), homemade or store-bought

Juice of 1 lemon (about 3 tablespoons)

2 tablespoons sugar

1 teaspoon kosher salt

6 pieces *helou s'farjal*
   (Candied Quince, page 290)
   for garnish (optional)

1. Stuff the eggplants with the *hashu*.

2. Place alternating layers of quince and stuffed eggplants in a large ovenproof saucepan.

3. To make the sauce, in a small bowl, combine the *ouͨ*, lemon juice, sugar, salt, and 1 cup water, and mix well. Pour the sauce over the stuffed eggplants and quince. Place a heat-proof plate over them to serve as a weight.

4. Cook over medium-low heat for about 10 minutes, or until the eggplants release moisture. Remove the saucepan from the heat. Add enough water to cover the eggplants three-quarters of the way. Keep the heat-proof plate on top as a weight. Bring to a boil over medium-high heat, then reduce the heat to low, cover, and simmer for 30 minutes, or until ¼ of the liquid remains.

5. Preheat the oven to 300°F.

6. Transfer the saucepan to the oven and braise for 45 minutes. Uncover and braise for 30 more minutes. Garnish with the candied quince, if desired.

Yield: 6 to 8 servings

Mehshi Banadoura

TOMATOES STUFFED
WITH GROUND MEAT AND RICE

If you are using fresh local tomatoes at their peak, they may be very juicy. After coring, strain the excess liquid through a fine-mesh strainer, reserving ½ cup to add to the dish in step 3. Plum tomatoes are preferred because they hold their shape better than larger tomato varieties; they are usually sweeter and less acidic as well. However, any type of tomato will suffice, especially vine-ripened tomatoes at the height of summer.

12 medium Italian plum tomatoes, pulp and seeds removed

1 pound *hashu* (Aleppian Ground Meat and Rice Filling, page 136)

2 tablespoons vegetable oil

1 teaspoon kosher salt

Juice of 1 lemon (about 3 tablespoons)

3 tablespoons *ouc* (tamarind concentrate, page 41), homemade or store-bought

2 teaspoons sugar (optional)

1. Preheat the oven to 350°F.

2. Fill the tomatoes loosely with *hashu*.

3. Drizzle 1 tablespoon of the vegetable oil into a large ovenproof saucepan or roaster. Place the stuffed tomatoes in the pan so they are upright. Sprinkle with the salt. Drizzle some of the lemon juice into the center of each tomato. Drizzle the remaining 1 tablespoon oil liberally around pan. Dollop a teaspoon of *ouc* over each tomato and sprinkle with the sugar, if desired.

4. Cover and roast in the oven for about 40 minutes. Remove the cover and cook for an additional 10 minutes, or until the juices have thickened.

Yield: 6 to 8 servings

Mehshi Kusa

ZUCCHINI OR YELLOW SQUASH
STUFFED WITH GROUND MEAT AND RICE

One tool that is essential for this recipe is the *ma'vdeh,* a squash corer used in the Middle East (see photo, page 139). This narrow utensil is used to core eggplant, zucchini and squashes, and potatoes, and comes in two lengths: a shorter one for coring smaller eggplant and zucchini, and a longer one to hollow out larger squashes. A narrow apple corer makes an acceptable substitute for the shorter corer. The more accomplished cook will strive to achieve a very thin shell when coring. Some cooks also decorate the zucchini or squash by peeling alternating vertical ¼-inch strips from the vegetable or by scoring lengthwise with a fork.

8 medium zucchini
  or yellow squash, cored

1 pound *hashu* (Aleppian Ground Meat
  and Rice Filling, page 136)

2 tablespoons vegetable oil

20 dried apricots

1 teaspoon kosher salt

3 tablespoons freshly squeezed lemon juice

3 tablespoons *ouᶜ* (tamarind concentrate,
  page 41), homemade or store-bought

1 tablespoon sugar (optional)

1. Loosely stuff the squash with *hashu.*

2. Pour the vegetable oil into a medium ovenproof saucepan. Place the stuffed squash inside and layer half the apricots on top. Place the saucepan over medium heat and cook the squash for about 8 minutes, or until they begin to release their liquid.

3. Add the remaining apricots in a layer and sprinkle with salt. Mix the lemon juice, *ouᶜ*, and, if desired, sugar, and add to apricots. Pour 1 cup water over the apricots and place a heat-proof plate on top as a weight. Bring the liquid to a boil over medium-high heat. Reduce the heat to low, cover, and simmer gently for 1 hour.

4. Preheat the oven to 350°F.

5. Transfer the saucepan to the oven and cook the squash for an additional 40 minutes to thicken the sauce, integrate the flavors, and caramelize the squash.

❧ *Variation* ❧

MEHSHI KUSA WITH TOMATO-MINT SAUCE
Omit the apricots and *ouᶜ* in step 3, substitute one 6-ounce can tomato sauce; 1 tablespoon dried mint; and 6 garlic cloves, chopped. To prevent the *mehshi* from sticking to the pan, cut a peeled potato into thin slices and layer on the bottom of the pan before adding the *mehshi.*

Yield: 6 to 8 servings

*Mehshi Kusa (Zucchini or Yellow Squash Stuffed
with Ground Meat and Rice, page 143)*

Mehshi Basal

CARAMELIZED ONIONS STUFFED WITH GROUND MEAT AND RICE

A cook's expertise can be discerned by the tightness of her rolled stuffed onions. A tray of tightly rolled *mehshi basal* arranged in uniform rows or randomly placed is a beautiful sight to see—and delicious either way! *Mehshi basal* and *mehshi malfuf* (Cabbage Stuffed with Ground Meat and Rice, page 148) are never served at the same meal because they are too similar.

3 Spanish or Vidalia onions

1 pound *hashu* (Aleppian Ground Meat and Rice Filling, page 136)

3 tablespoons *ouᶜ*
(tamarind concentrate, page 41),
homemade or store-bought

2 tablespoons freshly squeezed
lemon juice

1 teaspoon kosher salt

1 teaspoon sugar (optional)

1. Cut a vertical slit down the side of each onion and remove the outer skin. Put the onions in a large saucepan, cover with water, and bring to a boil. Reduce the heat to low and simmer for 20 minutes, or until the onion layers begin to soften and come apart.

2. Drain and remove the onions from the saucepan. Separate the individual layers of each onion.

3. Spoon a tablespoon of *hashu* into each onion layer and roll tightly. (The onions can be frozen on a baking sheet, if desired, and stored in a freezer bag.)

4. Preheat the oven to 350°F.

5. Place the stuffed onions in a medium ovenproof saucepan or roaster. In a small bowl, mix the *ouᶜ*, lemon juice, salt, 1 cup water, and sugar, if using. Pour over the onions. Top with an ovenproof plate to keep onions from opening. Bring to a boil over high heat, then reduce the heat to low, cover, and simmer for 30 minutes, or until the juices have thickened and the meat is fully cooked. Transfer to the oven and continue to cook the onions for 1 hour and 20 minutes.

Yield: 6 to 8 servings

Mehshi Malfuf محشي ملفوف

CABBAGE STUFFED
WITH GROUND MEAT AND RICE

Hashu (meat and rice stuffing) is augmented here with a chopped raw onion. This dish has a very distinct taste—tart, yet fruity and balanced—and is very different from the cabbage dishes of Eastern Europe.

1 head green cabbage (3½ to 4 pounds)

2 pounds *hashu* (Aleppian Ground Meat and Rice Filling, page 136)

1 onion, chopped (about ½ cup)

1 tablespoon vegetable oil

2 tablespoons tomato paste

1 tablespoon *ouᶜ* (tamarind concentrate, page 41), homemade or store-bought

¼ cup freshly squeezed lemon juice (1 to 2 lemons)

1 tablespoon kosher salt

1. Remove the hard stem of the cabbage and place the leaves in a large saucepan with enough water to cover them completely. Boil the cabbage leaves for 15 minutes, or until the leaves are just tender. Be careful not to overcook the cabbage. Remove the cabbage from the saucepan. Separate the leaves and rinse in cold water.

2. Combine the *hashu* and onion. Place 1 tablespoon of the mixture on the lower portion of a leaf. Fold in the sides and roll tightly. Repeat with the remaining *hashu* and cabbage leaves.

3. Drizzle the vegetable oil in a large saucepan. Add the rolled cabbage, seam side down, and cook, covered, over medium-low heat for about 15 mïnutes. Then add 1 cup water, along with the tomato paste, *ouᶜ*, lemon juice, and salt. Bring the liquid to a boil over high heat, then reduce to low heat, cover with a heat-proof plate for weight, and simmer for 40 minutes, or until the cooking juices have thickened. (Alternatively, place the saucepan in a preheated 350°F oven for 40 minutes.)

Yield: 6 to 8 servings

Mehshi Batata

POTATOES STUFFED
WITH GROUND MEAT AND RICE

One of the heartier *mehshis,* this dish appears less often on the Sabbath dinner table because it tends to be quite filling and thus competes with the multidish menus favored by most of today's ambitious Aleppian Jewish cooks. Nonetheless, it is quite a delicious, rich item brought to the table when potatoes are not served alongside *djaj mishwi* (Friday Night Roast Chicken with Potatoes, page 189).

12 medium potatoes (any variety), peeled	1 pound *hashu* (Aleppian Ground Meat and Rice Filling, page 136)	1 tablespoon kosher salt
1 cup vegetable oil	1 tablespoon ground allspice	

1. Flatten the top of each potato by trimming the rounded part. Core the potatoes, leaving about ¼ inch of the outer shell, reserving the interior flesh for step 3.

2. In a medium saucepan, heat the vegetable oil and cook over medium-high heat. It will be ready for frying when it sizzles upon contact with a drop of water. Deep-fry the potato shells in batches for 5 minutes per batch, or until they begin turning golden. Drain them upside down on paper towels.

3. Deep-fry the interior flesh of the potatoes for 5 minutes, or until golden-brown, and drain.

4. Stuff the cored potatoes with the *hashu* and place them in a medium ovenproof saucepan or roaster. Add the fried interior pieces to the pot and enough water to cover the potatoes halfway. Sprinkle the potatoes with the allspice and salt.

5. Bring to a boil over high heat. Reduce the heat to low, cover, and simmer for 1 hour. Meanwhile, preheat the oven to 350°F.

6. Transfer the saucepan to the oven for 30 minutes more, uncovered, or until the potatoes are golden brown.

Yield: 6 to 8 servings

Yebra

GRAPE LEAVES STUFFED WITH GROUND MEAT AND RICE, WITH APRICOT-TAMARIND SAUCE

Yebra is the distinctively Aleppian version of the popular Mediterranean stuffed grape leaves. Instead of using the lemon and garlic that accents the common Mediterranean version (page 66), Aleppian Jews flavor *yebra* with dried apricots and *ouᶜ* (tamarind concentrate). The Aleppian Jews' penchant for tangy and fruity dishes betrays the Persian influence on their cuisine. Unlike lemon-garlic stuffed grape leaves, which are almost always cooked on the stove top and are often served cold, *yebra* is served hot and may be cooked slowly in the oven to allow the apricots to melt and the *ouᶜ* to absorb into the *hashu*. *Yebra* is usually served as one of several substantial beef, poultry, and vegetable dishes on the Sabbath dinner table. For a conventional meal, *yebra* can be served as a main course or as an accompaniment to a meat or poultry entrée.

36 preserved grape leaves (one 8-ounce jar), stems trimmed, drained, rinsed, and patted dry

1 pound *hashu* (Aleppian Ground Meat and Rice Filling, page 136)

1 tablespoon vegetable oil

16 dried apricots (see Note)

6 tablespoons *ouᶜ* (tamarind concentrate, page 41), homemade or store-bought

¼ cup freshly squeezed lemon juice (1 to 2 lemons)

1 teaspoon kosher salt

1. Place one grape leaf on a wooden board or plate, vein side up. Place 1 heaping teaspoon of *hashu* in the center of the leaf, near the stem edge. Roll the leaf end to end, starting from the stem edge. As you roll, fold the sides of the leaf toward the center. The rolled leaf should resemble a small cigar about 2½ inches long. Repeat with the remaining leaves and filling. (*Yebra* may be frozen at this point on a baking sheet lined with wax paper. When firmly frozen, transfer to an airtight plastic bag and store for future use.)

2. Drizzle the vegetable oil into a medium saucepan. Place the filled grape leaves and apricots in the pot, alternating between the two. Cover and cook the stuffed grape leaves over low heat for 5 to 8 minutes, or until they begin to sweat.

3. Dollop the *ouᶜ* over the grape leaves. Add the lemon juice and salt. Fill the pan with water to cover the grape leaves three-quarters of the way. Weigh down the grape leaves

with a heat-proof plate to prevent them from unraveling. Cover and bring to a boil over medium-high heat. Reduce the heat to low and simmer for 35 to 40 minutes. Alternatively, place the saucepan in an oven preheated to 350°F and cook for 1 hour. Spoon cooking liquid over the *yebra* occasionally. When they are done, the *yebra* should be neither soupy nor dry; a moderate amount of reduced pan juices should surround them. To minimize tearing, turn the *yebra* and pan juices onto a serving platter without handling any of them individually.

❧ *Note* ❧
California apricots work best here. Avoid unsulfured or pale Turkish apricots; they simply do not impart the tartness and flavor required for this dish.

Yield: 6 to 8 servings

Medias Shawki

ARTICHOKE HALVES
STUFFED WITH GROUND MEAT

Medias appeared in Aleppo courtesy of Spanish Jews who arrived in the Ottoman lands after Ferdinand and Isabella's Edict of Expulsion (see page 3). The word *media* is Spanish for "half." The artichokes in this recipe are split in half lengthwise, filled with meat, and then cooked.

6 artichokes

Filling:

1 pound ground beef

2 eggs

1 teaspoon ground allspice

1 teaspoon kosher salt

1 cup *matzah* meal

1 cup vegetable oil

Sauce:

Two 8-ounce cans tomato sauce

Juice of 2 lemons (about 6 tablespoons)

1 teaspoon sugar

1 teaspoon kosher salt

2 tablespoons extra-virgin olive oil

1. Cut the artichokes in half lengthwise, remove the hairy choke, and trim 1 inch of bracts (leaves) from the top.

2. To make the filling, combine the beef, 1 egg, allspice, and salt in a medium mixing bowl and mix well. Fill the cavity of each artichoke with the filling.

3. Put the remaining egg in a shallow dish and beat it; put the *matzah* meal in another. Dip each artichoke in egg and then dredge in the *matzah* meal.

4. Heat the vegetable oil in a medium skillet over medium heat. Fry the artichokes, filling-side down, for 2 minutes, or until the breading is golden brown. Place the artichokes in a large skillet in a single layer. Do not stack.

5. To make the sauce, combine the tomato sauce, lemon juice, sugar, salt, and 1 cup water. Mix well.

6. Drizzle the olive oil into a medium ovenproof saucepan. Place the fried artichokes in the saucepan, filling-side up. Sprinkle the artichokes with salt. Cook over medium heat for 3 minutes, or until the artichokes begin to sweat. Pour the sauce over the artichokes. Bring to a boil over high heat, then reduce the heat to low, cover, and simmer for 30 minutes, or until the artichoke hearts are fork-tender.

Yield: 8 to 10 servings

Medias Shawki
(*Artichoke Halves Stuffed
with Ground Meat, page 153*)

Kibbeh

STUFFED SYRIAN MEATBALLS
WITH GROUND RICE

These uncooked meatballs are a staple in the Aleppian kitchen because they are used in many recipes. *Kibbeh* are often prepared with vegetables such as mushrooms and peas, and then added to sauce-based dishes such as *haloob* (Artichokes in Tamarind Broth with Sautéed Meatballs, page 98) and soups such as *shurba w'kibbeh* (Smooth Tomato-Rice Soup with Meatballs, page 104).

    Kibbeh combine two different kinds of meat: smooth, silky meat for the outer shell, and a seasoned meat for the filling. They absorb the liquid in which they are cooked, trapping surrounding flavors while maintaining a moist yet firm bite. Because *kibbeh* are used in so many recipes, most Aleppian Jewish cooks prepare them in large quantities and store them in the freezer. These *kibbeh* should not be confused with *kibbeh nabelsieh* (Golden Ground Meat–Filled Bulgur Shells, page 53) and *kibbeh bil sanieh* (Baked Bulgur–Ground Meat Pie, page 171).

Outer Shell:

1 pound very lean ground beef

½ cup ground long-grain white rice
   (see Note)

1 teaspoon kosher salt

Filling:

½ pound ground beef

¾ cup inner celery leaves, chopped

1 teaspoon ground allspice

1 teaspoon kosher salt

¼ cup vegetable oil,
     plus 1 optional teaspoon

1 teaspoon lemon juice

1. To make the outer shell, grind the lean meat in a meat grinder or a food processor equipped with a meat grinder attachment. Add the ground rice and salt to the meat and grind twice more, so that the mixture is well blended and smooth. Your butcher can easily do this for you.

2. To make the filling, in a medium mixing bowl combine the beef, celery leaves, allspice, salt, and the 1 teaspoon vegetable oil, if desired. Mix well by hand.

3. Roll the outer shell mixture into 1-inch balls. In a small dish, combine the ¼ cup oil and lemon juice.

4. Dip your finger into the oil and lemon mixture (this keeps the shell from sticking to it) and hollow each ball with your finger. The thinner you can make the shell, the better. This step requires some practice; use your finger to press the round ball against the palm of your hand, rotating your finger firmly. The shell should be thin, but not so thin that the filling will break through (about ⅛ inch).

5. Fill each hollowed-out shell with about 1 teaspoon of the filling. Close by pinching the shell firmly over the filling, smoothing with a little water. The meatballs may be frozen at this point.

∾ *Note* ∾

Ground rice is available at Middle Eastern groceries.

Yield: 6 to 8 servings, about 30 kibbeh

Bizeh b'Kibbeh

GREEN PEAS WITH ALLSPICE AND MEAT

Some Sabbath meals are considered incomplete without this dish. Families vary in how they like to prepare their peas. Some add them at the end of the cooking process, in order to preserve their bright green color and firmness. Others cook them for many hours for a mushier texture. It is worth using fresh peas when in season because they add unparalleled sweetness to this dish.

½ recipe *kibbeh* (Stuffed Syrian Meatballs with Ground Rice, page 156)

1½ tablespoons vegetable oil

3 garlic cloves, chopped (1½ teaspoons)

One 16-ounce bag frozen peas or 2 cups fresh peas

1 teaspoon ground allspice

½ teaspoon ground cinnamon

1 teaspoon kosher salt

In a medium skillet, sauté the *kibbeh* in the vegetable oil over medium heat for 5 minutes, or until brown. Add the garlic and cook for 1 minute. Add the peas, allspice, cinnamon, salt, and 1½ cups water. Cook, covered, over medium-low heat for 1 hour until ¼ cup of cooking liquid remains.

Yield: 4 to 6 servings

Fawleh b'Lahmeh

TENDER FLANKEN
WITH STRING BEANS

Cooks are encouraged to use fresh string beans. The flavor and texture they bring to the dish far surpasses the result achieved with frozen beans. Many prefer french-cutting the string beans so they will absorb more of the dish's flavors. To french-cut the beans, trim the ends and, using a sharp knife or a vegetable peeler with french-cutting blades at one end, cut the beans into thin strands.

1 pound flanken, cut in 2-inch cubes

2 to 3 tablespoons vegetable oil

2 onions, chopped (about 1 cup)

2 pounds string beans, trimmed, left whole or french-cut

2 large tomatoes, chopped (about 2 cups)

4 garlic cloves, chopped (about 2 teaspoons)

1 heaping tablespoon ground allspice

1 teaspoon ground cinnamon

1 tablespoon kosher salt

¼ teaspoon white pepper

1. In a large ovenproof saucepan, brown the flanken in the vegetable oil over medium-high heat for about 10 minutes. Add the onions to the meat and sauté for 10 minutes. Next, add 4 to 5 cups water, reduce the heat to low, and simmer, uncovered, for 30 minutes.

2. Add the string beans, tomatoes, garlic, allspice, cinnamon, salt, and white pepper. Simmer for 30 minutes, uncovered, or until about 1 cup of liquid remains.

3. Preheat the oven to 300°F.

4. To meld the flavors (and not disturb the appearance of the string beans), grasp the pan firmly with pot holders, cover, hold down the lid, and shake well. Transfer the saucepan to the oven, and braise, covered, for 1 to 1½ hours until meat is tender.

Yield: 8 to 10 servings

Kibbeh b'Fettair

MUSHROOMS AND SAUTÉED MEATBALLS

The *kibbeh* used in this dish should be somewhat larger than the ones prepared for *kibbeh hamdah* (Lemon-Mint Broth with Mixed Vegetables and Syrian Meatballs, page 97) and *haloob* (Artichokes in Tamarind Broth with Sautéed Meatballs, page 98). The meat cooks for a long time in the liquid released from the mushrooms and softens, absorbing the mushrooms' delicious flavor.

18 *kibbeh*, about 1¼ inches long
   (Stuffed Syrian Meatballs
   with Ground Rice, page 156)

2 tablespoons vegetable oil

2 pounds cremini mushrooms,
   button mushrooms, or desert truffles
   (see page 169)

1 teaspoon kosher salt

1 teaspoon ground allspice

¼ teaspoon white pepper
   (optional)

1. In a medium saucepan over medium heat, sauté the *kibbeh* in the vegetable oil for 5 minutes.

2. When the *kibbeh* are lightly browned, add the mushrooms and season with the salt, allspice, and white pepper, if desired. Reduce the heat to low and simmer, covered, for 45 minutes over low heat until the juices thicken. (Alternatively, place the saucepan into a 350°F oven for 45 minutes.)

Yield: 6 to 8 servings

Keftes

TAMARIND-STEWED MEATBALLS

Meatball dishes such as *keftes* are a tradition all over the Middle East. Some regions use turmeric and others use sumac or lemon and mint as flavoring accents for similar meatballs. Aleppian Jews like to use a combination of tomato sauce and tamarind, the proportions of which can vary according to a family's preference.

Meatballs:

1 pound ground beef

3 eggs

3 tablespoons *matzah* meal

1½ teaspoons kosher salt

1 teaspoon Aleppo pepper,
   or ½ teaspoon crushed red pepper

Sauce:

One 6-ounce can tomato paste,
   or two 8-ounce cans tomato sauce

1 tablespoon *ou^c*
   (tamarind concentrate, page 41),
   homemade or store-bought

Juice of 1 lemon
   (about 3 tablespoons)

1 teaspoon kosher salt

½ teaspoon sugar
   (optional)

2 tablespoons vegetable oil

1. To make the meatballs, combine the beef, eggs, *matzah* meal, salt, and Aleppo pepper. Mix well by hand. The mixture should be loose and moist so that it can best absorb the sauce and sustain a velvety texture. Shape the meat mixture into walnut-size balls.

2. To make the sauce, combine the tomato paste, *ou^c*, lemon juice, salt, 1 cup water, and, if desired, sugar. Mix well.

3. In a large ovenproof saucepan, brown the meatballs, one batch at a time, in the oil over medium-high heat for about 3 minutes per batch.

4. Return all the meatballs to the saucepan. Pour the sauce over the meatballs and bring to a boil. Reduce the heat to low and simmer, covered, for 30 minutes to thicken sauce and allow the flavors to integrate thoroughly.

☙ *Variation* ☙

For a tangier sauce, increase the *ou^c* by 1½ teaspoons and increase the water by ½ cup. Or omit the *ou^c* altogether for a lighter, more refreshing sauce, especially if you are serving another dish with *ou^c*.

Yield: 8 to 10 servings

Kebab Garaz

SWEET CHERRY–STEWED MEATBALLS

A small, bitter, crimson-colored cherry found near Aleppo, called the St. Lucie's cherry (*Prunus mahaleb* L.), is the featured flavor of two Aleppian Jewish dishes, this one and *kibbeh b'garaz* (Sweet Cherry–Stuffed Beef Slices, page 166). You can use either fresh pitted sour cherries or canned sweet cherries (though not the garish, syrupy sort used for pie filling). During the summer months, it is a good idea to pit cherries and freeze them for later use.

This dish, *kebab garaz,* is a stewlike preparation. It was traditionally served over open-faced Syrian flatbread and topped with chopped parsley and scallions. Today, many Aleppian Jews enjoy *kebab garaz* over rice because it is often served alongside other dishes that are complemented by rice.

Meatballs:

1 pound ground beef

½ cup pine nuts

½ teaspoon ground allspice

3 tablespoons vegetable oil

Sauce:

3 onions, chopped (about 1½ cups)

Two 15-ounce cans dark sweet pitted cherries, including liquid, or 1 pound fresh cherries, pitted

1 tablespoon *ouᶜ* (tamarind concentrate, page 41), homemade or store-bought

Juice of 1 lemon (about 3 tablespoons)

1 tablespoon sugar

1 teaspoon ground allspice

1 cup sweet red wine or Concord grape juice (optional)

1. To make the meatballs, combine the beef, pine nuts, and allspice in a medium mixing bowl. Knead thoroughly by hand. Form into 2-inch-long torpedo shapes.

2. In a medium saucepan, sauté the meatballs in 2 tablespoons of the vegetable oil over medium heat for 3 minutes or until lightly browned, turning gently to brown both sides.

3. Remove the meatballs and set aside. Use the same saucepan to make the sauce. Sauté the onions in the remaining 1 tablespoon vegetable oil over medium heat for 4 to 6 minutes, or until translucent. Add the liquid from the canned cherries, along with the *ouᶜ*, lemon juice, sugar, allspice, and ½ cup water (or 1 cup if using fresh cherries), and wine or juice, if desired. Give it a stir. Bring to a boil. Add the meatballs and cherries to the saucepan. Cover the saucepan, reduce the heat to low, and simmer for 1 hour, or until the sauce has thickened.

Yield: 6 to 8 servings

Kibbeh b'Garaz

SWEET CHERRY–STUFFED BEEF SLICES

This cherry-based dish is popular among Aleppian Jews. It is a relative newcomer to the repertoire of Aleppian Jewish cuisine, though it relies on traditional ingredients. It is composed of similar ingredients to those found in *kebab garaz* (Sweet Cherry–Stewed Meatballs, page 165), another beloved dish. The essential difference is the way it is prepared. Here, the meat portion of the dish is rolled end over end like a jelly roll. When the meat is sliced, it makes for quite a beautiful and appetizing display.

Outer Shell:

2 pounds *kibbeh* mixture (Stuffed Syrian Meatballs with Ground Rice, page 156)

Meat Mixture:

1 pound ground beef

½ cup finely chopped celery leaves

1 teaspoon kosher salt

½ teaspoon ground allspice

½ pound dried apricots

Sauce:

Three 15-ounce cans pitted sweet cherries, drained, reserving the liquid; or 3 pounds fresh cherries, pitted

9 tablespoons *ouᶜ* (tamarind concentrate, page 41), homemade or store-bought

1 tablespoon kosher salt

Juice of 2 lemons (about 6 tablespoons)

2 tablespoons vegetable oil

1. To make the outer shell, divide the *kibbeh* into 3 equal portions. Between 2 sheets of wax paper, roll each portion into an 8 x 11-inch rectangle that is ⅛ inch thick. Remove the top sheet of the wax paper.

2. In a medium mixing bowl, combine the ground beef, celery leaves, salt, and allspice. Divide into 3 equal portions. Spread ⅓ of the ground beef filling evenly across the top of one of the flattened *kibbeh* meats. Lay ⅓ of the apricots in a row across the bottom edge. Roll the *kibbeh* meat like a jelly roll, using the wax paper as a guide. Repeat with the remaining 2 flattened *kibbehs,* filling, and apricots. (The rolled meat may be frozen at this point, wrapped tightly.)

3. To make the sauce, in a medium mixing bowl combine the pitted cherries, *ouᶜ*, salt, lemon juice, and reserved cherry juice (or 1½ cups water if using fresh cherries). Mix well and set aside.

4. Preheat the oven to 375°F.

5. Brush each roll with vegetable oil. Pierce the rolls deeply with a fork. Place the rolls in a large roaster, seam side down. Cover the roaster and braise in the oven for 10 minutes, or until the meat is slightly browned.

6. Remove the rolls from the oven. Pour the sauce over them and reduce the oven temperature to 350°F. Return the roaster to the oven and braise the rolls, covered, for another 45 minutes, or until tender. Remove the roaster from the oven and let stand for 5 minutes.

7. Remove the rolls from the roaster and slice them thinly on the bias. Arrange the slices in a single layer in the roaster. Baste the slices and cherries with pan juices. Return the roaster to the oven, cover, and braise for 30 minutes or longer, until the sauce thickens.

*Yield: **8 to 10 servings***

Rubuh'

SUCCULENT ROAST VEAL STUFFED WITH SPICED GROUND MEAT AND RICE

This is one of the more elaborate dishes in the Aleppian Jewish repertoire, utilizing a broad array of ingredients and techniques. *Hashu,* the ground meat and rice stuffing, is enhanced by the addition of allspice and is then stuffed into a breast of veal that is slow-roasted until it achieves superb tenderness. Adding vegetables such as mushrooms, fava beans, carrots, peas, or desert truffles (*kamayeh,* see page 169) to the roaster further intensifies the rich cooking juices and makes for a wonderful accompaniment. Fava beans are one of the most popular choices. Some of the old-time Syrian women cook the beans with the pods to enhance the flavor of the recipe. Cut the bean pods on a diagonal, so that each bean remains in its own shell. This works well when the fava beans are small and tender, and makes for a tastier dish.

Another delicious twist is to surround the veal with up to 6 whole, uncooked eggs in their shells. The eggs come out with a brown finish and are traditionally enjoyed with salt and allspice.

3 to 4 pounds veal breast, bone in, slit crosswise to form a pocket (your butcher can do this)

1 pound *hashu* (Aleppian Ground Meat and Rice Filling, page 136)

1 tablespoon ground allspice

1 teaspoon kosher salt

2 to 3 garlic cloves, minced (1 to 1½ teaspoons)

¼ teaspoon ground white pepper (optional)

3 tablespoons vegetable oil

1 large onion, chopped (about 1½ cups)

4 ribs celery, including leaves, chopped (about 2 cups)

Choice of:

2 pounds shelled fava beans, fresh or frozen, or 2½ to 3 pounds fresh whole fava beans, cut diagonally

2 pounds shelled green peas, fresh or frozen

2 pounds fresh whole mushrooms, cleaned and trimmed

2 pounds artichoke hearts, quartered, fresh or frozen

2 pounds desert truffles

1. Preheat the oven to 350°F.

2. Loosely stuff the veal breast with the *hashu.* Place extra stuffing in a parchment envelope. Set the breast aside on a tray.

3. Combine the allspice, salt, garlic, and pepper, if desired. Rub 1 tablespoon of the oil all over the veal breast. Generously apply allspice mixture to the veal breast.

4. In a large roaster, sauté the onion and celery in the remaining 2 tablespoons oil for 3 minutes or until soft. Transfer to a small mixing bowl.

5. Sear the veal in the same large roaster over medium-high heat for 5 minutes, or until lightly browned, turning once. Add the onion-celery mixture to the pan, along with the parchment envelope and 1 cup water. Cover and braise for 1 hour, basting occasionally.

6. Remove from oven and add any of the optional vegetables to the roaster. Season with additional allspice, salt, and white pepper, if desired. Open the envelope of extra stuffing, breaking it up with a fork and discarding the parchment paper. Reduce oven temperature to 300°F. Add an additional ½ cup water and return to oven. Roast for another 1½ to 2 hours.

❧ *Note* ❧

You can freeze fresh fava beans and enjoy them near the peak of their flavor year-round. In a medium saucepan, place the fresh beans in enough water to cover them. Bring to a boil over medium heat, then remove the beans from the heat immediately. Pour the beans and the liquid into a plastic container, cool, then freeze.

Yield: 8 to 10 servings

❧ *Kamayeh*—Desert Truffles ❧

Syrian desert truffles, like the distantly related European black and white forest truffles, are quite rare and make equally exquisite additions to any meal, particularly as accompaniments to rich meat dishes. They resemble small potatoes and are available in red and white varieties, the former more prized than the latter. The flavor of desert truffles is deep and earthy, and the texture is firm yet pleasantly yielding to the bite.

These truffles appear in the Syrian desert only after the rains of winter and spring. Some argue that the prevalence of truffles in a given season depends on whether there were extensive thunderstorms during the preceding autumn. Though it sounds like a laughable old wives' tale, scientists have indeed found that lightning enriches rain with nitrogen, which apparently triggers the growth of *kamayeh.*

In Syria, the Bedouin are skilled at locating desert truffles, which they collect near rockrose shrubs. They simply look out on the dunes for the desert truffles, which peek their heads out after ripening, appearing as little bumps in the sand. The truffles are brought to market in Damascus and Aleppo and as far as Beirut, where they sell for as much as fifteen dollars per pound, a small fortune in the Middle East.

If you ever have a chance to try them, do not hesitate. *Kamayeh* are truly a luxurious and uncommon treat. Desert truffles begin losing their flavor immediately after they are harvested. They can be frozen for 2 weeks in a glass jar.

Kibbeh bil Sanieh

BAKED BULGUR–GROUND MEAT PIE

This meat pie, sometimes cut in a diamond pattern, uses the same ingredients as *kibbeh nabelsieh* (Golden Ground Meat–Filled Bulgur Shells, page 53), but is easier to make. The recipe was traditionally prepared with a stone mortar and heavy pestle called the *hon* or *jorn* and *modaqqa*, but today we can easily use a food processor.

Filling:

½ cup pine nuts

1 pound *tadbileh* (Spiced Ground Beef Filling, page 55)

Crust:

½ pound ground beef

2 cups fine bulgur (cracked wheat), rinsed in cold water and drained

1 onion, grated (about ½ cup)

1 teaspoon tomato paste

1 teaspoon ground allspice

1 tablespoon ground cumin

1 teaspoon Aleppo pepper, or ½ teaspoon crushed red pepper

1 tablespoon kosher salt

2 tablespoons vegetable oil or margarine

1. Preheat the oven to 350°F.

2. To make the filling, fold the pine nuts into the *tadbileh*.

3. To make the crust, combine the ground beef and bulgur in a medium mixing bowl. Pass the mixture through a meat grinder. (Alternatively, you can use a food processor for 1 minute.) Return to the bowl and add the grated onion, tomato paste, allspice, cumin, Aleppo pepper, and salt. Mix well.

4. Grease a round 12-inch baking dish (or a 13 x 9-inch pan). Cover the bottom of the dish with half the crust mixture to a depth of ¼ inch. Press down to form a smooth surface. Spread the filling evenly over the bottom crust. Top with the remaining crust.

5. Cut into wedges if using a round pan. In a rectangular pan, score diagonally to make a diamond pattern, or slice vertically and horizontally to make squares. Be sure to use a sharp knife. Dip the knife occasionally in cold water to ensure clean and even cut lines.

6. Pour the vegetable oil or dot the margarine over the crust and bake for 1 hour. Serve hot or at room temperature, with *tehineh* (Sesame Spread, page 26), lemon wedges, or *salata arabi* (Basic Syrian Salad with Lemon-Cumin Dressing, page 30).

Yield: 6 to 8 servings

Lahmeh fil Makleh لحمة بالمقلي

ALEPPIAN BEEF STEW

This hearty, nourishing dish, which resembles ratatouille with meat, helped many families through the chilly Aleppo winters. If you prefer, substitute chicken pieces for the beef, or make the stew as a vegetarian dish. Additional vegetables may also be used, such as green beans, yellow squash, acorn squash, butternut squash, and yams.

1 large onion, chopped (about 1 cup)

1 tablespoon vegetable oil

1 pound ground beef or beef chuck
   or flanken, cut in 2-inch cubes

One 29-ounce can stewed tomatoes

One 8-ounce can tomato sauce

1 large potato, peeled and cubed

1 large carrot, sliced

½ large eggplant, peeled and cubed

1 green bell pepper, sliced

¼ cup *ou*ᶜ (tamarind concentrate, page 41),
   homemade or store-bought

¼ cup freshly squeezed lemon juice
   (1 to 2 lemons)

Pinch of sugar

1. In a medium saucepan, sauté the onion in the vegetable oil over medium heat for 6 to 8 minutes, or until translucent. Add the ground meat to the onion mixture and cook for about 20 minutes, stirring occasionally. Or, if using cubed meat, add 2 cups water and cook over medium-low heat, covered, for about 30 minutes.

2. Reduce the heat to low, and add the tomatoes, tomato sauce, potato, carrot, eggplant, bell pepper, *ou*ᶜ, lemon juice, and sugar to the meat mixture and cook for about 1 hour, or until the vegetables are fork-tender and the liquid has thickened.

Yield: 8 to 10 servings

Ma'udeh

HEARTY BEEF STEW

This recipe is a centuries-old classic. An unusually rich dish, *ma'udeh* calls for many types of meat, which meld over low heat into a delectable and hearty stew. The longer *ma'udeh* simmers on the stove, the more tender and delicious it becomes—and its flavor only improves when reheated the next day. Amazingly, this dish does not call for salt. *Ma'udeh* is simple to prepare and perfect for a winter Sabbath dinner or lunch.

1 lamb shank

2 pounds flanken, cut in 2-inch cubes

1½ pounds boneless veal,
    cut in 2-inch cubes

1½ pounds beef chuck steak,
    cut in 2-inch cubes

½ head celery, cut into 4-inch segments

3 onions, sliced

20 *kibbeh* (Stuffed Syrian Meatballs
    with Ground Rice, page 156)

Cook the lamb shank, flanken, veal, beef, celery, onions, and 1 cup water in a large heavy saucepan, covered, over low heat for 1 hour. Add the *kibbeh* and continue to cook for 4 more hours, or until the meat is tender and the onions and juices are caramelized. After the first 2 hours, shake the pot to distribute juices and coat the meat. To avoid shredding the meat, never stir with a spoon .

Yield: 8 to 10 servings

Salajahn

SPICY GRILLED MEAT KABOBS

These kabobs make a fantastic summer barbecue meal, served with warm Syrian flatbread and *salata arabi* (Basic Syrian Salad with Lemon-Cumin Dressing, page 30). Many families are so enamored of this dish that during the colder seasons, cooks will grill the kabobs right over a stove-top flame.

1 pound ground beef or lamb	2 tablespoons chopped fresh flat-leaf parsley	1 teaspoon ground cinnamon
1 onion, finely chopped (about ½ cup)	1 teaspoon ground allspice	1 teaspoon kosher salt

1. Combine the beef, onion, parsley, allspice, cinnamon, and salt in a medium mixing bowl. Mix well. Form the mixture into cigar shapes around skewers.

2. Prepare a medium-hot grill or preheat a broiler.

3. Cook the kabobs for 8 to 10 minutes, turning once, until the meat is slightly charred and well done.

Yield: 4 to 6 servings

Salchicha

SPICY SAUSAGE

In the old days, Aleppian Jewish cooks made sausage by stuffing spiced meat into casings made from cattle intestines (*taa'* in Arabic) and then hanging them to dry in the cool air of their cellar. *Salchicha* is Spanish for "sausage." As its name indicates, this recipe represents another contribution to Aleppian Jewish cuisine by Spanish Jews. It is a delicacy that depends on the preservative power of salt (*sal* in Spanish). Today, *salchicha* remains much adored, especially with scrambled eggs on Sunday morning. However, most prefer to spare their families and buy *salchicha* from a Syrian grocer instead of festooning their basements with ropes of sausage. Aleppian Jews usually substitute synthetic casings for the natural ones because natural kosher casings are extremely difficult to obtain.

3 yards sausage casing	2 tablespoons ground cinnamon	¼ cup black pepper
2 pounds ground beef	2 tablespoons ground nutmeg	1 tablespoon kosher salt
¼ cup ground allspice		

1. Soak the casing in cold water for 1 hour, changing the water frequently.

2. Combine the beef, allspice, cinnamon, nutmeg, black pepper, and salt in a large mixing bowl. Mix thoroughly.

3. Roll one yard of casing onto the opening of a sausage-stuffing attachment for a stand mixer.

4. To begin, pinch the casing with your fingers. Force the meat into the feeder at medium speed until an entire yard of casing is full. Twist the casing every 4 inches to form sausages. Remove from the attachment and repeat this process with the remaining casing 2 more times. Hang the sausages overnight. (The sausages may be frozen at this point.)

5. To cook the *salchicha*, place on a hot grill or in an oven preheated to 375°F. Cook for 8 to 10 minutes, turning once. Do not overcook; the sausages should remain juicy.

Yield: 27 sausages

Inferekeh

GROUND MEAT WITH
SCRAMBLED EGGS AND MUSHROOMS

In Aleppo, a pot of steaming *inferekeh* was usually served for lunch on the eve of Passover. By then all signs of bread were long gone from the house. *Inferekeh* was served over rice because Jewish law required that the Passover *matzah* not be eaten until the evening meal, which still holds true today.

1 pound ground veal or beef

5 eggs, beaten

½ teaspoon ground allspice

¼ teaspoon ground cinnamon

½ teaspoon kosher salt

1 tablespoon vegetable oil

1 pound cremini or white button mushrooms or one 15-ounce can whole mushrooms, drained

1. Combine the veal, eggs, allspice, cinnamon, and salt in a medium mixing bowl, breaking up the veal with a fork until the mixture is smooth and well blended.

2. Heat the vegetable oil in a large skillet over medium-high heat. Put the meat mixture in the skillet. Cook, stirring constantly, for 3 to 4 minutes or until it loses its pink color.

3. Add 1¼ cups water and bring to a boil. Add mushrooms and reduce heat to medium. Cover and simmer for 15 minutes, stirring occasionally. The consistency of *inferekeh* should be soft, with about ½ cup cooking liquid in the final dish. The mushrooms should remain plump and juicy.

Yield: 6 to 8 servings

Zeroa

ROASTED LAMB SHANKS

Although these lamb shanks are traditionally served on the Passover tray during the *seder* meals (see page 349), they are a savory meat that can be enjoyed on any occasion.

6 pounds lamb shanks

2 tablespoons vegetable oil

6 garlic cloves, minced
  (about 1 tablespoon)

4 teaspoons kosher salt

1 teaspoon Aleppo pepper,
  or ½ teaspoon crushed red pepper

1 teaspoon paprika

1 teaspoon ground allspice

3 ribs celery

1. Put the lamb in a large stockpot, add 2 quarts water, and bring to a boil over high heat. Reduce the heat to medium-low and cook for 30 minutes, uncovered, periodically skimming the surface of the cooking liquid.

2. Preheat the oven to 375°F.

3. Transfer the lamb to a platter. Combine the vegetable oil, garlic, salt, Aleppo pepper, paprika, and allspice in a small dish and rub the mixture all over the lamb.

4. Put the celery ribs on a rack in a shallow roasting pan and lay the shanks on top. Roast, uncovered, for 30 minutes or until tender. Discard the celery before serving.

Yield: 6 to 8 servings

Muhah

BRAINS IN OLIVE OIL AND LEMON

Though it may sound odd to the Western ear, calf's brains are a favorite delicacy in the Middle East. The dish has a fine, tender quality and is highly receptive to spices. In this version, the lemon really shines through as a welcome accompaniment to the flavorful organ meat. It is a simple but lovely dish, smooth and rich in texture. Be sure to seek out a trustworthy butcher and insist on the highest quality. Fresh brains must be used within 24 hours of purchase.

1 teaspoon kosher salt

1 tablespoon freshly squeezed
   lemon juice

1 pound calf's brains, rinsed (see Note)

Ice

1 cup *matzah* meal

3 garlic cloves, chopped
   (about 1½ teaspoons)

½ teaspoon ground allspice

½ teaspoon ground cinnamon

Pinch of white pepper

2 eggs, beaten

½ cup extra-virgin olive oil

Lemon wedges for serving

1. In a large saucepan, combine the salt, lemon juice, and 1 quart water. Bring to a boil over high heat. Add the brains and return to a boil. Reduce the heat to low, cover, and simmer for 20 minutes.

2. Meanwhile, fill a medium mixing bowl with ice and cold water.

3. Remove the brains from the cooking liquid and plunge into the ice-water bath. With a sharp knife, remove the membrane from the calf's brains. Chop the brains into 2-inch dice.

4. Combine the *matzah* meal, garlic, allspice, cinnamon, and white pepper in a shallow dish. Dip the diced brains into the beaten egg, then dredge in *matzah* meal.

5. In a medium saucepan, fry the breaded diced brains in the olive oil over medium-high heat until golden. Serve with the lemon wedges.

❧ *Note* ❧
Before cooking brains, blanch them briefly to firm them, or soak in several changes of cold, acidulated water, made by adding a small amount of vinegar or lemon juice to water.

Yield: 6 to 8 servings

Lissan w'Zbeeb

SPICED TONGUE WITH RAISIN SAUCE

Tongue is a fascinating cut of meat that is often overlooked. The muscular texture allows for assertive spicing to create a strong but not overpowering flavor. The density of the meat also permits a long simmering time, giving the cook an opportunity to marry several flavors and produce a subtle and original sauce.

Meat:

1 cow's tongue (about 2 pounds)

1 onion

1 cup chopped celery (about 2 ribs)

4 whole cloves

1 bay leaf

12 peppercorns

Sauce:

One 15-ounce can tomato sauce

One 8-ounce can pineapple chunks, including liquid

¾ cup seedless raisins

½ cup brown sugar

1. To prepare the meat, cover the tongue with water in a medium stockpot over medium-high heat. Add the onion, celery, cloves, bay leaf, and peppercorns to the pot. Bring to a boil, reduce the heat, cover, and simmer over low heat, allowing 1 hour for each pound of tongue.

2. Remove the tongue from the water. Cut the membrane and peel it off carefully. Remove the bone and gristle at the thick end. Let cool.

3. Preheat the oven to 350°F.

4. Slice the tongue crosswise. Place the slices in a shallow ovenproof casserole, overlapping the slices.

5. To prepare the sauce, in a medium saucepan over medium-high heat, mix the tomato sauce, pineapple, raisins, and brown sugar in ½ cup water. Bring to a boil, then reduce the heat to low. Cook, stirring constantly, until the mixture bubbles and thickens. Pour the sauce over the tongue.

6. Cover and bake the tongue in the oven for 20 minutes, or until caramelized.

Yield: 6 to 8 servings

Halablabat

BRAISED SWEETBREADS
IN TOMATO SAUCE

Sweetbreads are the meaty portion of the thymus gland in the neck of a calf or young lamb. A delectable, soft organ meat, sweetbreads are considered a real treat because they must be prepared within 24 hours of purchase.

2 pounds sweetbreads, rinsed and dried	2 tablespoons vegetable oil	¼ teaspoon white pepper
1 rib celery, finely chopped	1 tablespoon tomato paste	½ teaspoon kosher salt

1. In a medium saucepan, sauté the sweetbreads and celery in the vegetable oil over medium heat for 8 to 10 minutes, or until the meat appears cooked through.

2. Remove the celery and add 1 cup water, along with the tomato paste, white pepper, and salt. Bring to a boil over medium heat. Reduce the heat to low and simmer, uncovered, until very little liquid is left in the saucepan.

3. Let the sweetbreads cool. Slice the sweetbreads and serve with the cooking liquid.

Yield: 6 to 8 servings

Halablabat wa Fettair

BRAISED SWEETBREADS
WITH MUSHROOMS

When choosing your sweetbreads, make sure to pick ones that are firm and white. Be sure to prepare them within 24 hours of purchase because all organ meats are extremely perishable. Mushrooms are a fantastic complement, adding a deep, earthy flavor to the silky-smooth-textured sweetbreads. Braising makes the meat very tender while ensuring a melodious balance of flavors in each bite.

2 pounds sweetbreads (see Note)	1 onion, finely chopped (about ½ cup)	2 tablespoons vegetable oil
4 ribs celery, finely chopped	1 pound cremini mushrooms	1 teaspoon kosher salt

1. In a medium saucepan, boil the sweetbreads in 2 cups water over medium heat for 2 to 3 minutes. Drain the sweetbreads and set aside.

2. In another medium saucepan, sauté the celery, onion, and mushrooms in the vegetable oil over medium-high heat for 8 to 10 minutes, or until the mushrooms begin to plump. Add the sweetbreads, salt, and enough water to cover. Cook, covered, for 30 minutes, or until the sweetbreads are tender.

❧ *Note* ❧

Before preparing this dish, the sweetbreads should be soaked in several changes of acidulated water (made by adding a small amount of vinegar or lemon juice to the water) to maximize their flavor.

Djaj Mishwi
(*Friday Night Roast Chicken with Potatoes, page 189*)

Djaj wa Samak

دجاج وسمك

POULTRY AND FISH

Poultry dishes are second to meat in the Aleppian Jewish culinary hierarchy. Chicken dishes are almost always eaten during the Aleppian Sabbath dinner. *Djaj mishwi* (Friday Night Roast Chicken with Potatoes, page 189) is served with fried potatoes, which are added to the roaster to absorb the flavorful cooking juices. Another notable poultry recipe with a similar cooking method is *djaj wa rishta* (Roast Chicken with Crispy Spaghetti, page 192), a delightfully crispy and richly flavored spaghetti accompanied by moist roast chicken.

Fish recipes comprise a very small portion of the Aleppian repertoire because fresh fish was not commonly available to the inland-dwelling Aleppian community. However, when reliable Mediterranean fish could be purchased, there was no shortage of delightful ways to prepare it.

POULTRY AND
FISH RECIPES

الوجبات

Djaj Mehshi

STUFFED CHICKEN

This is an elaborate roast chicken dish reserved for special holiday meals. The stuffing, studded with almonds, pistachios, and pine nuts, adds a rich and extravagant note to this dish.

Marinade:

¼ cup vegetable oil

3 garlic cloves, minced
(about 1½ teaspoons)

1 teaspoon ground cardamom

1 teaspoon paprika

1 tablespoon kosher salt

1 teaspoon ground nutmeg (optional)

One 3- to 4-pound chicken

Stuffing:

1 cup short-grain white rice

1½ teaspoons kosher salt

½ cup almonds, blanched and peeled
(see page 310)

½ cup pistachios, shelled, blanched,
and peeled (see page 310)

½ cup pine nuts

1 pound ground beef
or boneless lamb, chopped

1 teaspoon ground allspice

½ teaspoon ground cinnamon

1. Preheat the oven to 350°F.

2. To make the marinade, combine the vegetable oil, garlic, cardamom, paprika, salt, and, if desired, nutmeg in a large baking dish. Mix thoroughly. Put the chicken in the dish and let it marinate in the refrigerator for at least 30 minutes and up to 2 hours.

3. Meanwhile, prepare the stuffing. In a small saucepan, bring ¾ cup water to a boil. Add rice and ½ teaspoon of the salt, cover, and simmer for 10 minutes.

4. Place nuts on parchment-lined baking sheet. Bake until slightly golden, approximately 5 to 7 minutes. Cool. Combine the nuts with the beef, parboiled rice, allspice,

cinnamon and the remaining 1 teaspoon salt in a medium mixing bowl. Mix thoroughly.

5. Loosely stuff the chicken cavity. Extra stuffing should be placed into parchment paper and folded into an envelope.

6. Add 1 cup water to a roaster, add the chicken, and place the packet of stuffing alongside it. Cover and roast in the oven for 1 hour. Remove the stuffing from the parchment envelope and fluff with fork in pan. Spoon juices onto the stuffing and roast for 1 more hour, or until the chicken is fork-tender and the stuffing is moist and fluffy.

Yield: 8 to 10 servings

Djaj Mishwi

FRIDAY NIGHT ROAST CHICKEN
WITH POTATOES

The potatoes in this dish are fried before they are added to the chicken. After absorbing the pan drippings, they become absolutely addictive. When the chicken is done roasting, one tradition is to cut it into eighths and serve it layered among the potatoes.

One 3- to 4-pound chicken

3 cups plus 3 tablespoons
    vegetable oil

3 garlic cloves, minced
    (about 1½ teaspoons)

1 teaspoon paprika

1 teaspoon kosher salt

1 onion

3 pounds of potatoes, peeled
    and cut into 1½-inch wedges

1. Preheat the oven to 350°F.

2. In a large roaster, coat the bottom of the pan with 1 tablespoon of the oil. Rub the entire chicken with 2 tablespoons oil, the garlic, paprika, and salt.

3. Add the onion to the roaster. Place the roaster into the oven, covered, and roast the chicken for 1 hour.

4. Meanwhile, deep-fry the potatoes, 1 to 1½ cups at a time, over medium heat in a deep fryer or medium saucepan

filled with the 3 cups vegetable oil. Fry each batch for 4 to 5 minutes, or until the potatoes are golden. Drain on paper towels.

5. Add the potatoes to the roaster. Give them a stir in the pan drippings, making sure that they are well coated. Roast the chicken for 1 more hour, or until the chicken is golden.

Yield: 8 to 10 servings

Djaj w'Sfiha

ROAST CHICKEN
WITH STUFFED BABY EGGPLANT

This recipe calls for *banjan meqli* (Fried Eggplant Slices, page 91), and *s'fiha* (Stuffed Baby Eggplants with Ground Meat and Rice, page 138). A favorite for Sabbath dinners and holidays, this dish is especially good when made with fresh stuffed eggplants rather than dried ones. Fresh eggplants, okra, and fava beans were not available in Syria year-round because of the cool winters in the region of the Anti-Lebanon Mountains. This is why Aleppian Jews are accustomed to using dried eggplant skins. Today, even dried okra is used; it can be found along Atlantic Avenue in Brooklyn and at other Middle Eastern markets that still carry the traditional vegetables commonly used in the Arab world.

One 8-ounce can chickpeas, drained, or ½ cup dried chickpeas, soaked overnight or for 6 to 8 hours, drained, and peeled

1 onion, chopped (about ½ cup)

½ bunch flat-leaf parsley, chopped

½ recipe *hashu* (page 136)

12 small fresh eggplants, cored, or 12 dried eggplant skins, softened in boiling water for 1 minute

One 3- to 4-pound chicken, whole or cut into eighths

3 tablespoons vegetable oil

4 garlic cloves, minced (about 2 teaspoons)

1 teaspoon paprika

½ tablespoon ground allspice

8 fried eggplant slices (about 1 eggplant) (*banjan meqli*, page 91)

2 tablespoons kosher salt

1. Preheat the oven to 350°F.

2. Fold the chickpeas, onion, and parsley into the *hashu* filling.

3. Stuff each eggplant with *hashu*.

4. In a large skillet, fry the stuffed eggplants in 2 tablespoons of the vegetable oil over medium heat for 3 minutes, tossing to ensure all sides are cooked. Remove carefully with a slotted spoon and drain on paper towels.

5. Rub the chicken with the remaining vegetable oil, 1 teaspoon of the garlic, and the paprika. Place the chicken in a roaster.

6. Sprinkle the allspice over the stuffed eggplant and the eggplant slices. Lay the eggplant slices over the stuffed eggplants in the roaster.

7. Season the contents of the roaster with the salt and the remaining garlic.

8. Roast in the oven, covered, for 1 hour. Add 1 cup water to the roaster. Reduce the oven temperature to 300°F and continue to roast for 1 more hour. Uncover and continue roasting for 30 minutes, or until the stuffed eggplants appear toasted and the chicken is golden.

Yield: 8 to 10 servings

Djaj Riz w'Hummus

ROAST CHICKEN WITH RICE
AND CHICKPEAS

This combination of chicken, vermicelli, rice, and chickpeas creates a hearty one-pot meal and complements *Salata Banadoura* (Fresh Tomato Salad with Allspice-Lemon Dressing, page 34).

One 3- to 4-pound chicken

2 onions, diced (about 1 cup)

4 to 6 garlic cloves, chopped
   (about 2 to 3 teaspoons)

2 tablespoons vegetable oil

1 cup dry vermicelli, cut in half

3 cups long-grain rice

Two 15½-ounce cans chickpeas, drained,
   or 1½ cups dried chickpeas,
   soaked overnight or for 6 to 8 hours
   and drained

2 teaspoons ground allspice

¼ teaspoon white pepper

2 teaspoons kosher salt

1. In a large stockpot, cover the chicken with water, about 3½ quarts. Bring to a boil over high heat, then reduce heat to medium-low. Simmer for 1 hour or until it is fork-tender. Skim the cooking liquid periodically, if necessary.

2. Remove the chicken and let stand for 30 minutes. Reserve 4 cups of the broth for step 4 and store the rest for another use (for example, for *beida bi'lemouneh*, Velvety Lemon Sauce, page 198). Bone the chicken and cut into 2-inch chunks.

3. In a large saucepan, sauté the onions and garlic in the vegetable oil over medium heat for 4 to 6 minutes, or until soft. Add the vermicelli and rice and sauté for 1 minute.

4. Add the chicken chunks, chickpeas, 4 cups of the chicken broth plus 2 cups water, allspice, white pepper, and salt. Bring to a boil over medium heat, then reduce the heat to low, and simmer, covered, for 30 minutes, or until the rice is fluffy.

Yield: 8 to 10 servings

Djaj wa Rishta دجاج ورشتا

ROAST CHICKEN
WITH CRISPY SPAGHETTI

A quirky taboo accompanies this dish: it should never be served for Sabbath dinner. Why? There is no clear reason, but many Aleppian Jewish brides learned this early in their marriages and have superstitiously stuck to it. Leaving old-world taboos aside, it is still preferable to serve this dish for Sabbath lunch or weekday suppers so that it can stand alone, undiminished by the fancier Sabbath dinner dishes. As the chicken roasts, the pasta absorbs the cooking juice of the chicken, achieving a heavenly flavor. With its perfect balance of protein and starch, *djaj wa rishta* is the Aleppian Jewish version of the meat-and-potatoes supper, albeit with crunchy allspice-dusted pasta as a mouthwatering counterpoint to the tender roast chicken. The dish is designed to sate the hunger of work-weary spouses and homework-frazzled kids; your family will be even more grateful if you make extra for the next day's lunch.

One 3- to 4-pound chicken

3 tablespoons vegetable oil

3 garlic cloves, chopped
(about 1½ teaspoons)

1 tablespoon paprika

2 tablespoons kosher salt

1 onion, diced (about ½ cup)

1 pound dried spaghetti

1 teaspoon ground allspice

1 teaspoon ground cinnamon
(optional)

One 6-ounce can tomato paste

1 green bell pepper, seeded
and quartered (optional)

1. Preheat the oven to 350°F degrees.

2. Place the chicken in a medium roaster. Season the chicken with the vegetable oil, garlic, paprika, and 1 tablespoon of the salt. Add 1 cup water along with the onions. Cover and roast for 1 hour. Remove the chicken and let cool, reserving the cooking juices for step 4. The chicken may be left whole or can be boned at this point. Reduce the oven temperature to 300°F.

3. While the chicken cools, boil the spaghetti in a large pot of salted water for about 8 minutes. It should be firmer than al dente. Drain the spaghetti.

4. Add the allspice, cinnamon, and the remaining 1 tablespoon salt to the cooking juices in the roaster. Add the tomato paste and mix well. Add the bell pepper, if desired, and boiled spaghetti and combine with the seasoned cooking juices. Place the chicken in the roaster, breast side down, over the seasoned spaghetti. Or, if using chicken pieces, tuck in among the spaghetti strands. Cover and bake in the oven for 2 hours, or until the chicken is well roasted and the spaghetti begins to crisp.

Yield: 8 to 10 servings

Riz w'Djaj

RICE WITH CHICKEN

For this dish, the rice is cooked in the chicken broth to achieve a rich flavor. Another Arabic variation to this dish is to perfume the stock with 1 teaspoon ground cinnamon and 1 teaspoon cardamom. Cardamom has an intense aroma and an exotic, earthy flavor. This is a simple, filling chicken dish that is enhanced with the addition of *beida bi'lemouneh* (Velvety Lemon Sauce).

3 onions, chopped (about 1¾ cups)

2 tablespoons vegetable oil

One 3- to 4-pound chicken

1 tablespoon kosher salt

Pinch of white pepper (optional)

1 heaping teaspoon ground allspice

1 teaspoon ground cinnamon (optional)

1 teaspoon ground cardamom (optional)

1 teaspoon ground turmeric (optional)

3 cups long-grain white rice

Beida bi'lemouneh (Velvety Lemon Sauce, page 198)

1. In a large pot, sauté the onions in the vegetable oil over medium heat for 4 to 6 minutes, or until translucent. Add 3 quarts water, along with the chicken. Add the salt and white pepper, if using. Bring to a boil over medium heat, then reduce the heat to low and simmer for 40 minutes, or until fork-tender.

2. Remove the chicken and transfer to a platter. Drain off all but 4½ cups of cooking liquid from the pot. Reserve the excess for the Velvety Lemon Sauce.

3. Bone the chicken. Return the chicken meat to the pot. Add the allspice and, if desired, cinnamon and cardamom. If you want a bit of bright yellow color, add turmeric. Bring to a boil over medium-high heat. Add the rice and stir. When the liquid comes to a boil again, reduce the heat to low and cover. Simmer for 45 minutes, or until the rice is fluffy and all liquid is absorbed. Serve with *beida bi'lemouneh*.

Yield: 8 to 10 servings

Djaj w'Rishta b'Loz

CHICKEN, RICE, AND PASTA

Orzo is the ideal pasta for this recipe because it absorbs the cooking juices fabulously. Broken up vermicelli is a suitable substitute.

One 3- to 4-pound chicken

¾ cup vegetable oil

2 onions, finely chopped (about 1 cup)

1 cinnamon stick

4 teaspoons kosher salt

¾ cup dried chickpeas, soaked overnight
  or for 6 to 8 hours, and drained,
  or one 15½-ounce can chickpeas

½ cup slivered almonds

1 pound ground beef

½ teaspoon ground cinnamon

½ teaspoon black pepper

1 garlic clove, chopped

¾ cup orzo or vermicelli, slightly broken up

1 cup rice

1. In a large pot, brown the chicken in ¼ cup of the vegetable oil over medium heat for about 20 minutes, turning once. Add 2 quarts water, half the onions, the cinnamon stick, and 2 teaspoons of the salt. Bring to a boil and cover. Reduce heat to medium-low and simmer for 40 minutes until the chicken is fall-apart tender. Set the broth aside.

2. Meanwhile, put the soaked chickpeas (if using dried) in a large saucepan, add 2½ quarts water, and bring to a boil over high heat. Reduce the heat and simmer, covered, for 20 minutes, or until tender. Drain and set aside.

3. In a small dry skillet, toast the almonds over medium heat for 10 minutes. Set aside.

4. In a medium saucepan, sauté the beef with ¼ cup vegetable oil over medium heat, occasionally breaking up with a fork, until brown. Reduce the heat and simmer for 15 minutes, or until nearly tender. Stir in the ground cinnamon, black pepper, the remainder of the onions, garlic, and the remaining 2 teaspoons salt, and cook for 25 more minutes. Transfer to a medium mixing bowl.

5. Pour the remaining ¼ cup vegetable oil in the saucepan and sauté the orzo or vermicelli until golden brown. Add the rice and sauté for 5 more minutes.

6. Pour 5 cups broth from the cooked chicken over the rice, adding water if necessary. Bring to a boil, and add the cooked beef and onion mixture, and the chickpeas. Stir well, cover, reduce the heat to low, and simmer for 40 minutes, or until the rice is fluffy. Remove from the heat and let stand for 10 minutes. Transfer the chickpea-rice mixture to a platter. Top with the chicken pieces and garnish with almonds.

Yield: 4 to 6 servings

Farrju Mashwi

GRILLED CHICKEN

Although the preferred method for cooking this dish is to grill it over charcoal, roasting or broiling it will also produce delicious results. A piece of Syrian flatbread dipped in the drippings is absolutely delectable—you may actually enjoy it just as much as the grilled chicken itself. *Farrju mashwi* is wonderful served with *mehalal lemouneh* (Pickled Lemons, page 71).

One 3- to 4-pound chicken, cut into eighths	6 garlic cloves, minced (about 1 tablespoon)	Juice of 3 lemons (about ½ cup)
¼ cup vegetable oil	1 tablespoon kosher salt	

1. Place the chicken in a large glass baking dish or bowl. Add the vegetable oil, garlic, salt, and lemon juice. Marinate for 30 minutes in the refrigerator.

2. Prepare a medium-hot grill. Grill the chicken for 30 minutes, or until the liquid runs clear when a thigh is pierced. (Alternatively, place the chicken in a baking pan in a single layer and roast in a 350°F oven for 45 minutes, or until brown and crispy.)

Yield: 6 to 8 servings

Shish Tawuq شيش طاووق

CHICKEN, PEPPER, AND TOMATO KABOBS

During the summertime in Aleppo, families or groups of friends would very often go to the countryside or the Anti-Lebanon Mountains. The favorite dishes for those summer nights were *salchicha* (Spicy Sausage, page 175) and grilled meats such as *salajahn* (Spicy Grilled Meat Kabobs, page 174), and these zesty kabobs, which were enjoyed with a wide selection of salads.

Marinade:

2 tablespoons freshly squeezed
   lemon juice

3 garlic cloves, chopped
   (about 1½ teaspoons)

3 tablespoons extra-virgin olive oil

1 tablespoon kosher salt

1 teaspoon Aleppo pepper,
   or ½ teaspoon crushed red pepper

2 pounds boneless chicken,
   cut into 2-inch chunks.

1 red bell pepper, cut in chunks

1 yellow bell pepper, cut in chunks

1 green bell pepper, cut in chunks

2 large onions, quartered

18 cherry tomatoes (about 1 pound)

1. To make the marinade, combine lemon juice, garlic, oil, salt, and Aleppo pepper in a glass bowl or baking dish. Place the chicken chunks in the dish and marinate for 2 hours in the refrigerator.

2. Prepare a medium-hot grill.

3. Remove the chicken from the marinade. Spear the chicken, bell peppers, onions, and tomatoes onto skewers, alternating chicken and vegetables.

4. Place the skewers on the grill and cook for 10 minutes, turning once, or until the chicken is tender.

Yield: 6 to 8 servings

Beida bi'Lemouneh بيضة بالليمونة

VELVETY LEMON SAUCE

This sauce is a staple on the eve of Yom Kippur, the Day of Atonement. During this sacred day in the Jewish calendar, it is customary for Jews to undertake the positive commandment of *kaparot,* which is derived from the Hebrew word meaning "to forgive." *Kaparot* is a process by which one sponsors the slaughtering of a chicken as a substitute punishment for the sins one committed during the year. Given the number of chickens available as a result of *kaparot,* it isn't surprising that *beida bi'lemouneh,* which uses chicken broth, appears on the pre-fast table alongside roast chicken, rice, and *bizeh b'jurah* (Green Peas and Rice with Coriander and Meat, page 118). For many Aleppian Jewish families, *beida bi'lemouneh* is a staple at the Friday night Sabbath dinner table as well.

2 eggs	2 cups Chicken Stock (recipe follows) cooled to room temperature or cooler	2 tablespoons all-purpose flour combined with 2 tablespoons water
Juice of 1 lemon (about 3 tablespoons)		

1. Using a fork, beat the eggs with the lemon juice in a medium mixing bowl for 1 minute, or until they are thoroughly combined.

2. Stir the stock into the beaten egg mixture. Pour into a medium saucepan and bring to a boil over medium-high heat. Promptly add the flour paste to the stock. Cook, stirring constantly, for 2 to 3 minutes, or until the mixture reaches a thick, velvety consistency. Pour into a medium serving bowl and serve at room temperature.

Yield: 2 cups sauce

Chicken Stock

While store-bought chicken stock usually suffices, it cannot compete with the fresh homemade version. Stock can be stored in the freezer for many months.

One 3- to 4-pound chicken

1 rib celery, chopped (about ½ cup)

1 onion, chopped (about ½ cup)

2 teaspoons kosher salt

1. Combine the chicken, celery, onion, salt, and 6 cups water in a large stockpot. Bring to a boil over high heat. Reduce the heat to low and simmer for 1 hour.

2. Remove the chicken and reserve for another use—for example, *riz w'djaj* (Rice with Chicken, page 194).

Strain the stock through a fine-mesh strainer into a large bowl. It can be refrigerated for up to 1 week.

Yield: 10 servings, 2 cups of stock

Samak Meqli

FRIED FISH

In the Middle East, frying is the most common way of preparing fish. Fried fish is a simple Thursday night staple, usually served with *filla spanekh b'jibn* (Spinach and Cheese with *Filla,* page 229) and *tehineh* (Sesame Spread, page 26) on the side for dipping. A squeeze of lemon over the fish adds a bright note of freshness.

3 pounds white-flesh fish, whole or filleted (for example, trout, sole, flounder, red or gray mullet, or sea bass)

4 garlic cloves, minced (about 2 teaspoons)

2 cups all-purpose flour

½ tablespoon kosher salt

½ teaspoon ground cumin

½ teaspoon Aleppo pepper, or ¼ teaspoon crushed red pepper

3 cups vegetable oil

1. Rinse the fish and pat with paper towels until completely dry. Rub the fish with the garlic.

2. Combine the flour, salt, cumin, and Aleppo pepper in a shallow dish. Dredge the fish in the flour mixture, then shake off the excess.

3. Pour the vegetable oil into a large saucepan and heat over medium heat until the oil sizzles upon contact with a drop of water. Make sure that the oil is very hot so that the flour does not simply soak it up and become soggy.

4. Fry the fish in batches for 3 to 4 minutes, depending on the size of the fish. Turn over and fry for another 3 to 4 minutes. Remove the fish and drain on paper towels.

Yield: 4 to 6 servings

Samak bi'Tehineh

FISH WITH SESAME SPREAD

This very popular dish is prepared for festive occasions or luncheon affairs for which a dairy meal is preferred. The fish meat is flaked and combined with *tehineh,* then sculpted into the shape of a fish. Additional *tehineh* is then carefully spread over the fish like icing on a cake. Because of its interesting presentation, *samak bi'tehineh* is an attention grabber and is one of the first dishes to disappear from the table.

2 pounds flounder fillets

1 tablespoon vegetable oil

1 teaspoon kosher salt

¼ teaspoon white pepper

1 cup *tehineh*
   (Sesame Spread, page 26)

1 black olive

1 green bell pepper, cored, seeded,
   and cut lengthwise into strips

One ½-inch strip roasted red bell pepper

2 Kirby cucumbers, cut into ⅛-inch rounds

1. Preheat the oven to 350°F.

2. Brush the fish with the vegetable oil and sprinkle with the salt and white pepper. Line a baking pan with parchment paper and place the fish on the paper. Bake for 30 minutes. Let cool.

3. Place the fish in a medium mixing bowl and flake with a fork. Add 2 tablespoons of the *tehineh* and toss.

4. On a serving platter, form the fish mixture into the shape of a fish. Spread the remaining *tehineh* over the fish like icing on a cake. Garnish the fish with a black olive or cherry tomato for the eye, strips of green pepper for the spine or Kirby cucumbers for the scales, and the strip of red pepper for the mouth.

Yield: 6 to 8 servings

Samak Mehshi b'Snobar

WHOLE STUFFED FISH
WITH PINE NUTS

This dish is served on special occasions. If available, a whole fish is preferred because the bones add a richer, fuller flavor. The fish usually becomes so tender that lifting it out of the pan causes it to break apart. Lining the the baking pan with parchment paper will help you keep the fish intact for an attractive presentation.

Marinade:

⅓ tablespoon vegetable oil

2 tablespoons lemon juice

3 garlic cloves, minced
   (about 1½ teaspoons)

1 teaspoon Aleppo pepper,
   or ½ teaspoon crushed red pepper

1 tablespoon kosher salt

One whole 3-pound white-flesh fish
   (for example, sea bass, mullet,
   or sea bream)

Stuffing:

1 cup short-grain white rice, parboiled
   (see Note, page 67)

3 garlic cloves, chopped
   (about 1½ teaspoons)

1 rib celery, chopped
   (about ½ cup)

1 onion, chopped (about ½ cup)

1 cup pine nuts, toasted
   (see Note)

½ teaspoon ground cinnamon

½ teaspoon ground allspice

½ teaspoon Aleppo pepper,
   or ¼ teaspoon crushed red pepper

1 teaspoon kosher salt

2 cups vegetable oil

2 pounds potatoes,
   peeled and cut into 1-inch dice

1. To make the marinade, combine the vegetable oil, lemon juice, garlic, Aleppo pepper, and salt in a large glass baking dish. Mix well. Coat the fish liberally with the marinade and refrigerate for 20 minutes.

2. To make the stuffing, combine the rice, garlic, celery, onion, pine nuts, cinnamon, allspice, Aleppo pepper, and salt in a large mixing bowl. Mix until well blended and set aside.

3. Preheat the oven to 400°F.

4. To fry the potatoes, heat the oil in a deep fryer or medium saucepan over medium heat until it sizzles upon contact with a drop of water. Fry the potatoes in batches, 1 to 1½ cups at a time, for 4 to 5 minutes, or until golden. Drain on paper towels.

5. Stuff the fish with the stuffing, and wrap the leftover stuffing in a packet of parchment paper.

6. Line the large baking pan with parchment paper or lightly oiled foil. Place the fish and parchment paper packet in the pan and add ½ cup water. Surround the fish with the fried potatoes.

7. Roast the fish for 15 minutes, covered. Reduce the oven temperature to 350°F, remove the lid, and continue roasting, uncovered, for another 30 minutes, or until the fish is flaky and the stuffing is fluffy. To transfer from the pan, lift the parchment paper and slide the fish onto a serving platter. Put the extra stuffing in a serving dish.

∽ *Note* ∾

Pine nuts can be toasted by tossing in a dry pan over medium-low heat or heating them in a 300°F oven. Toast for 10 minutes or until golden brown.

Yield: 6 to 8 servings

Samak b'Batata

BAKED MIDDLE EASTERN
WHOLE FISH WITH POTATOES

When fish was available in Aleppo, it was purchased whole. After the fish was cleaned, it was marinated in anything from cumin and lemon juice to garlic and green peppers.

1 whole 3-pound white-flesh fish
(for example, cod, sea bass, mullet,
or sea bream)

3 garlic cloves, minced
(about 1½ teaspoons)

2 tablespoons extra-virgin
olive oil

1 onion, chopped (about ½ cup)

1 green bell pepper, chopped

2 ribs celery, chopped

2 potatoes, peeled and cubed

2 carrots, sliced

½ teaspoon chopped fresh flat-leaf parsley

½ teaspoon Aleppo pepper,
or ¼ teaspoon crushed red pepper

1 teaspoon ground cumin

1 teaspoon kosher salt

1 cup tomato sauce

1. Preheat the oven to 350°F.

2. Rub the fish liberally with the garlic and olive oil, then put the fish in a large baking pan. Place the onion, bell pepper, celery, potatoes, and carrots around the fish. Sprinkle the fish and vegetables with parsley, Aleppo pepper, cumin, and salt. Add the tomato sauce and ½ cup water to the pan.

3. Cover the pan with foil and bake for 45 minutes, or until the vegetables are tender and the fish is flaky.

Yield: 6 to 8 servings

Samak Meshwi

GRILLED FISH KABOBS

Grilling is a popular method of preparing fish in the summertime. Make sure the grill rack is hot to prevent the fish from sticking to it.

Marinade:

1 cup freshly squeezed lemon juice
  (4 to 6 lemons)

2 onions, chopped (about 1 cup)

1 teaspoon Aleppo pepper,
  or ½ teaspoon crushed red pepper

1 teaspoon kosher salt

1½ pounds cod fillets,
  cut into 2-inch chunks

2 green bell peppers,
  cut into 2-inch chunks

2 tomatoes, cut into 8 wedges,
  or 8 to 10 cherry tomatoes

6 tablespoons vegetable oil

Lemon wedges for serving

1. For the marinade, combine the lemon juice, onions, Aleppo pepper, and salt in a medium glass baking dish. Mix well. Place the fish chunks in the dish and marinate for about 20 minutes in the refrigerator.

2. Prepare a medium-hot grill.

3. Remove the fish chunks from the marinade. Spear the fish chunks, green peppers, and tomatoes onto skewers, alternating the fish and vegetables in an attractive pattern. Brush the skewers with the vegetable oil and grill for 4 to 6 minutes, turning once. Serve immediately with the lemon wedges.

Yield: 4 to 6 servings

Jibneh Shelal
(*Twisted White String Cheese
with Nigella Seeds, page 236*)

Jibneh wa Beid

جبنة وبيض

DAIRY AND EGGS

In Aleppo, milk and yogurt were delivered fresh to every house. The milkman would sing, "*laban tasa!*" ("fresh yogurt!") and "*zibbeh!*" ("butter!"). Many favorite treats, such as *jibneh shelal* (Twisted White String Cheese with Nigella Seeds, page 236), *sambousak* (Buttery Cheese-Filled Sesame Pastries, page 212), and all manner of *jibn* (frittatas), were made with the milk and cheese that he brought to each home.

Dairy has a special place in the cuisine of Aleppian Jews. According to Jewish dietary law, it is forbidden to eat dairy and meat together. In fact, it is even forbidden to cook the two with the same utensils. Kosher kitchens always contain two sets of pots and pans: one for meat and one for dairy. This law derives from the Torah, in which it is commanded, "You shall not boil a kid [baby goat] in its mother's milk" (Exodus 23:19, 34:26, Deuteronomy 14:21).

الوجبات

DAIRY AND EGG RECIPES

Sambousak

BUTTERY CHEESE-FILLED SESAME PASTRIES

Sambousak has quite a lineage. As early as the thirteenth century, it was included in classic medieval Arab cookbooks by al Baghdadi and Ibn al Adim. Its name is derived from the Persian *sanbusa,* which denotes anything triangular. *Sambousak* is also related to the *samosa* of Indian cuisine.

Like the *samosa, sambousak* is a snack food served with midday tea or to guests. The ideal *sambousak* shell is thin and redolent of butter, with a lightly browned bottom. The cheese inside should be light and airy, completely filling the interior of the shell. Almost every Aleppian Jewish household has a few *sambousaks* in the freezer to have on hand for guests and for children to take for school lunches.

Dough:

2 cups all-purpose flour

1 cup *smead* (semolina)

2 sticks butter (½ pound),
   at room temperature

Dash of kosher salt

Filling:

1 pound Muenster cheese, grated

2 eggs, beaten

2 tablespoons sesame seeds

1. To make the dough, mix the flour, *smead,* butter, and salt in a large mixing bowl. Be sure to beat the butter first to avoid clumps in the dough mixture. Add ½ cup warm water in small measures, allowing the dough to incorporate more of the butter after each addition. Mix well. Dough should be soft and moist. Cover and set aside.

2. To make the filling, combine the cheese and eggs in a medium mixing bowl. Stir gently.

3. Preheat the oven to 350°F.

4. Divide the dough into thirds. Take one-third and further divide it into walnut-size balls. Dip one side of each ball in the sesame seeds.

5. With a tortilla press or a rolling pin, flatten each ball, sesame-seed side down, into a 2-inch round. Place 1 teaspoon of the filling in the center of each round. Fold each round in half, covering the filling, so that the sesame-seed side faces up. Firmly pinch the ends closed. If you like, form the traditional twisted edge. Start at one end and press the edge of the dough between the thumb and forefinger twisting inward, creating 5 to 6 twists. Repeat steps 4 and 5 two more times with the remaining dough and filling. (At this point the *sambousak* can be frozen for later use.)

6. Place the filled pastries on an ungreased baking sheet. Bake for about 15 minutes, or until the *sambousak* are lightly browned. (Frozen *sambousak* should be baked at 400°F for about 20 minutes.)

Yield: 50 to 60 pastries

Sambousak
(Buttery Cheese-Filled
Sesame Pastries, page 212)

Sarine Kattan,
Aleppo, Syria, circa 1947
(courtesy of author)

Imwarrah b'Jibn

أم ورق بجبين

CHEESE-FILLED *FILLA* TRIANGLES

This is one of the most delicious cheese pastries prepared with *filla* (phyllo, a thin pastry dough), especially when eaten hot straight out of the oven. The sesame seeds add a light nutty flavor. Purchase the *simsom* (sesame seeds) from a Middle Eastern grocer; chances are that they will be fresher and less expensive.

When working with *filla*, it is important to keep it covered to prevent it from drying out and breaking. If the *filla* sheets look dry, they are no longer usable and will crumble when you attempt to make the triangles. If you buy frozen *filla*, defrost it in the refrigerator before using.

Filling:

1½ pounds Muenster cheese, grated

3 eggs, beaten

24 sheets *filla* (about 1 pound)

¾ cup (1½ sticks) unsalted butter, melted

¾ cup sesame seeds

1. Preheat the oven to 375°F.

2. To make the filling, combine the cheese and eggs in a medium mixing bowl. Stir gently. Set aside.

3. Cut all the *filla* sheets with a sharp knife crosswise into 3 rectangular sections about 3 inches wide. Work with only one strip of *filla* at a time. Cover the rest with wax paper and a damp towel. Brush the strip of *filla* with melted butter, then fold in half lengthwise.

4. Spoon a heaping teaspoon of filling near one end of a *filla* strip, about 1 inch from the short edge. Fold one corner over the filling, making a triangle. Continue folding over the *filla*, making a triangle each time, until the whole strip is used. Tuck the loose end neatly into the triangular shape. Repeat with the remaining *filla* strips. Then brush the top of each triangle with butter and dip into the sesame seeds. Place on a baking sheet.

5. Bake for 20 to 25 minutes, or until the triangles are crisp and lightly browned.

Yield: 72 pieces

Ejjeh b'Jibneh

CHEESE FRITTERS

This is the basic recipe for *ejjeh;* the following pages cover many common variants. Muenster works especially well with this recipe, but you can use whatever cheese you prefer.

3 eggs, beaten	1 teaspoon kosher salt
½ pound Muenster cheese, grated	1 cup vegetable oil

1. Combine the eggs, cheese, and salt in a large mixing bowl, and mix until well blended. The batter should be loose.

2. Heat the vegetable oil in a skillet over medium heat. When the oil sizzles upon contact with a droplet of water, drop 1 tablespoon of the egg batter into the pan. Flatten the mound of batter slightly with the back of a spoon. Continue adding as many mounds of the batter mixture as the skillet will allow. Fry for 2 minutes or until golden, turning once. Drain the fritters on paper towels. Repeat this process with the remaining batter, and if necessary, add more oil.

Yield: 4 to 6 servings

Ejjeh Bakdounez

PARSLEY AND ONION FRITTERS

Traditionally, mothers would prepare *ejjeh* for their kids' school lunches because it could be eaten hot or cold and it kept well. It is a great snack anytime, but it is best enjoyed straight out of the pan tucked in warm Syrian flatbread with a slice of fresh tomato. For this recipe, Aleppians prefer finely chopped parsley. Leaves that are too large tend to wilt during cooking and become less aesthetically pleasing.

1 bunch fresh flat-leaf parsley, finely chopped

1 onion, chopped (about ½ cup)

1 tablespoon kosher salt

1 tablespoon ground allspice

5 eggs, beaten

1 cup vegetable oil

1. In a large bowl, combine the parsley, onion, salt, allspice, and eggs. Mix well.

2. Heat the vegetable oil in a skillet over medium heat. When the oil sizzles upon contact with a droplet of water, drop 1 tablespoon of the egg batter into the pan. Flatten the mound of batter slightly with the back of a spoon. Continue adding as many mounds of the batter as the skillet will allow. Fry for 2 minutes, or until golden, turning once. Drain the fritters on paper towels. Repeat this process with the remaining batter, and if necessary, add more oil.

Yield: 4 to 6 servings

Ejjeh Batata

POTATO FRITTERS

The next time Hanukkah rolls around, try this *ejjeh* as a simpler and lighter alternative to the potato *latke* of Ashkenazi cookery. Similar to the *latke, ejjeh batata* features potato, eggs, and onion, but it does not need flour or *matzah* meal to hold it together. This dish is great to serve on wintry nights, but it's tasty year-round, stuffed in a loaf of flatbread with pickled green pepper or fresh tomato.

3 large potatoes, peeled
   and coarsely grated (shredding disc
   of food processor may be used)

5 eggs, beaten

1 onion, finely chopped (about ½ cup)

1 teaspoon ground allspice

1 teaspoon kosher salt

1 cup vegetable oil

1. Put the grated potatoes in a colander and press firmly against the perforated surface to extract water. Alternatively, the potatoes can be gathered in cheesecloth and wrung several times.

2. In a large bowl, combine the potatoes, eggs, onion, allspice, and salt. Mix well.

3. Heat the vegetable oil in a skillet over medium heat. When the oil sizzles upon contact with a droplet of water,

drop 1 tablespoon of the batter into the pan. Flatten the mound of batter slightly with the back of a spoon. Continue adding as many mounds of the batter as the skillet will allow. Fry for 2 minutes, or until golden, turning once. Drain the fritters on paper towels. Repeat this process with the remaining batter, and if necessary, add more oil.

Yield: 4 to 6 servings

Ejjeh Kusa

ZUCCHINI FRITTERS

Some people like to add cinnamon to this particular *ejjeh,* a summertime favorite when zucchini are in season.

3 zucchini or yellow squash, coarsely grated (shredding disc of food processor may be used)

4 eggs, beaten

2 onions, finely chopped (about 1 cup)

1 teaspoon ground allspice

1 teaspoon kosher salt

1 teaspoon ground cinnamon (optional)

1 cup vegetable oil

1. To extract water from the zucchini, place it in a colander and press it down against the perforated surface.

2. Combine the zucchini, eggs, onions, allspice, salt, and cinnamon, if desired, in a medium mixing bowl. Mix well.

3. Heat the vegetable oil in a skillet over medium heat. When the oil sizzles upon contact with a droplet of water, drop 1 tablespoon of the egg batter into the pan. Flatten the mound of batter slightly with the back of a spoon. Continue adding as many mounds of the batter as the skillet will allow. Fry for 2 minutes, or until golden, turning once. Drain the fritters on paper towels. Repeat this process with the remaining batter, and if necessary, add more oil.

Yield: 4 to 6 servings

Ejjeh b'Kerrateh

LEEK FRITTERS

Ejjeh b'kerrateh is featured on the dinner table during the New Year festival of Rosh Hashanah. The smooth, savory notes of the sautéed leeks are balanced with the eggs, imparting to this *ejjeh* a simple but elegant flavor.

1 cup plus 2 tablespoons
   vegetable oil

1 pound leeks, chopped
   (white and light green parts)

1 teaspoon kosher salt

6 eggs, beaten

1 teaspoon allspice

1 teaspoon cinnamon (optional)

½ teaspoon Aleppo pepper
   or ¼ teaspoon crushed red pepper
   (optional)

1. In a medium skillet, heat 2 tablespoons of the vegetable oil over medium-high heat. Add the leeks and sauté for 2 to 3 minutes, or until soft. Add the salt.

2. In a medium mixing bowl, combine the leeks, eggs, allspice, and, if desired, cinnamon and Aleppo pepper. Mix well.

3. Heat the remaining 1 cup vegetable oil in a skillet over medium heat. When the oil sizzles upon contact with a droplet of water, drop 1 tablespoon of the egg batter into the pan. Slightly flatten the mound of batter with the back of a spoon. Continue adding as many mounds of the batter as the skillet will allow. Fry for 2 minutes, or until golden, turning once. Drain the fritters on paper towels. Repeat this process with the remaining batter, and if necessary, add more oil.

Yield: 4 to 6 servings

Krefsiyeh

SWISS CHARD FRITTERS

If you cannot find Swiss chard, you can use its close relative: beet greens. This is a heavier egg dish than most egg dishes, so many prefer to have it as a lunch course or an early dinner.

2 bunches Swiss chard, stems trimmed	½ teaspoon ground allspice	1 cup vegetable oil
4 eggs, beaten	1 teaspoon ground cinnamon	
1 onion, finely chopped (about ½ cup)	1 teaspoon kosher salt	

1. In a medium stockpot, bring 1 inch of water to boil. Add the Swiss chard, cover, and cook for 2 minutes. Drain the Swiss chard thoroughly and chop it.

2. Combine the eggs, onion, allspice, cinnamon, and salt in a medium mixing bowl. Mix well and stir in the Swiss chard.

3. Heat the vegetable oil in a skillet over medium heat. When the oil sizzles upon contact with a droplet of water, drop 1 tablespoon of the egg batter into the pan. Flatten the mound of batter slightly with the back of a spoon. Continue adding as many mounds of the batter mixture as the skillet will allow. Fry for 2 minutes, or until golden, turning once. Drain the fritters on paper towels. Repeat this process with the remaining batter, and if necessary, add more oil.

Yield: 4 to 6 servings

Spanekh b'Jibn

SPINACH-CHEESE FRITTATA

A *jibn* is basically a quiche without the pie crust. It is made easily and quickly with eggs, cheese, and a vegetable. Spinach is the most popular variety of *jibn* in the Aleppian Jewish repertoire, and is often enjoyed with a dollop of *laban* (Yogurt, page 241) on top.

1 onion, chopped (about ½ cup)

1 tablespoon vegetable oil

Two 10-ounce packages frozen chopped spinach, thawed and drained, or 2½ pounds fresh spinach, trimmed and chopped

6 eggs, beaten

1¾ pounds Muenster cheese, grated

1 teaspoon kosher salt

½ pound cottage or farmer cheese (optional)

1. Preheat the oven to 350°F.

2. Sauté the onion in oil in a large skillet over medium heat for 4 to 6 minutes, or until translucent. Add the spinach and sauté for 5 more minutes, or until the spinach is wilted.

3. In a large mixing bowl, combine eggs, Muenster cheese, salt, and cottage cheese, if desired. Add the spinach to the egg-cheese mixture and mix well.

4. Pour the mixture into a 2-quart baking dish. Bake, uncovered, for 40 minutes, or until lightly browned.

Yield: 4 to 6 servings

Kusa b'Jibn

ZUCCHINI-CHEESE FRITTATA

The natural sweetness of squash combined with savory onions makes this a particularly wonderful, homey dish.

2 pounds zucchini or yellow squash, chopped (about 5 cups)

1 onion, finely chopped (about ½ cup)

3 tablespoons vegetable oil

6 eggs, beaten

1 pound Muenster cheese, grated

1 teaspoon kosher salt

1 tablespoon butter, cut into 6 pieces

1. Preheat the oven to 350°F.

2. In a large skillet, sauté the squash and onion in the vegetable oil over medium heat for 6 minutes, or until the squash is crisp-tender.

3. In a large bowl, combine the eggs, cheese, squash-onion mixture, and salt. Stir well.

4. Pour the contents into a 2-quart baking dish. Dot the top of the mixture with butter. Bake, uncovered, for 40 minutes, or until lightly browned.

Yield: 4 to 6 servings

Shawki b'Jibn

ARTICHOKE FRITTATA

This *jibn* has a different personality from the others because it calls for garlic instead of onions. The strong flavor profile of garlic is a better counterpoint to the nutty, earthy character of artichokes. Although frozen artichokes are perfectly fine for this dish, fresh are ideal. Avoid marinated artichokes; they do not have the right texture or flavor for this dish.

6 garlic cloves, finely chopped (about 1 tablespoon)

2 tablespoons vegetable oil

Two 10-ounce packages frozen artichoke hearts, or 6 fresh artichokes hearts, chopped

6 eggs, beaten

1 pound Muenster cheese, grated

1 teaspoon kosher salt

2 tablespoons butter, cut into 6 pieces

1. Preheat the oven to 350°F.

2. In a medium skillet, sauté the garlic in the vegetable oil over medium heat for 2 minutes, or until soft. Add the artichoke hearts. Sauté for 2 more minutes if the artichokes are frozen, or 4 more minutes if they are fresh.

3. Combine the eggs, cheese, and salt in a medium bowl. Mix well.

4. Add the artichokes to the egg-cheese mixture and pour the contents into a 2-quart baking dish. Dot with butter over the surface of the *jibn*. Bake for 40 minutes, or until lightly browned on top.

Yield: 4 to 6 servings

Filla Spanekh b'Jibn

SPINACH AND CHEESE WITH *FILLA*

This is a beautiful dish and a favorite dairy treat. The elegant, diamond-shaped *filla* is served at luncheons and special brunches, often accompanied by *laban* (Yogurt, page 241). Fresh spinach is readily available all year, and is preferable to frozen. Select small, sturdy spinach leaves with good color. Look for stems that are fairly thin and firm. Thick stems indicate overgrown spinach, which may be leathery and bitter. If you buy frozen *filla* (phyllo dough), defrost it in the refrigerator before using.

2 onions, chopped (about 1 cup)

2 tablespoons vegetable oil

4 pounds fresh spinach, trimmed and chopped, or one 32-ounce package frozen chopped spinach, thawed and drained

3 eggs, beaten

1 pound Muenster cheese, grated

1 teaspoon kosher salt

24 sheets *filla* (about 1 pound)

¾ cup (1½ sticks) unsalted butter, melted

¼ cup sesame seeds

1. Preheat the oven to 350°F.

2. In a medium saucepan, sauté the onions in the vegetable oil over medium heat for 4 to 6 minutes, or until soft. Add the spinach and sauté for 2 minutes. It should remain bright green.

3. Drain the spinach-onion mixture in a strainer. Transfer the mixture to a large mixing bowl. Add the eggs, cheese, and salt, and give the mixture a stir.

4. Brush 12 of the *filla* sheets, one at a time, with melted butter and layer them in a flat 3-quart baking dish. (Keep the untended sheets covered with plastic wrap and a towel so they do not dry out.) Pour the spinach-onion mixture onto the *filla*. Brush the remaining 12 sheets of *filla* with the remaining melted butter. Place the sheets onto the spinach-onion mixture.

5. Sprinkle the top *filla* sheet with the sesame seeds and refrigerate the baking dish for 5 minutes. Remove the dish from the refrigerator. With a very sharp knife, cut diagonally through the *filla*, creating diamond shapes. Bake, uncovered, for about 40 minutes, or until the top is lightly browned.

Yield: 10 to 12 servings

Beida Franji بيضة فرنجي

EGGS SCRAMBLED WITH TOMATOES

Beida franji is a soul-soothing dish that is simple to prepare and quite versatile since it is suitable for breakfast, lunch, or dinner. It is perfect with warm Syrian flatbread, a sprinkle of *za'atar* (page 20) or Aleppo pepper, and a dish of olives.

Beida is Arabic for "egg." The word *franji* (Arabic for "foreigner," but literally, "French") denotes that this recipe contains tomato, one of the "foreign," New World ingredients that appeared in Syria during the seventeenth century. With its ample use of tomato and onion and its rapid preparation time, this recipe has much in common with the Spanish dish *huevos revueltos* (scrambled eggs).

1 large onion, diced (about 1 cup)

4 tomatoes, chopped (about 4 cups)

2 tablespoons vegetable oil

8 eggs

1 teaspoon kosher salt

1 teaspoon ground allspice

½ teaspoon Aleppo pepper, or ¼ teaspoon crushed red pepper (optional)

1. In a large skillet, sauté the onion and tomatoes in the vegetable oil over medium-high heat for 4 to 5 minutes.

2. Crack the eggs into a medium mixing bowl. Add the salt but do not beat. Pour the eggs into the onion-tomato mixture and reduce the heat to medium-low. Let the eggs set. This will take about 1 minute.

3. Scramble the eggs gently with a fork, breaking up the yolks. Switch to a large spoon, and mix well, continuing to cook for 2 to 3 minutes.

4. Sprinkle the allspice over the surface of the eggs. Bring the pan right to the table and serve with piping hot Syrian bread. Sprinkle with Aleppo pepper, if desired.

Yield: 4 to 6 servings

Beid Ru'and

EGGS SCRAMBLED WITH RHUBARB

In this unique dish, rhubarb is treated as a vegetable, rather than an accompaniment to sweeter fruit such as strawberries. The eggs and seasonings mellow the tartness of the rhubarb.

2 garlic cloves, finely chopped
   (about 1 teaspoon)

1 tablespoon vegetable oil

1 pound rhubarb, peeled and cut into
   1-inch segments (2 cups)

6 eggs, beaten

½ teaspoon ground allspice

2 teaspoons kosher salt

1 teaspoon dried mint leaves

1. In a medium skillet, sauté the garlic in the vegetable oil over medium heat for 2 minutes, or until soft. Add the rhubarb and cover. Reduce the heat to low and cook for 10 to 15 minutes, or until the rhubarb is soft.

2. In a medium mixing bowl, combine the eggs, allspice, and salt. Give them a stir.

3. Uncover the skillet, raise the heat to medium, and pour the eggs into the rhubarb mixture. Stir with a large spoon for 2 to 3 minutes, or until the eggs set. Before serving, sprinkle the mint over the eggs.

Yield: 2 to 4 servings

Beid Hamine بيض همينة

SLOW-COOKED EGGS
WITH ONION PEELS

These hard-cooked eggs were traditionally prepared the day before Passover for use at the *seder* (see page 350) and throughout the holiday. Make a large quantity to have on hand. These distinctive eggs are not the usual white color of hard-boiled eggs; they turn light beige as a result of the onions, which caramelize slightly in the cooking water. To produce an even darker shade, just add a pinch of ground coffee.

12 eggs	2 tablespoons vegetable oil
Skins from 12 onions	

Combine the eggs and onion skins in 4 quarts of water in a large stockpot over high heat. Bring to a boil, and reduce the heat to low. Add the vegetable oil to the stockpot (it prevents the water from evaporating). Simmer for at least 6 to 8 hours, or overnight. Alternatively, the eggs may be baked at 200°F for 6 hours or overnight.

Yield: 4 to 6 servings

Mehshi b'Laban محشي بلبن

RICE-STUFFED ZUCCHINI
WITH BUTTER SAUCE

Unlike the more common *mehshis,* which are vegetables stuffed with ground meat, this variation gets its unique flavor from butter. Aleppian Jewish women take pride in making this dish with slender zucchini, which makes an attractive presentation. When shopping, look well for these narrow zucchini, though they're not easy to find because zucchini tend to grow large quickly.

When scooping out the pulp, be sure to avoid breaking through the skin or opening the other end. Leave only one side open for stuffing. With a proper corer (see page 143) and little practice, you can master this technique.

When *mehshi b'laban* is being prepared, it is a sure sign that *lib kusa* (Sautéed Squash Pulp), is on the way. This sweet dish—prepared from the pulp and eaten with warm flatbread—is an all-time favorite.

1 cup long-grain white rice

One 15½-ounce can chickpeas, drained, or ¾ cups dried chickpeas, soaked overnight or for 6 to 8 hours, then drained and cooked

1 cup (2 sticks) butter, at room temperature

2 teaspoons kosher salt

9 medium zucchini, cored, reserving the pulp for *lib kusa* (Sautéed Squash Pulp)

1. Preheat the oven to 350°F.

2. In a small saucepan, bring ¾ cup water to a boil. Add rice, reduce heat to low, and simmer for 10 minutes. Allow to cool.

3. Combine ½ cup of the chickpeas, the cooked rice, 1 stick of the butter, and the salt in a medium mixing bowl. Stir to mix well.

4. Stuff each zucchini three-quarters full with the chickpea-rice mixture. Arrange the stuffed zucchini side by side in a 2-quart baking dish. Sprinkle the remaining chickpeas over the stuffed zucchini. Dot the zucchini with the remaining 1 stick butter. Add ½ cup water to the baking dish.

5. Place the stuffed zucchini in the oven and bake, covered, for 45 minutes. Uncover the dish and continue cooking for 15 more minutes, or until the liquid has been absorbed. Remove the zucchini carefully; they are extremely delicate.

Yield: 4 to 6 servings

Lib Kusa—Sautéed Squash Pulp

1 onion, chopped (about ½ cup)

2 tablespoons vegetable oil

Pulp from 9 zucchini or yellow squash

1 teaspoon sugar

1 teaspoon kosher salt

1. In a medium saucepan, sauté the onion in the vegetable oil over medium heat for about 2 minutes, or until translucent.

2. Add the squash pulp, sugar, and salt to the saucepan. Sauté on medium-low heat for 4 more minutes. Serve alongside *mehshi b'laban*.

Yield: 4 to 6 servings

Jibneh Shelal جبنة سلل

TWISTED WHITE STRING CHEESE
WITH NIGELLA SEEDS

Syrian string cheese is still made at home on a regular basis, and "stringing the cheese" is still a common sight in Aleppian Jewish kitchens. Strands of the cheese and sliced cucumber tucked into Syrian flatbread was an old standby in Aleppo and is still adored by young and old alike.

The tiny aromatic black nigella seeds (*hebit il berekeh,* page 366) impart a distinct and special flavor to this cheese—nutty with a slight but pleasant bitterness. The seeds don't release much aroma until they're heated, which is why they are boiled with the starter cheese (curd). They are also known as "black cumin."

5 pounds curd (12 cups), cut into 1-inch dice (see Note)	2 teaspoons nigella seeds	6 teaspoons kosher salt, to taste

3. Transfer to a colander. Add another ⅛ teaspoon nigella seeds and ¼ teaspoon of the salt while forming into a ball. Then pick up the cheese with your hands (be careful, it will be hot). Make a hole in the middle of the cheese and pull it outward slowly, shaking the excess water from the sides at the same time. Stretch the cheese, like pulling taffy, until the hole is about 10 inches wide, or until it is as large as possible.

4. Twist the cheese in the form of a figure-8 and keep twisting until you cannot twist anymore, then knot the two ends together. The cheese will be cool and no longer pliable.

5. Immediately submerge the cheese into the ice bath for at least 20 minutes to stop the cooking process. Repeat steps 1 to 4 for the remaining curd. Remove all the cheese from the ice bath and place on a tray. Coat with remaining salt. At this point, the cheese may be refrigerated or frozen whole. The twists can be stored in sealed plastic bags for up to 1 week in the refrigerator and 3 weeks in the freezer. Before serving, pull, or "string," individual strands from the cheese.

1. Fill a large bowl with ice and cold water.

2. Bring 1 cup water to a boil in a large saucepan over high heat. Lower to a simmer, then add 1½ cups of the curd and ⅛ teaspoon of the nigella seeds. Mix with a wooden spoon until it has an elastic consistency.

➻ *Note* ↣

Curd is the semisolid matter remaining after milk sours or an acid or enzyme is added to it. Curd is available upon request from high-quality cheese shops.

Yield: 8 twisted cheeses

Jibneh جبنة

SYRIAN WHITE CHEESE

Jibneh is a fresh white cheese that is eaten without any aging. It is a staple on the Middle Eastern breakfast table, usually accompanied by warm flatbread, cucumbers, tomatoes, and olives.

Homemade cheese was traditionally kept in a *temekeh,* a large metal container filled with plenty of water and salt, which was left in a cool, dry place in the basement. Sometimes it was buried in the ground until the cheese was ready.

1 gallon whole milk

1 teaspoon vegetarian rennet gel,
   diluted in ¼ cup cold water (see Note)

Kosher salt to taste

1.   Pour the milk into a large stockpot over medium heat. Remove the milk when it is lukewarm, about 10 minutes. Do not allow the milk to get hot. Add the rennet to the milk and give it a stir. Let the milk rest for about 2 hours, uncovered, or until foam forms around the edges.

2.   Stir the milk once, then cover the pot with a large piece of cheesecloth. Weigh the cheesecloth down with a glass so that the liquid rises. Remove the liquid that has risen to the top.

3.   Pour the milk through a strainer lined with cheesecloth. Pick up the ends of the cheesecloth and twist to release the excess liquid. Hold for a few minutes, or until the cheese is formed.

4.   Remove the cheese from the cheesecloth and transfer to a medium mixing bowl. Sprinkle with salt. The cheese will release more liquid. Cool and pour off the excess liquid, leaving a little amount for the cheese to set in. Refrigerate for up to 1 week.

✎ *Note* ✐

Rennet is the common name for the substance used by cheese makers to coagulate milk and form curds. In the past, rennet was mostly derived from animal sources. In Aleppo, due to their observance of *kashrut* (page 10), Jews prepared cheese with vegetable rennet derived from plants. It was not easy to obtain and was usually imported from the United States in a powdered form. Vegetarian rennet is now commonly available in supermarkets, in the pudding section, or you can purchase liquid rennet from a cheese maker's supply house. Rennet must be refrigerated.

Yield: 4 to 6 servings (1 pound)

Laban

YOGURT

Unlike the sweetened single servings sold here in America, yogurt in the Middle East has a notable sour tang. Aleppians like to mix cucumbers, mint, and sometimes minced garlic into a bowl of *laban* to kick up the flavor. Yogurt is also a common side dish at the supper table; for some, it is even the main course.

1 quart low-fat or whole milk

1 cup nonfat dry milk (not instant)

1 cup unflavored yogurt

1. Combine the milk and dry milk in a saucepan, and heat to just below boiling. Remove from the heat and cool until lukewarm. Put the yogurt in a large bowl and add a small amount of the milk. Beat lightly with a fork. Add the remaining cooled milk and mix briefly.

2. Pour the mixture into a yogurt maker or a glass jar. Cover and put in a warm place. If you are not using a yogurt maker, put the jar in an oven with a pilot light, or near a radiator or heating duct. Whatever method you use to keep the jar warm, it is important that the yogurt not be disturbed. An average batch should be thickened in 6 to 8 hours. Chill several hours before using. Yogurt will stay fresh for about 2 weeks. Save 1 cup of yogurt to use as a starter for the next batch.

Yield: 4 to 6 servings, about 1½ quarts

Lebneh

لبنة

YOGURT SPREAD

Lebneh is simply a thickened version of *laban* (Yogurt, page 241). Its flavor is therefore more concentrated and its texture rich and creamy. *Lebneh* is served as a spread or dip, drizzled with vegetable oil and sprinkled with *za'atar* (page 20). It makes a great breakfast with Syrian flatbread alongside *hummus* (Chickpea-Sesame Spread, page 27), *baba ghanooj* (Eggplant-Sesame Puree, page 29), olives, sliced cucumbers, and tomatoes.

Another popular way of preparing *lebneh* is by forming it into 1½-inch balls, placing them in a jar, and completely covering them with vegetable oil. The oil acts as a preservative, and the *lebneh* balls last up to a month in the refrigerator. They are nice to have on hand for unexpected breakfast guests or as an everyday snack.

1½ quarts *laban* (see recipe on page 241) or store-bought yogurt

1½ teaspoons ground cumin

1½ teaspoons dried mint

½ teaspoon Aleppo pepper

1½ teaspoons kosher salt

1 cup plus ½ teaspoon vegetable oil

---

1. Place a strainer inside a glass bowl. Line the strainer with cheesecloth. Pour the yogurt into the strainer and fold in the corners of the cheesecloth. Drain overnight or until the yogurt reaches a thick, creamy consistency. As the yogurt drains, occasionally pour the excess liquid from the bowl. Alternatively, you can drain the liquid by knotting the corners of the cheesecloth over the shaft of a sink faucet. The cheesecloth should be suspended over the sink into which the liquid will drain.

2. To prepare the balls, place the yogurt spread in a bowl and add cumin, mint, Aleppo pepper, and salt. Mix well. Fill a pint-size jar with ½ cup of the oil. Lubricate hands lightly with ½ teaspoon oil and form 1½-inch balls. Gently drop the balls into the jar. Fill the jar with the remaining oil. Cover the jar tightly and refrigerate. The yogurt spread will stay fresh for about 2 weeks.

Yield: 1 pint

Helou Hindi
(Candied Coconut with Pistachios, page 289)

Hilweyat wa Mashareeb
حلويات ومشاريب
SWEETS AND BEVERAGES

Aleppo has always been famous for the quality of its sweets. They are quite sugary and dainty, similar to those found in Indian cuisine. Unlike Western desserts, Aleppian confections do not appear at the end of meals. In fact, there is no Arabic word for "dessert." With the bountiful fruits of the Levant, most meals conclude with fresh fruit. Sugary treats are usually an accompaniment to tea or coffee during a midafternoon break and are also enjoyed on very special occasions, such as engagement parties and weddings. There are a great variety of sweets. Many, such as *eras b'ajweh* (Date-Filled Crescents, page 268) and *kra'bij* (Marshmallow-Dipped Nut-Stuffed Pastry, page 269), demand nuts, dried fruits, and floral water of the highest quality. The first and most important step in all these recipes is to obtain the freshest ingredients available.

Aleppian Jews still preserve the custom of having fresh and dried fruit and traditional sweet pastries available in their homes at all times in case an unexpected guest arrives. Oranges, grapefruits, pears, apricots, figs, olives, plums, grapes, pistachios, walnuts, hazelnuts, and fresh or dried almonds were all offered for sale at the roadside or heaped on grocers' carts in Aleppo, and they are still cherished in Aleppian Jewish communities today. Melons of all kinds are also prized, especially as a refreshing counterpoint to a large repast. Preserved fruits, particularly apricots, are a specialty of Damascus, while Aleppo is noted for its almond paste. Scrumptious apricot sweetmeats and pastries stuffed with pistachios and dripping with honey beckon from the windows of Syrian sweetshops.

A great many citrus fruits are available almost year-round in Aleppo. One unusual type of orange, *laymoon helou*, is a smooth-skinned yellow orange with a sweet taste. Many people believe it is the only cure for the common cold. In the springtime, almonds take over the markets of Aleppo. They are eaten whole and unripe, with their crunchy, furry green skin. Plums are also eaten unripe, dipped in salt to enhance the sour flavor. Apricots (*meshmosh*) are harvested at this

time as well. Dried apricots are tossed into candy dishes along with mixed nuts and, occasionally, red and white mulberries (*toot*).

Summer fruits include a vast array of cherries (*karaz*), white and dark plums (*janarek*), apples (*teffah*), pears (*n'jass*), peaches (*derra*), and grapes. *Maqassi*, the golden grape, is the sweetest. *Al-bayadi* is a white grape that is shapelier, while *enab zayni* is a refreshing pale red. Unripe grapes, or *hosrun*, are eaten with a little salt.

During the summer, some of the most unusual fruits begin to appear in the clay and enamelware bowls of Syrian vendors. Prickly pears (*sobbyayr*) can be purchased at roadside stands, cut open and ready to eat, while jujube (*'ennab*), a deep red olive with a gooey green center, and myrtle (*henblass*), a dry green fruit, are savored at home.

In the late summer, many of the classic Middle Eastern fruits begin to appear. Pomegranates, sweet or sour, are a special treat alone or as an enhancement for many dishes, such as *kibbeh nabelsieh* (Golden Ground Meat–Filled Bulgur Shells, page 53). Figs of all kinds (*teen*) are available, from bright green to deep crimson to nearly black, as are melons (*bateesh asfar*), watermelons (*batteekh ahmar*), persimmons (*kaki*), and quinces (*s'farjal*).

From the wealth of the market, Aleppian Jewish cooks prepared *helou*, homemade candied fruit, for friends and relatives who dropped by. They were stored and often served in pretty containers called *bau'the*, with miniature spoons and forks for guests to help themselves.

There is also a variety of interesting and refreshing Aleppian beverages that can be enjoyed alone or as an accompaniment to sweets. Along with heady *'ahweh* (Arabic Coffee, page 318) and refreshing *chai b'nana* (Mint Tea, page 322), there are special beverages, such as *shrab al loz* (Sweet Almond Milk, page 312), which is regularly served at engagement parties to symbolize a sweet marriage, and *arak*, the Syrian version of anisette and the beverage of choice at *sebbits* (festive Sabbath luncheons, see page 334).

الوجبات

SWEETS AND
BEVERAGE RECIPES

continued

Shira شيرا

FRAGRANT ALEPPIAN
DESSERT SYRUP

This simple syrup is a component of so many Aleppian desserts that it is a fixture in Aleppian refrigerators. The addition of rose or orange blossom water imbues it with an exotic flavor for which the Middle East is renowned.

When preparing *shira,* it is important to get the right consistency. For some Syrian sweets, a thicker syrup may be necessary. To thicken the syrup, keep it on the heat a bit longer; if it is too thick, add some water and simmer again. When pouring *shira* over hot pastries, the syrup should be cold so the pastries stay crisp.

3 cups sugar

1 teaspoon freshly squeezed lemon juice

½ teaspoon orange blossom water
or rose water

1. Combine the sugar, lemon juice, orange blossom water, and 1 cup water in a medium saucepan over medium heat. Stir constantly with a wooden spoon until the mixture boils. Reduce the heat to low and simmer for 15 minutes, or until the syrup slides slowly down the back of a spoon.

2. Allow the syrup to cool. Use immediately or pour into a glass jar and refrigerate. It will keep for up to 2 months.

❧ *Note* ❧
All *helou* recipes use orange blossom water; rose water is used for other sweets.

Yield: 2 cups

Zalabieh

FRIED PASTRY BALLS
WITH SUGAR SYRUP GLAZE

In the Middle East, it is believed that eating sweet things will ward off the evil eye. Whether that is true or not, you can always play it safe with *zalabieh,* a honey-sweet pastry that is soaked in warm syrup and usually eaten while hot. It is essentially identical in form and name to the Indian sweet known as *jalebi. Zalabieh* is usually served on Hanukkah. It is one of the most kid-friendly sweets and is very addictive—to walk away after having just one would be a true demonstration of willpower!

1 teaspoon sugar

Pinch of kosher salt

2 teaspoons active dry yeast
   dissolved in 1 cup warm water

2 cups all-purpose flour

2 cups vegetable oil

1 cup *shira* (Fragrant Aleppian
   Dessert Syrup, page 249)

1. Combine the sugar, salt, and yeast mixture in a large bowl, and let stand for 15 minutes, until it begins to bubble. Add the flour and 1 cup water to the yeast mixture and mix by hand in bowl, until a batter forms with a pancakelike consistency. Cover with wax paper. Let the mixture stand in a place warmer than room temperature for 2 hours to rise until double the original size.

2. Heat the vegetable oil in a deep fryer or medium saucepan over medium heat until it sizzles upon contact with a drop of water.

3. Warm the *shira* in a small saucepan over low heat.

4. Drop the *zalabieh* mixture, 1 teaspoon at a time, into the oil. Fry them in batches of 10 until golden. Drain the *zalabieh* briefly on paper towels.

5. While still hot, submerge the *zalabieh* in the warm *shira* to glaze. Place on flat platter. Serve hot or at room temperature.

Yield: 4 dozen balls

Baklawa

PISTACHIO *FILLA* WEDGES
IN ROSE WATER SYRUP

In a quality sweetshop, *baklawa* can be quite a beautiful sight: it is cleanly cut into elegant diamond shapes, with a hint of the delicious pistachio peeking out from the crisp golden layers of *filla*. Each piece shines like a gem. The sheen on the surface of *baklawa* comes from the *shira* (Fragrant Aleppian Dessert Syrup, page 249).

Proud Aleppians call this sweet *baklawa halabi* (Aleppian *baklawa*) because in Syria it is made with the unparalleled pistachios grown in the hinterlands of Aleppo. Even though this sweet originated with the Turks, Aleppians found ways to make it better.

In the Levant, *filla* was rolled by hand, a time-consuming and exhausting task. It is now predominantly manufactured by machines; it is rare to find hand-rolled *filla* outside the Eastern Mediterranean.

As for the choice of pistachios, connoisseurs from Aleppo now residing abroad prefer Sicilian, Turkish, Iranian, or Afghan varieties—never Californian—but for them, *baklawa* will never be perfect without the superior flavor and crunch of elegant Aleppian pistachios. To enjoy pistachios from Aleppo, one must travel to Syria because they are no longer exported in great numbers. Nonetheless, you can achieve absolutely wonderful results with this recipe.

1½ pounds pistachios, shelled, blanched, peeled, and finely chopped (see page 310)

2 tablespoons confectioners' sugar

1¼ pounds (5 sticks) unsalted butter or margarine, melted

24 sheets *filla* (about 1 pound)

1 cup cold *shira* (Fragrant Aleppian Dessert Syrup, page 249)

1. Combine the pistachios, sugar, and ¼ cup of the melted butter in a medium mixing bowl.

2. Working with half the *filla*, brush each sheet, one at a time, using slightly less than half the remaining melted butter. Stack them evenly, one on top of the other. (Keep the untended sheets covered with wax paper and a towel to prevent them from drying out.) Fit the buttered *filla* sheets into a 14-inch round or 10 x 12-inch baking pan, folding the sides over to create a round or straight edge.

3. Preheat the oven to 350°F.

4. Spread the nut mixture over the *filla*. Repeat step 3 for the remaining sheets of *filla*, covering the nut layer and brushing the top sheet with a generous amount of butter. Refrigerate, covered, for 20 minutes. Cut the pastry into diamond, square, or rectangular pieces.

5. Bake for 1 hour, or until the *baklawa* is puffy and golden.

6. After removing the *baklawa* from the oven, pour the cold *shira* over it. Let the *baklawa* cool.

Yield: 30 pastry wedges

Kanafe

RICOTTA-FILLED
SHREDDED WHEAT PASTRY

Kanafe, the main ingredient for which this sweet is named, starts as a thin mixture of flour and water. The mixture is sprinkled into an immense copper pan. As the batter touches the hot metal, it crackles and solidifies into long threads. These are scooped up in crisp bundles that resemble loops of yarn. The final product is available at Greek and Middle Eastern grocery stores.

    Kanafe is one of the most popular sweets served at life-cycle events such as the celebration of a *bar mitzvah* or a *brit milah* (ritual circumcision). They are traditionally prepared in a round tray, but today other versions have become popular, such as three-tiered *kanafe* and *kanafe* balls. The secret to successful *kanafe* is getting the consistency of the pudding just right, neither too thick nor too thin. Luckily, it freezes beautifully; *kanafe* is time-consuming to prepare, and having it on hand makes for a very rewarding treat with a fresh pot of *'ahweh* (Arabic Coffee, page 318).

½ cup whole milk

1 pint heavy cream

2 tablespoons sugar

2 tablespoons cornstarch

1 teaspoon rose water

1 teaspoon orange blossom water

2 pounds whole-milk ricotta cheese

1 pound *kanafe*
(unprocessed shredded wheat)

1½ cups (3 sticks) unsalted butter

1 cup *shira* (Fragrant Aleppian
Dessert Syrup, page 249)

1. Combine the milk, cream, sugar, and cornstarch in a medium saucepan over medium heat. Using a wooden spoon, stir the mixture until dissolved. When it reaches its boiling point, stir in the rose water and orange blossom water. Reduce the heat to low and simmer for 5 minutes, or until the mixture is thickened and velvety. Remove and cool thoroughly. Stir the ricotta cheese into the milk mixture until well blended.

2. Preheat the oven to 350°F.

3. Shred the *kanafe* in a large bowl. Melt the butter in a small saucepan over low heat. Do not let the butter brown. Pour the butter over the *kanafe* and mix until the *kanafe* is well coated.

continued

4. Spread half the *kanafe* onto the bottom of a 3-quart baking dish. Flatten with the palm of your hand to make an even layer. Spread the ricotta-cream mixture over the *kanafe* and top with the remaining *kanafe*. Bake for 1 hour and 15 minutes, or until the top of the dish is golden.

5. Remove the *kanafe* from the oven and pour the cold *shira* over it immediately. When the dish is cool, cut it into pieces and serve.

Yield: 40 pastries

Basbusa

SWEET COCONUT
AND ALMOND DESSERT

Basbusa is one of the most famous sweetmeats made in Aleppo. These semolina squares covered with *shira* (Fragrant Aleppian Dessert Syrup) are easily prepared and are perfect with coffee or tea. Typically, *basbusa* is eaten warm, but it can be enjoyed chilled and will keep for several days in the refrigerator.

1 cup (2 sticks) unsweetened butter, at room temperature

1½ cups sugar

2 cups *smead* (semolina)

1 cup finely grated fresh coconut meat (see page 289)

2½ cups heavy cream

2 teaspoon baking powder

1 cup cold *shira* (Fragrant Aleppian Dessert Syrup, page 249)

1 cup almonds, blanched, peeled, and slivered (see page 310)

1. Preheat the oven to 375°F.

2. Cream the butter with the sugar by hand in a medium mixing bowl. Add the *smead,* coconut, and cream to the butter mixture and blend well. Fold in the baking powder.

3. Pour the coconut mixture into two greased 9 x 13-inch baking pans. Bake for 35 minutes.

4. Remove the mixture from the oven and pour the *shira* over it. Top with almonds. Return to the oven to bake for another 20 minutes, or until golden. When cooled, cut into 1½-inch squares. Serve at room temperature. (The dessert may be frozen when cooled.)

✎ *Note* ✐

For those seeking a *pareve* (nondairy) dish, substitute margarine for the butter and nondairy creamer or soy milk for the cream. The result will not be as flavorful, however.

Yield: 108 squares

'Ataiyef

قطايف

STUFFED SYRIAN PANCAKES

'Ataiyef is not your ordinary Sunday morning pancake. Filled with ricotta cheese, deep-fried, dipped in chopped pistachio nuts, and topped with *shira* (Fragrant Aleppian Dessert Syrup), it is more like a five-star dessert. Aleppian Jews eat *'ataiyef* on happy occasions such as engagement parties.

These pancakes are one of the dairy foods customarily eaten during Shavuot (Festival of the Giving of the Torah). King Solomon's "Song of Songs," particularly the words "honey and milk are under your tongue," inspired this dish. The sweetness of *shira* shares a symbolic connection with the sweetness of the Torah, which the Jews received on Shavout. *'Ataiyef* is also served on Hanukkah because it is fried, and thus symbolizes the miracle of oil celebrated on that holiday.

While this recipe offers a way to make the batter from scratch, you may find commercial pancake mixes more convenient than homemade.

Batter:

2 cups all-purpose flour

1 teaspoon baking soda

1 tablepoon sugar

½ teaspoon baking powder

½ teaspoon salt

1 large egg, lightly beaten

1 cup ricotta cheese

1 cup vegetable oil

1 cup *shira* (Fragrant Aleppian Dessert Syrup, page 249)

1 cup pistachios, shelled, blanched, peeled, and finely chopped (see page 310)

1. Preheat a griddle pan over medium heat. Wipe the pan with a paper towel dipped in vegetable oil.

2. Combine the flour, baking soda, sugar, baking powder, and salt in a large mixing bowl. Add the egg and 2½ cups water to the mixture. Stir the mixture until the batter is smooth and there are no lumps.

3. Make the pancakes by pouring the batter, 1 tablespoon at a time, onto the griddle. Shape the batter into 3-inch-wide pancakes, much like a thin crepe. Cook on one side only. Remove the pancake when bubbles appear on its surface. Keep the cooked pancakes moist by covering them with a clean towel.

4. Place 1 teaspoon ricotta cheese in the uncooked center of each pancake. Fold the pancake in half and pinch the sides firmly closed. Fill the pancakes as quickly as possible so they do not dry out. (At this point, the pancakes may be frozen for later use.)

5. In a medium saucepan over medium heat, heat the vegetable oil until it sizzles upon contact with a drop of water. Deep-fry the filled pancakes in batches for 3 minutes, or until brown. Coat the fried pancakes in the cold *shira*. Dip the point of each pancake in pistachio nuts. To ensure a crispy texture, place the pancakes on a tray in a single layer; do not stack or cover them.

⤳ *Variation* ⤶

For a non-dairy version, combine 2 cups finely chopped walnuts, ½ cup sugar, and 1 teaspoon cinnamon and substitute for the ricotta.

Yield: About 4 dozen pancakes

أصابع بسوتلاج

Assabih b'Sutlaj

CUSTARD-FILLED FINGERS
IN *FILLA*

Assabih is Arabic for "fingers." These dainty, fingerlike desserts are quite impressive. The textural contrast of the luscious custard and the delicate, crisp *filla* is divine. Though it can be tricky to work with *filla,* once you get the hang of it the rest of this recipe is extremely simple. When these sweets bring exuberant praise from your family and friends—and they will—you might not want to admit how easy this recipe really is.

1 quart milk	½ teaspoon orange blossom water or rose water	1 pound (4 sticks) unsalted butter, melted
½ cup cornstarch		Pinch of ground cinnamon (optional)
2 tablespoons sugar	24 sheets *filla* (about 1 pound)	Pinch of confectioners' sugar (optional)

1. To make the custard, combine the milk, cornstarch, and sugar in a large saucepan. Stir thoroughly with a wooden spoon until the cornstarch is completely dissolved. Cook over medium-high heat. Bring to a boil. Reduce the heat to low and simmer, stirring constantly, for 10 minutes, or until the mixture reaches a velvety consistency. Stir in the orange blossom or rose water.

2. Pour the custard into a 15½ x 10½-inch rimmed baking sheet and let cool. Refrigerate for 1 hour, or until firm.

3. Remove the custard from the refrigerator, and slice into 2 x 1-inch bars.

4. Preheat the oven to 350°F.

5. Cut through all the *filla* sheets with a sharp knife crosswise into 3 rectangular sections about 3 inches wide. Work with only one strip of *filla* at a time. Cover the remaining *filla* strips with wax paper and a damp towel to keep them from drying out. Brush one strip of *filla* with melted butter. Place a custard bar from step 4 about 1 inch from the short edge of the *filla* strip. Fold the edge over the custard, then fold in the two sides of the sheet over the filling to prevent it from oozing out. Roll the strip like a cigar. Fill and roll the remaining *filla* strips.

6. Bake for 20 to 30 minutes, or until the tops are slightly golden. Serve warm with a sprinkle of cinnamon and confectioners' sugar, if desired.

Yield: 72 fingers

Assabih b'Loz

NUT-FILLED *FILLA* FINGERS

Assabih b'loz is a favorite in the Aleppian Jewish community and is served at parties and special occasions. It keeps well in the freezer, so if you wish, freeze the pastries and prepare the *shira* (Fragrant Aleppian Dessert Syrup) in advance.

Filling:

1 pound walnuts or pistachios, shelled and chopped (page 310)

1 cup sugar

1 tablespoon butter, melted

1 teaspoon rose water

24 sheets *filla* (about 1 pound)

1 pound (4 sticks) butter, melted

1 cup *shira* (Fragrant Aleppian Dessert Syrup, page 249)

1. Preheat the oven to 350°F.

2. To make the filling, combine the nuts, sugar, butter, and rose water in a small mixing bowl.

3. Cut *filla* sheets lengthwise into thirds. You'll be working with one strip at a time. Cover the other sheets with wax paper and a damp towel to keep from drying out.

4. Brush each *filla* strip with melted butter. Spoon 1 teaspoon of the filling about ½ inch from the short edge of a *filla* strip. Fold the edge over the filling, then fold in the sides. Continue to roll the strip like a cigar. Place on a baking sheet. Repeat with the remaining *filla* strips and filling.

5. Bake for 20 minutes, or until the tops of the pastries are slightly golden. Pour the *shira* over the pastries before serving.

Yield: 72 fingers

Ka'ak bi'Loz كعك بلوز

ALMOND COOKIE WREATHS

These edible wreaths are as lovely as handcrafted pieces of jewelry. With the delicate twists of the pastry and the small rose decorations at the joint, they are truly works of art. A traditional part of engagement (*swanee*) parties (see page 362), and the *mikveh* (ritual bath) required of a young bride, *ka'ak bi'loz* are served on beautiful trays along with an array of other pastries. The almonds in this sweet symbolize fertility. Whether you decide to leave them in their natural almond color or tint half of them green or pink, they will truly be a feast for the eyes. If you are looking for a more streamlined preparation, commercial almond paste and icing are widely available.

Almond Paste:

2½ cups almonds, blanched in boiling water for 3 to 4 minutes and peeled

1¼ cups sugar

¼ cup rose water

5 drops green or pink food coloring

Icing:

¾ cup confectioners' sugar

2 tablespoons freshly squeezed lemon juice

1 drop red food coloring or color of your choice

1. To make the almond paste, blend the almonds, sugar, and rose water in a food processor for 3 to 5 minutes, or until it forms a paste. Separate the paste into two equal mounds and transfer to medium mixing bowls. Stir the food coloring into one of the bowls and mix until the color is even.

2. Roll the colored paste into strands ¼ inch wide and 7 inches long. (Moisten palms with a small amount of cold water if consistency is too sticky when rolling.) Roll on a flat surface with your hands. Twist two colored or uncolored strands together 7 to 8 times. Then bring the ends of each interlaced strand together, forming a circle. Gently pinch the ends to close the joint. Place on a tray. Repeat the process with the remaining paste.

3. Prepare the icing by mixing the confectioners' sugar with the lemon juice (if it seems too dry, add a few drops of water). Then add the food coloring. Place icing mixture in a pastry tube fitted with a #12 tip. Form a conical shape for the base of a rose. Change to a #104 tip for the petals. Carefully form two concentric layers of rose petals around the base. Then form two leaves on each side. This step is a bit advanced, and may take some practice. Don't worry if you feel the need to skip it your first few times around— these cookies are quite a sight without the icing as well.

4. Air-dry the wreaths for 8 to 10 hours. They should be soft and chewy; do not overdry. You may store in an airtight container or freeze for up to 3 months.

Yield: 48 cookies

Loz w'Arus

INITIAL WEDDING COOKIES

"Initial cookies," inscribed with the initials of a couple's first names, play an important role in Aleppian Jewish engagement celebrations. It is a time-honored tradition to serve them at the Meeting of the Family (see page 362).

1 recipe Almond Paste
  (see page 263, step 1)

½ cup granulated sugar

1 cup confectioners' sugar

4 egg whites

Icing:

¾ cup confectioners' sugar

2 tablespoons freshly squeezed lemon juice

1 drop food coloring of your choice

1. Preheat oven to 325°F.

2. Line two cookie sheets with lightly greased foil.

3. Mix the almond paste and granulated sugar in a food processor until smooth. Add the confectioners' sugar and 2 of the egg whites. Process until smooth.

4. Whisk the remaining 2 egg whites in a small bowl until frothy. With lightly floured hands, roll dough into 1 to 1½ inch balls. Coat balls in egg whites, shaking off excess. Arrange balls on cookie sheets and flatten lightly to 2-inch-long flat ovals. Place the cookies 2 inches apart on the cookie sheet.

5. Bake 20 minutes, or until lightly browned. Let stand on the cookie sheet for 1 minute. Transfer to a wire rack to cool.

6. Prepare the icing by mixing the confectioners' sugar with the lemon juice (if it seems too dry, add a few drops of water), then add the food coloring. Transfer the icing mixture to a pastry tube fitted with a #2 tip. Inscribe each cookie with the initials of the couple's first names.

Yield: approximately 36 cookies

Ka'ak b'Sukar

BRAIDED SUGAR COOKIES

Like the candy *amar e'deen* (Apricot Fruit Paste, page 306), *ka'ak b'sukar* is a favorite childhood memory for many Aleppian Jews. These are the very basic cookies with which Aleppian Jewish mothers commonly fill their cookie jars. Children are quick to discover all the secret stashes of *ka'ak b'sukar* and ruin their appetites on many occasions with this sweet, simple treat.

4 large eggs

1½ cups sugar

2 tablespoons grated orange zest
(about 2 oranges)

2 teaspoons vanilla extract

1 cup vegetable oil

5 cups all-purpose flour

3 teaspoons baking powder

1. In a medium bowl, beat the eggs, 1 cup of the sugar, the orange zest, vanilla extract, and oil. Then gradually add the flour and baking powder to the mixture to form a sticky dough. Mix about 2 minutes, until well blended. Refrigerate for 15 minutes.

2. Preheat the oven to 350°F.

3. Roll the dough into strands 4 inches long and ½ inch thick. Take 2 strands and twist them together 5 to 6 times. Gently pinch the ends. Repeat the process with the remaining dough.

4. Lightly dip each cookie in the remaining sugar. Place the cookies on a greased baking sheet about 1 inch apart. Bake for 8 to 10 minutes. The cookies should remain pale.

Yield: 40 cookies

Graybeh

SWEET BRACELET-SHAPED BUTTER COOKIES

These delicious butter cookies are delicate and melt in your mouth. Their name comes from the Arabic word meaning "to swoon," which is appropriate for these crowd-pleasers. *Graybeh* can be found all over the Mediterranean these days, often with hints of orange flavor from orange zest or orange blossom water.

3 sticks (¾ pound) unsalted butter, at room temperature, then clarified (see step 1)	1 cup superfine sugar 3 cups all-purpose flour	1 cup pistachios, shelled, blanched, and peeled (see page 310)

1. To clarify butter, in a medium saucepan melt the butter very slowly over low heat. Do not stir. Skim the foam off the top, and discard the foam.

2. In a large bowl, combine sugar and 1 cup clarified butter. Mix well. Refrigerate for 30 minutes. Beat sugar-butter mixture for about 5 minutes, or until it is the consistency of whipping cream. With a wooden spoon, add the flour, 1 cup at a time. Knead by hand for 10 minutes, or until the batter is very soft.

3. Preheat the oven to 300°F.

4. To form the pastries, on a wooden cutting board, pinch off a walnut-size chunk of the dough, and form into a strand ½ inch wide and 4 inches long. Join the ends of the strand to form a bracelet, and place a whole pistachio at the joint. Form the remaining dough into bracelets and place the bracelets on an ungreased baking sheet 1 inch apart. Work quickly, handling the dough as little as possible. Wipe often to keep the surface clean.

5. Bake the bracelets for 10 minutes, or until the bottoms are lightly browned but the tops are still pale. Do not remove from the baking sheet until cool. The cooled cookies may be frozen for up to 3 weeks. Handle with extreme care because *graybeh* are very fragile.

Peeling skins off shelled pistachios

Yield: 70 cookies

Eras b'Ajweh   قراص بعجوة

DATE-FILLED CRESCENTS

A supply of *eras b'ajweh* is usually kept on hand to serve with tea or coffee to guests. Be sure to use Medjool dates—much of the flavor of this sweet depends on the quality of the dates. Avoid those with rigid meat or thick, tasteless skins. These sweets should melt in your mouth to reveal a soft, almost puddinglike consistency.

Dough:

2 cups all-purpose flour

1 cup *smead* (semolina)

2 sticks unsalted butter (½ pound), at room temperature

Dash of kosher salt

½ teaspoon rose water (optional)

Filling:

1 pound Medjool dates, pitted

1 cup chopped walnuts (optional)

½ teaspoon grated orange or lemon zest or ½ teaspoon orange blossom water

Confectioners' sugar

1. To make the dough, combine the flour, *smead*, butter, salt, and rose water (if desired) in a large mixing bowl. Add ½ cup warm water, ¼ cup at a time, mixing until well blended after each addition. Cover and set aside.

2. To make the filling, in a medium saucepan, place the dates in enough water to cover them. Bring the water to a simmer over medium heat, reduce the heat to medium-low, and cook for 15 minutes, or until the dates are soft.

3. Remove the dates from the heat and transfer them to a medium mixing bowl. Mash the dates with a fork until a smooth, jamlike consistency is achieved. Stir in the walnuts and zest. Let cool.

4. Preheat the oven to 350°F.

5. Pinch off walnut-size pieces of the dough and flatten them into 2-inch rounds on a work surface. Place 1 teaspoon of the date filling in the center of each round. Then, with your hands, roll the pastry into a fluted shape with open ends. Turn the ends of the fluted pastry toward one another to form a crescent shape. Continue in this way with the remaining dough and filling. Transfer the finished pastries to an ungreased cookie sheet.

6. Bake the pastries for about 15 minutes, or until only the bottoms are light brown. Make sure that the tops of the pastries remain pale. Sprinkle with confectioners' sugar just before serving.

Yield: 48 cookies

Kra'bij

MARSHMALLOW-DIPPED
NUT-STUFFED PASTRY

On the holiday of Purim (The Festival of Lots), Aleppian Jews eat *kra'bij* and *ma'amoul* (Nut-Stuffed Pastry, page 272). During the commotion of entertaining guests during this joyous festival, it is very important to keep an eye on these sweets. *Kra'bij* are topped with *natif,* a white marshmallow spread, which is perfect for clandestine finger-swiping by little boys and girls. Commercial marshmallow cream is widely available and can be substituted for homemade *natif.*

Natif spread:

3 cups granulated sugar

½ teaspoon freshly squeezed lemon juice

3 egg whites

¼ teaspoon vanilla extract,
   or ½ teaspoon rose water

Dough:

2 cups all-purpose flour

1 cup *smead* (semolina)

½ teaspoon rose water (optional)

1 cup (2 sticks) unsalted butter
   or margarine

Filling:

1 pound pistachios, shelled, blanched,
   and peeled, and chopped (see page 000)

2 tablespoons confectioners' sugar

½ teaspoon orange blossom water

1 tablespoon butter or margarine, melted

¼ cup finely chopped pistachios

1. To make the *natif,* combine the sugar, 1 cup water, and the lemon juice in a medium saucepan over medium-high heat. Bring to a boil and cook for 8 minutes, or until the mixture achieves a syrupy consistency.

2. Using an electric mixer, begin beating the egg whites. Gradually add the steaming hot syrup, beating constantly until stiff peaks form. Add the vanilla extract.

3. To make the dough, combine the flour and *smead* in a large mixing bowl. Add rose water, if desired. Fold in the butter and pour in ¼ to ½ cup lukewarm water (see Note). Knead the dough well (in the bowl) and cover.

4. To make the filling, combine the 1 pound pistachios, sugar, orange water, and butter in a large bowl and stir to mix well.

5. Preheat the oven 450°F.

6. To form the pastries, divide the dough into 4 portions. Work with 1 portion at a time, keeping the rest covered as you work. Pinch a walnut-size ball from the dough. Press down on the center of the ball with your finger, forming a ½-inch indentation. Fill the indentation with ¾ teaspoon of the filling. Close the pastry over the filling with your thumb and forefinger. Place it on a baking sheet lined with parchment paper. Repeat with the remaining dough and filling.

7. Bake the pastries for 15 minutes, or until the bottoms of the pastries are lightly browned and the tops are still pale. Cool completely.

8. Top the pastries with about 1 teaspoon of the *natif* spread, and finish them with a dusting of finely chopped pistachios.

✿ Note ✿

Don't make the dough too thin, or it will stiffen after baking. A thicker dough will be flakier and moister.

Yield: 48 pastries

Kra'bij *(Marshmallow-Dipped Nut-Stuffed Pastry, page 269)*

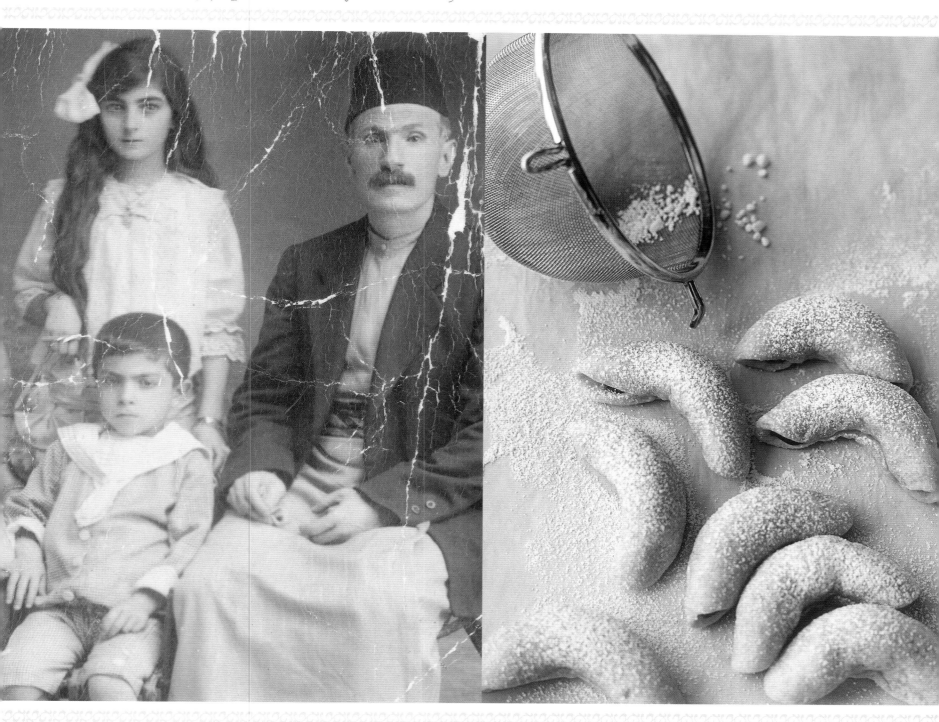

Selim and Frieda Dweck and family, circa 1905
(courtesy of Sephardic Community Center Archives)

Eras b'Ajweh *(Date-Filled Crescents, page 268)*

Ma'amoul

NUT-STUFFED PASTRY

The definition of the Arabic word *ma'amoul* is "filled." It is a small rounded pastry made with decorative molds called *tabe'*. The nut filling is inserted into a hollow shell in the pastry and then closed. The filled pastry is then placed inside the mold. Each mold shape indicates a different type of *ma'amoul* filling. A flat-topped pastry usually means a date filling, while a pointy top usually means some kind of nut filling.

When the *ma'amoul* are baked, the embossed design becomes more prominent and very beautiful. Another option is to decorate the *ma'amoul* with a special pincher (called *mulaht*) with a serrated edge. Using this tool, which is sold at Middle Eastern groceries, you can crimp the top of the rounded pastry about six times. *Ma'amoul* is a Purim staple, along with *kra'bij* (Marshmallow-Dipped Nut-Stuffed Pastry, page 269).

Dough:

2 cups all-purpose flour

1 cup *smead* (semolina)

½ teaspoon rose water (optional)

1 cup (2 sticks) unsalted butter
   or margarine

Filling:

1 pound pistachio nuts, shelled, blanched,
   peeled, and chopped (see page 310)

3 tablespoons confectioners' sugar

1 tablespoon unsalted butter, melted

½ teaspoon orange blossom water

1. To make the dough, combine the flour and *smead* in a large mixing bowl until the mixture has a crumbly consistency. Add rose water, if desired. Fold in the butter and add ¼ to ½ cup lukewarm water. Knead the dough well and cover.

2. To make the filling, combine the pistachios, 2 tablespoons of the sugar, the butter, and orange blossom water.

3. Preheat the oven to 350°F.

4. To form the pastries, divide the dough into 4 portions. Work with 1 portion at a time, keeping the rest covered as you work. Pinch a walnut-size ball from the dough. Press down on the center with your finger, forming a ½-inch indentation. Fill the indentation with ¾ teaspoon of the filling. Close the pastry with your thumb and forefinger. If using the special *ma'amoul* mold, press the top of the pastry firmly against the mold to impress the desired pattern onto the pastry. Lightly tap the mold on a hard surface to remove the pastry. Place the pastry on a baking sheet lined with parchment paper. Repeat with the remaining dough and filling.

5. Bake for 12 minutes, or until the bottoms of the pastries are lightly browned and the tops remain pale. Sprinkle the *ma'amoul* with the remaining 1 tablespoon confectioners' sugar before serving.

Yield: 30 pastries

Khu'shaf

APRICOTS, ALMONDS, AND PISTACHIOS IN SWEET SYRUP

The vibrant orange apricots, bright green pistachio nuts, and stark white almonds create a colorful, elegant dish. The greener the nut, the better the flavor. The fragrance of the floral water adds a lush, romantic touch. *Khu'shaf* is often served at happy occasions; it is presented in a deep crystal bowl and spooned into shallow dessert bowls so that guests can fully enjoy the contrast of the syrup, fruit, and nuts. This dish can be stored in a covered glass jar in the refrigerator for several weeks.

2 cups sugar

1 pound dried apricots

1 cup pistachios, shelled, blanched, and peeled (see page 310)

1 cup almonds, blanched and peeled (see page 310)

½ teaspoon rose water or orange blossom water

1. Mix the sugar and apricots with 1 cup water in a medium mixing bowl. Soak overnight.

2. Add the pistachio nuts, almonds, and rose water to the bowl. Refrigerate until ready to serve.

Yield: 5 cups

Al Mazieh المارية

PUDDING WITH ROSE WATER
AND NUTS

This fabulous sweet is served at special occasions and *sebbits* (festive Sabbath luncheons, page 334). The neutral flavor of the cornstarch allows the taste of the pistachios and the fragrance of the floral waters to shine through. Traditionally served cold after it has jelled, *al mazieh* is also enjoyed piping hot.

1 cup cornstarch

2 cups sugar

1 cup pistachios, shelled, blanched,
   and peeled (page 310)

1 cup almonds, blanched and peeled
   (page 310)

½ teaspoon rose water
   or orange blossom water

1. In a large saucepan, combine the cornstarch, sugar, and 9 cups water until the cornstarch is completely dissolved.

2. Cook the dissolved cornstarch mixture over medium-high heat, stirring often with a wooden spoon. Bring to a boil. Reduce the heat to low and simmer for 1 hour, stirring occasionally until it obtains a puddinglike consistency.

3. Add the pistachios, almonds, and rose water to the saucepan. Stir until well blended.

4. Pour the pudding into a 2-quart nonstick mold or a large glass serving bowl. Let the pudding cool thoroughly. Refrigerate, uncovered, for at least 2 hours. Remove from the mold and serve. To unmold, press sides gently to loosen the pudding from the mold. Place a platter on top of the mold and turn over.

Yield: 6 to 8 servings

Heta'li'eh

COLD PUDDING

A combination of a drink and dessert, this is a refreshing treat prepared for warm summer afternoons.

Pudding:

1 cup cornstarch dissolved
    in 2 cups water

1 cup sugar

Syrup:

3 cups sugar

4 teaspoons rose water
    or orange blossom water

1 cup pistachios, shelled, blanched, peeled,
    and chopped (see page 310)

1 cup almonds, shelled, blanched, peeled,
    and chopped (see page 310)

1. To make the pudding, bring 7 cups water to a boil in a medium saucepan. Reduce the heat to medium, add the dissolved cornstarch and sugar, and cook for about 1 hour, stirring occasionally until it reaches a puddinglike consistency.

2. Let stand until cool. Pour the cornstarch mixture into a 13 x 9-inch baking pan. Pour ½ cup water into the pan. Do not stir. Let stand until cool. Refrigerate for 3 hours.

3. To make the syrup, combine the sugar, rose water, pistachios, almonds, and 4½ cups water in a medium mixing bowl. Refrigerate.

4. To serve, remove the pudding and syrup from the refrigerator. Cut the pudding into 1-inch squares. Pour the syrup over the pudding squares and refrigerate again. Serve chilled.

Yield: 6 to 8 servings

Sutlaj

MILK PUDDING WITH ROSE WATER
AND ORANGE BLOSSOM SYRUP

This pudding is also known as *muhallabeya,* a dessert enjoyed in Syria and other parts of the Arab world. Although the name *sutlaj* originated in Turkey and the Balkans, the Aleppian community adopted this version of the recipe. This dish is traditionally served on Shavuot, the Jewish festival that honors the giving of the Torah at Mount Sinai. *Sutlaj* is usually preferred hot, but it can also be eaten at room temperature or cold.

4 cups whole milk

½ cup cornstarch

3 tablespoons sugar

½ teaspoon rose water
  or orange blossom water

Combine the milk, cornstarch, and sugar in a large saucepan. Using a wooden spoon, stir until the cornstarch has fully dissolved. Over medium-high heat, bring to a boil, then reduce the heat to low and simmer, stirring constantly, for 10 minutes. Stir in the rose water. Pour the mixture immediately into a serving bowl.

Yield: 6 to 8 servings

Mamounieh

SEMOLINA PUDDING
WITH BUTTER

Aleppian Jewish women have a custom of eating *mamounieh* right after giving birth in order to gird their nursing newborns with strength. A common dessert at luncheons and special occasions, *mamounieh* may also be eaten for breakfast because of the nutritional value of the semolina. It's quick and easy to prepare.

1 cup sugar

¼ cup (½ stick) unsalted butter

1 cup semolina (*smead*)

½ teaspoon ground cinnamon

1 tablespoon pistachios, shelled, blanched, peeled, and chopped (see page 310)

1. In a medium saucepan, combine 1 cup water with the sugar. Bring to a boil, then reduce the heat to low, and simmer for 10 minutes, or until the mixture slides slowly down the back of a spoon.

2. Melt 2 tablespoons of the butter in a small saucepan over low heat. Make sure it does not brown. Add the semolina and cook for 3 minutes, stirring constantly. Do not let the semolina brown.

3. Add the cooked semolina to the hot syrup. Bring the mixture to a boil, add the remaining 2 tablespoons butter, and stir well. Remove from the heat.

4. Pour the mixture into a bowl and let stand for 5 minutes. Sprinkle with the cinnamon and pistachios. The pudding can be served warm or at room temperature.

Yield: 6 to 8 servings

Sliha

SWEETENED WHOLE WHEAT GRAINS WITH MIXED NUTS

When a baby begins to teethe, at about three to nine months, Aleppian Jewish moms and grandmoms rush out to procure the ingredients for *sliha*. This dessert is served to celebrate a child's first tooth, an event that Aleppian Jews treat as an omen of good health and normal development. This is a relatively healthful snack with whole-grain wheat and a variety of nuts.

1 cup sugar

1 teaspoon ground cinnamon

1 cup coarsly chopped walnuts

1 cup pistachios, shelled, blanched, and peeled (page 310)

1 cup pine nuts

1 cup husked whole wheat kernels, picked over and rinsed

2 tablespoons anise seeds

1 teaspoon rose water

3 tablespoons grated fresh coconut meat

3 tablespoons pomegranate seeds, (½ pomegranate; optional)

1. Combine the sugar, cinnamon, walnuts, pistachios, and pine nuts in a large mixing bowl. Set aside.

2. Boil the whole wheat kernels and anise seeds in 2 quarts water in a medium saucepan over medium-high heat. Reduce the heat to low and simmer for 1 hour, or until the kernels begin to open. Remove from the heat and drain.

3. Add the wheat–anise seed mixture to the cinnamon-nut mixture and mix thoroughly. Stir in the rose water and mix well. Top with the coconut and pomegranate seeds, if desired, before serving. This dish will keep, refrigerated, for 1 week.

Yield: 8 to 10 servings

Riz ib Haleb

ALEPPIAN RICE PUDDING

This pudding was prepared almost every day in old-time Aleppian Jewish homes. Enjoyed either hot or cold, it is a nutritious breakfast and a welcome accompaniment to daily meals. It is also a great snack to have around for the children. In the old days, Aleppians added ¼ teaspoon mastic at the end of the preparation along with ½ teaspoon of rose water. Mastic is pulverized tree resin native to the Mediterranean region and is available in Middle Eastern groceries. Mastic enhances the flavor of the pudding, but be careful not to use too much because it can impart an unpleasant taste.

1 cup long-grain white rice

2 quarts whole milk

¾ cup sugar

1 tablespoon vanilla extract

1 teaspoon rose water

¼ teaspoon ground cinnamon, ground cardamom, or freshly grated nutmeg (optional)

1. Combine the rice and 2 cups water in a large saucepan and bring to a boil over medium-high heat. Reduce the heat to low and simmer for 30 minutes, or until the rice is fluffy.

2. Add the milk, sugar, vanilla extract, and rose water to the pot. Raise the heat to medium-low and cook, stirring often, for about 1½ hours, or until the mixture thickens. Pour the rice pudding into a serving dish. Sprinkle with the spice, if desired. The pudding may be eaten warm or chilled.

Yield: 6 to 8 servings

Ríz b'Asal

HONEY-RICE PUDDING

Ages ago, Aleppian Jewish cooks devised this recipe, prepared with honey instead of milk, so their families could enjoy rice pudding after meat suppers while observing the Jewish prohibition of eating dairy after meat. This lip-smackingly sweet version turned out just as smooth and silky as the milk-based pudding.

½ cup white long-grain rice

¼ cup honey

⅛ teaspoon kosher salt

Bring 4 cups water to a boil in a medium saucepan. Add the rice, salt, and honey. Return the mixture to a boil, reduce the heat to very low, and simmer for 45 minutes, stirring occasionally. Pour into a bowl or individual serving dishes. Refrigerate until the pudding is set, and serve chilled.

Yield: 4 to 6 servings

Helou Mishmosh

CANDIED APRICOTS WITH PISTACHIOS

The best apricots for this apricot sweet are from California. They are five times the price of Turkish apricots, but worth it for their concentrated notes of sweet and sour flavors. The bright green of the pistachios contrasts with the vibrant orange of the apricots, making for quite a beautiful presentation. This is one of the essential sweets every Aleppian household has on hand.

½ pound pistachios, shelled, blanched, and peeled (see page 310)

3 pounds dried apricots

1 cup cold *shira* (Fragrant Aleppian Dessert Syrup, page 249)

1. Using a steamer basket suspended over a pot of boiling water, steam the apricots in batches for 4 to 5 minutes, tossing occasionally to ensure that they are evenly softened.

2. While the apricots are hot, process a few of them at a time in a food processor, pulsing several times, or until they are smooth. Repeat with the remaining apricots.

3. Combine the cold *shira* and the apricot paste in a medium saucepan. Toss in the pistachios. Bring to a boil over medium-high heat. Reduce the heat to low and simmer for about 15 minutes, or until the mixture forms a paste.

4. Line the bottom of a 15½ x 10½-inch rimmed baking sheet with parchment paper. Pour the mixture into the tray. To dry the apricot paste, leave the tray out, uncovered or lightly covered with foil, for 1 week.

5. Slide a sharp knife along the edges of the tray. Turn out the paste onto a flat cutting surface and cut diagonally to make diamond shapes about 1¼ inches wide. These sweets last for 3 to 4 weeks in a candy dish covered with aluminum foil (plastic wrap will make them soggy).

Yield: 3 pounds

Helou Banjan حلو باذنجان

CANDIED EGGPLANT WITH CLOVES

Besides your own garden, farmers' markets are practically the only source for the tiny eggplants required for this sweet. The *shira* used in this recipe does not contain floral water because the cloves are the main flavoring component. This sweet is often stuffed with pistachios or walnuts. In order to preserve the eggplants for years, the sugar syrup has to be very thick and heavy. It is not uncommon for Aleppian Jewish cooks to hold on to their *helou banjan* for several years, waiting for just the right occasion. Amazingly, a woman could serve a tray of *helou banjan* at her daughter's engagement party and present some *helou banjan* from the very same batch at the engagement party of her granddaughter many years later. To ensure maximum preservation, store the sweets in a cool dry place or in the refrigerator.

20 miniature Japanese eggplants (at most, 3 inches long), stems and caps trimmed	2 cups cold *shira* (Fragrant Aleppian Dessert Syrup, page 249), made without rose water or orange blossom water	1 tablespoon whole cloves

1. With a fork, prick each eggplant in two places.

2. Boil 3 cups of water in a large saucepan. Add the eggplants and boil for 3 minutes. Remove the eggplants and rinse them under cold water. Let stand to cool.

3. Nestle a colander or strainer in a medium mixing bowl. Place the eggplants in the colander and pour 1 cup of the *shira* over them. Let the eggplants stand for 10 minutes in order for the *shira* to fully saturate them. The excess *shira* is discarded.

4. Combine the remaining 1 cup *shira*, eggplants, and cloves in a medium saucepan over medium-high heat. Bring to a boil, reduce the heat to low, and simmer for approximately 40 minutes, or until the *shira* is thick.

5. Remove the eggplants from the heat. Let stand and cool. The *shira* should be a syruplike consistency. If it is thin, reheat the eggplants and *shira* for about 10 more minutes, and let cool again. Take care not to overcook the eggplants or they will become hard and inedible. When cooled, pour the eggplants and syrup into a glass jar. When ready to serve, cut the eggplants crosswise into ½-inch slices.

Yield: 1 pint whole eggplants

Helou Hindi

CANDIED COCONUT WITH PISTACHIOS

The name for this sweet, *hindi*, derives from the Arabic word for India, which was the source for the coconuts that were available in Aleppo. *Helou hindi* was and still is the traditional sweet of choice for Passover. It emerged as a replacement for chocolate, which could not be eaten because the ingredient lecithin is not kosher for Passover. *Helou hindi* highlights the enormous gap in flavor between store-bought grated coconut and freshly grated coconut meat. It is a little more work to crack open a fresh coconut, but it is well worth it. (To crack one open, pierce the eyes with an ice pick and drain out the water. Break open the coconut with a hammer and pry the meat from the coconut shell with a dinner knife. Then peel off the thin, brown skin with a sharp knife.) The snowy white meat sprinkled with bright green pistachios is lovely, and the fragrance of the floral water is nearly intoxicating.

2 pounds fresh coconut meat, shredded (about 2 to 3 coconuts), or store-bought unsweetened coarsely shredded coconut (see Note)

3 cups sugar

1 tablespoon freshly squeezed lemon juice

1 teaspoon orange blossom water

1 cup pistachios, shelled, blanched, and peeled (see page 310)

In a medium saucepan, combine the coconut meat, sugar, lemon juice, 1 cup water, and the orange blossom water and bring to a boil over medium-high heat. Reduce the heat to low and simmer for 8 to 10 minutes, stirring the mixture occasionally with a wooden spoon. While the coconut mixture is still hot, stir in the pistachios. Mix well, and cool before serving.

❧ Note ❧

If you use store-bought unsweetened shredded coconut, place it in a mixing bowl and add cold water. Gently fluff the coconut with your hands and let stand for 1 hour to plump and moisten the flakes. Drain before using.

Yield: 40 servings (2 quarts)

Helou S'farjal حلو سفرجل

CANDIED QUINCE

This is a traditional Turkish dish, served during the holiday of Rosh Hashanah. Quinces are often mistakenly tasted raw and therefore disliked. In fact, quince should only be eaten cooked because cooking removes the bitter taste and extracts the sweet and aromatic flavor from the fruit. Once cooked, quince has a wonderfully sharp taste that infuses everything around it. Marmalades, for example, were once made exclusively with quince, and the word "marmalade" actually comes from the Portuguese *inannelo* or *marmelo,* meaning "quince." When shopping for quince, examine the skin; the down of a ripe quince can be easily rubbed off by hand.

Helou are traditionally served in two dishes on a special tray, along with a small bowl of water, small forks, and cups for drinking water. After eating a piece of *helou* with a fork, place the utensil in the water to prevent it from getting too sticky. Traditionally, the set was used for special occasions, including the arrival of a prospective suitor to the home of a young woman's family. During the latter occasion, the young woman would hold the tray as her suitor and the girl's father would partake of the sweets. Coffee would be served later.

3 to 4 quinces, cored, peeled, and cut in 1-inch-thick slices (about 3 cups)

3 cups sugar

1. In a medium saucepan, cover the quinces with the sugar and cook over medium-low heat. The sugar will melt and liquefy, and the quinces will start to turn a beautiful dark and rosy color.

2. When the mixture bubbles, reduce the heat to low and simmer, stirring occasionally, for 1 hour, or until the quinces are thoroughly coated with a thick, gooey syrup. Transfer the quince and syrup to a jar, and store in the refrigerator for up to 2 months.

❧ *Note* ☙

You can use the pits of the quince in the cooking process to achieve a deeper color, but discard them before serving.

Yield: 2 ½ cups

Helou Griffon

CANDIED GRAPEFRUIT PEEL

The sign of a successful *helou griffon* is the elimination of any trace of bitterness. The trick to achieving this result is to repeatedly soak the peels, squeezing the water out of them between each soak. At the market, be sure to pick thick-skinned grapefruits. These sweets require a lot of work and are highly prized as gifts.

Peels of 4 grapefruits,
  sliced into 1-inch strips

1 cup *shira* (Fragrant Aleppian
  Dessert Syrup, page 249)

1. To extract the bitterness from the grapefruit peels, put them in a large saucepan with water to cover, and bring to a boil over medium-high heat. Reduce the heat to low and simmer for 1 hour, or until the skins can be easily pierced with a fork.

2. Using a slotted spoon, transfer the skins to a bowl of water. Change the water as often as 10 times during the day, or once every hour. Before each change of water, wring out the skins thoroughly. After the last soak, allow the skins to drain for 3 to 4 hours or overnight, until very dry.

3. Roll the peels against a work surface, white pith side up, until they form spirals. Tie every six or seven spirals together with a piece of thread to prevent them from unraveling.

4. Bring the *shira* to a boil in a medium saucepan over medium-high heat. Add the grapefruit skins, return to a boil, and then immediately reduce the heat to low. Simmer gently for about 1 hour, or until the peels are fork-tender.

5. Remove the grapefruit peels from the heat and let them cool to room temperature in the syrup. Remove threads. Transfer the grapefruit peels and syrup to a glass jar and refrigerate for up to 6 months. Turn the jar upside down periodically to make sure that the peels are always coated with the sugar syrup.

❧ *Note* ❧

A nice touch is to add a slice or two of tangerine rind to the *shira* in step 4.

Yield: 3 ½ cups

Helou Burtuqal

CANDIED ORANGE PEEL

Bitter Seville oranges are preferable for this recipe because of their thick skins. The bitter orange has been part of Mediterranean and Middle Eastern cuisine for centuries. Most traditional dishes using oranges are therefore based on this type of orange rather than the sweeter navel variety, which was introduced later from China. The navel orange and many of its variants are the common oranges available in American markets. Feel free to substitute them in this recipe—they won't diminish the splendor of these wonderful sweets.

Peels of 6 oranges,
  cut into 1-inch slices

4 cups sugar

Juice of 1 lemon
  (about 3 tablespoons)

½ teaspoon orange blossom water

1. Roll the peels, white pith side up, against a work surface until they form spirals. Tie every six or seven spirals together with a piece of thread to prevent them from unraveling. Place the peels in a bowl and cover them with water. Let stand for 2 days, changing the water twice daily.

2. Drain and transfer the strips to a large saucepan with enough water to cover them. Bring to a boil over medium-high heat. Reduce the heat to low, and simmer for 15 minutes. Drain without removing the peels from the saucepan.

3. Add the sugar, lemon juice, orange blossom water, and 2 cups water to the peels, and bring to a boil over medium-high heat. Reduce the heat to low, and simmer for 2 hours, or until the skins are well coated in thick syrup. Remove threads. Transfer the peels and syrup to a jar. Store in the refrigerator for up to 1 year.

Yield: 1 quart candied orange peels

Helou Kusa Sha'riyya

CANDIED SPAGHETTI SQUASH

This dish is served on Rosh Hashanah as an alternative to trumpet gourd, one of the traditional symbolic foods of the New Year. Spaghetti squash is a small, watermelon-shaped squash, ranging from two to five pounds. Its flesh is golden yellow and has a mildly sweet, nutty flavor. When cooked, the flesh separates in strands that resemble spaghetti. The depth of a spaghetti squash's yellow color is an indication of its ripeness; the nearly white ones are not very ripe and should be passed over. *Helou kusa sha'riyya* is a durable "keeper" that will last months if stored in a cool place.

1 large spaghetti squash
(3 to 4 pounds)

1 cup *shira* (Fragrant Aleppian
Dessert Syrup, page 249)

1. Preheat the oven to 350°F.

2. To prepare the squash, cut it in half lengthwise and remove the seeds, reserving them for another use (for example, roast them for *bizr,* Roasted Seeds, page 311). Place the squash halves on a baking sheet and roast for 30 minutes, or until the flesh is tender.

3. Scoop out the flesh from the squash halves and transfer it to a medium mixing bowl.

4. Add the *shira* to the squash and mix until well blended. Transfer the squash and syrup to a jar, and let stand at room temperature until cool. Serve in small bowls. This sweet can be refrigerated for up to a year.

Yield: 8 to 10 servings (1 quart)

Helou Kerrateh حلو كرات

CANDIED TRUMPET GOURD

This sweet often makes an appearance on the Rosh Hashanah table. The word *kerrateh* resembles the Hebrew word *karet,* meaning "to banish," which is used in a blessing that asks G-d to banish our enemies in the coming New Year. A little *miskeh,* or mastic, lends an exotic taste to this dish. Mastic is a resin collected from the *Pistacia lentiscus* tree, which is native to the Mediterranean region. There is an old Syrian saying that on Rosh Hashanah, the white is for good luck and the green is for fertility.

1 trumpet gourd (about 3 pounds), peeled and grated

1½ tablespoons freshly squeezed lemon juice (about ½ lemon)

4 cups hot *shira* (Fragrant Aleppian Dessert Syrup, page 249)

1 drop green food coloring (optional)

⅛ teaspoon mastic gum, available in Middle Eastern groceries (optional)

1. Place the gourd in a medium saucepan with the lemon juice and enough water to cover completely. Cook over medium-high heat for 15 minutes, or until tender.

2. Nestle a colander in a medium bowl. Put the gourd in the colander and press firmly to drain. Let stand so that the grated gourd drains thoroughly. The drier the gourd, the firmer the *helou.*

3. Return the gourd to the saucepan and add the *shira.* Bring to a boil over medium-high heat, then reduce the heat to low and simmer, stirring occasionally, for about 1 hour until it reaches a jamlike consistency.

4. Just before removing from the heat, stir in the food coloring and the mastic gum, if desired. Remove from the heat and let stand until cool. Transfer the gourd and syrup to a jar and store in the refrigerator for up to 1 year. When ready to serve, place in a small bowl with whole, peeled almonds and pistachios.

Yield: 10 to 12 servings (1 quart)

Helou Etrog

CITRON PRESERVES

Etrog is the Hebrew name for the wonderfully aromatic citron, a citrus fruit used exclusively in the *hoshana* ceremonies on the holiday of Sukkot (The Festival of Booths, page 342). After the close of Sukkot, Aleppian Jewish cooks collect leftover citrons, not a very palatable raw fruit, and make these preserves. *Helou etrog* is often given to pregnant Aleppian Jewish women because the *etrog* is considered to be a protective remedy (*segulah* in Hebrew) that will bring an easy birth and a healthy baby.

1 citron, seeded and cut lengthwise
into thin slices

1 orange, seeded and cut lengthwise
into thin slices

2 cups sugar

1. In a medium bowl, cover the citron and orange slices with water. Soak the fruit for 8 hours or overnight.

2. Drain the water and place the fruit in a medium saucepan. Cover with water and bring to a boil over medium-high heat. When it reaches a boil, drain the water.

Add the sugar, and cook over low heat for about 45 minutes, or until the sugar liquifies and the fruit begins to break down into a jamlike consistency. Let cool, transfer to a jar with the syrup, and store in the refrigerator for up to 1 year.

Yield: 1 cup

Membrillo ممبريللو

QUINCE PASTE

Membrillo is a type of candied quince. The addition of cloves to this recipe makes the flavor considerably strong and peppery.

3 to 4 pounds quince, cored, peeled, and cut into 1-inch slices

2 teaspoons lemon concentrate combined with 1 cup water for acidulated water

2 cups sugar

3 whole cloves

2 teaspoons freshly squeezed lemon juice

½ cup pistachios, shelled, blanched, peeled, and chopped (see page 310)

1. While preparing the quince slices, put them into the acidulated water so that they do not turn brown.

2. Combine the quince and 1 cup water in a large saucepan and cook, covered, over medium-high heat for 15 minutes. Add the sugar, cloves, and lemon juice, and cook for 45 minutes more, or until the syrup thickens. Stir in the pistachios while the mixture is still hot.

3. Pour the quince mixture onto a 15½ x 10½-inch rimmed baking sheet lined with parchment paper. Let it stand for 3 to 5 days, or until the mixture has congealed into a paste that is easily cut. Cut the paste into 1¼-inch squares with a sharp knife, dipping the knife occasionally into warm water to ensure clean, even lines.

Yield: About 3 pounds

Raha

TURKISH DELIGHT

This popular confection, dating back to the tenth century, is a specialty for which the sweetshops of Aleppo were renowned. *Raha,* known in English as Turkish Delight, is a pliable, gummy sweet made from sugar and mastic (today, some use cornstarch). Invented by Turkish confectioners during the Ottoman Empire, the sweet is known in Turkey as *lokum* or *raha lokum.* The sweetmakers of the Arab world became enamored of this recipe and quickly developed many flavors for it. Aleppian sweetmakers are renowned for their pistachio *raha.*

    Raha is quite difficult to master and is primarily made by professional confectioners. The ingredients are mixed over high heat in a three-foot-wide copper pot. The challenge is achieving a texture that is neither too runny nor too stiff.

4 cups sugar	1 teaspoon cream of tartar	1 cup pistachios, shelled and chopped
1 teaspoon lemon juice	1 tablespoon rose water	¾ cup confectioners' sugar
1¼ cups cornstarch		

1. Combine the sugar, 1½ cups water, and the lemon juice in a sturdy medium saucepan. Stir over low heat until sugar dissolves, making sure to brush sugar crystals off the side of the pan using a bristle brush dipped in cold water.

2. Bring mixture to a boil. Boil for 6 to 8 minutes to the soft-ball stage, which is 240°F on a candy thermometer (see Note). Remove from heat.

3. In another sturdy saucepan, blend 1 cup of the cornstarch, the cream of tartar, and 1 cup cold water until smooth. Add another 2 cups water. Increase heat to high and bring to a boil, stirring constantly until thick and bubbling. Whisk to remove lumps.

4. Pour the hot syrup (prepared in step 2) gradually into the mixture, stirring constantly. Bring to a boil and simmer for 1¼ hours, stirring occasionally with a wooden spoon. Cook until the mixture reaches a pale golden color.

5. Stir in the rose water. Add the pistachios, and remove from heat.

6. Pour the mixture into an oiled 9-inch-square cake pan. Allow to set, uncovered, for 12 hours at room temperature.

7. Combine confectioners' sugar and the remaining ¼ cup cornstarch in a flat dish.

8. Cut the *raha* into 1½-inch squares with an oiled knife and toss into the sugar mixture. Layer the *raha* in a sealed container with the remaining sugar mixture sprinkled between the layers.

❧ *Note* ❧

It's called the "soft-ball stage" because if you were to drop a bit of the syrup at this temperature into cold water, it would form a soft ball.

Yield: 2 pounds, or about 3 dozen pieces

Raha
(Turkish Delight, page 299)

Masapan
(*Marzipan, page 302*)

Masapan

MARZIPAN

Aleppian Jews serve marzipan at life-cycle events such as weddings or the celebration of a *brit milah* (ritual circumcision), and at holidays such as Passover and Purim. Though marzipan is similar to other sweetmeats that originated in the Levant, it is unclear whether it originated in the Middle East or in Europe. Toledo, Spain, was a medieval center of marzipan production, and one can speculate that the Arabs or the Jews, who were a major presence in Toledo, brought marzipan to Spain. The Jews definitely helped popularize marzipan in southern Europe and in the Middle East after their exodus from the Spanish kingdom. Regardless of where it originated, marzipan is now adored the world over. It is also one of the more popular sweets prepared in Aleppo, which has a reputation for hosting some of the Middle East's best confectioners.

The trick to great marzipan is grinding the almonds thoroughly—the finer, the better. To ensure a consistent powder when using a food processor, be sure to continually remove the cover and fold stray almond chunks into the bottom of the bowl. Grinding the nuts and sugar to a fine powder releases the nuts' oil, which binds the mixture, allowing it to achieve the texture of a soft, smooth paste.

2 cups almonds, blanched, peeled, and finely ground (see page 310)	1 cup sugar 1 teaspoon rose water	1 cup pistachios, shelled blanched, peeled, and finely chopped (see page 310)

1. Stir together the ground almonds, sugar, ¼ cup water, and rose water in a medium bowl. Transfer to a food processor and process until the mixture forms a paste.

2. Take 1 teaspoon of this almond paste and shape it into a walnut-size ball. Repeat. Press down on the center of each ball with your finger, making a ½-inch indentation. Fill the indentation with a pinch of pistachios. Close the pastry with your thumb and forefinger. Press the pastry into the middle of a fancy cookie mold, tap it out of the mold, and place on a baking sheet to dry.

Yield: 25 pieces

❧ Labas—Candy-Coated Almonds ❧

Labas can be made with raw or roasted almonds. The sugar coating comes in two varieties: dull and shiny. The dull-finish coating is of higher quality and preferable to the bright, shiny coating. For special occasions and holidays, beautiful silver platters are lavished with an array of *labas,* a selection of *helou* (candied fruit and vegetables), and high-quality chocolate. *Labas* are available in bright turquoise for a *brit milah* (ritual circumcision), pink for the birth of a girl, and silver for *swanees* (see page 362) and weddings. In the old days, many people got hitched at "*labas* weddings," which were far more modest than today's lavish catered receptions. The guests were happy to part with a package of *labas* as a good omen.

Halweh (Halvah)

SESAME SWEETMEAT

Halweh is a crumbly sweetmeat made from sesame paste. Many people eat it with hot Syrian flatbread and tea for breakfast, while others enjoy it before an evening meal or as a tasty morsel afterward. The closest thing in the Middle East to peanut butter, *halweh* is often packed into a pita pocket for kids to snack on. As a meal or as a little snack, *halweh* is a convenient, comfortable, and downright delectable option.

2 cups sugar

1 pound *tahini*
(see Note on page 26)

1 clove, ground in a spice grinder,
or pinch of ground cloves

⅛ teaspoon ground cinnamon

1 teaspoon freshly squeezed
lemon juice

1 teaspoon vanilla extract

1. Combine the sugar and ⅓ cup water in a medium saucepan. Bring to a boil, lower the heat, and simmer for about 20 minutes, or until the syrup slides slowly down the back of a spoon.

2. Place the *tahini* in a blender, and add the sugar syrup, clove, cinnamon, lemon juice, and vanilla extract. Blend until smooth. Transfer the mixture to a 13 x 9-inch baking pan or a 9-inch bundt pan and press flat. Let the mixture cool, then cut it into cubes. Store in a tightly sealed container for 1 week at room temperature. May be frozen up to 1 month.

Yield: 30 pieces

Simsemiyeh

SESAME CANDY

Simsemiyeh was originally made on a large baking sheet and broken into pieces, like a peanut brittle. Now it is sold commercially as small wrapped candies. The chewy, nutty treat lasts a long time and is a candy dish staple as well as a perennial favorite to hand out to kids during the festival of Simhat Torah (The Festival of the Torah, see page 342).

1 cup sugar	1 teaspoon ground cinnamon	1 teaspoon freshly squeezed lemon juice
½ cup sesame seeds	Pinch of ground cloves	

1. Combine the sugar and 1 cup water in a medium saucepan. Cook over medium heat for 10 minutes, or until the sugar is caramelized. Stir in the sesame seeds, cinnamon, cloves, and lemon juice, and cook for 3 minutes. Remove from the heat.

2. Pour the sesame mixture onto a wet, smooth work surface, or onto a greased baking sheet. Spread out to a thickness of 1 inch. Using a sharp knife, cut the mixture into diamond shapes or let it harden and then break into chunks. Store in a tightly sealed container for 2 weeks at room temperature. May be frozen up to 2 months.

Yield: 30 pieces

Amar e'Deen قمر الدين

APRICOT FRUIT PASTE

This Syrian specialty, a sticky sheet of candy made with a sweetened dried apricot puree, is the equivalent of a lollipop for Middle Eastern children. It is usually not made at home, but rather bought in a sweetshop and stored in the pantry. It keeps well for a very long period in a cool, dry place.

Most Aleppian Jews grew up on *amar e'deen.* It is still exported from Aleppo as a round sheet, 10 to 12 inches in diameter, wrapped in orange cellophane. *Amar e'deen* is available in both thick and thin versions.

4 cups dried apricots, peeled, pitted, and chopped	1 cup sugar

1. Line 2 large rimmed baking sheets with clear plastic wrap and secure the edges with tape.

2. Puree the apricots and sugar in a food processor until smooth.

3. Pour half the puree onto each baking sheet and spread to your desired thickness. Cover with a towel.

4. Set the baking sheets outside in full sunlight until the puree is dry enough to peel off easily. If it is not dry enough after the first day, keep the sheets in the sun until the mixture is dry. If the climate is just too humid for the sheets to dry, place them in a 150°F oven with the door left open. Be careful not to let the sheets get too dry, or they will crack.

5. Roll up each sheet of fruit paste, along with the plastic, and twist the ends to seal. Pieces can be any size. Wrap with an additional piece of plastic. The apricot paste can be stored in a cool, dry place at room temperature for up to 1 month. It can be kept in the refrigerator for 3 to 4 months or in the freezer for up to 1 year.

Yield: two 9 x 13-inch sheets

Helou Teen

CANDIED FIGS

Another popular delicacy enjoyed on Passover, *helou teen* is a simple yet wonderfully presentable dish consisting of poached, undressed figs.

1 pound dried figs, stems trimmed	1 tablespoon sugar	½ cup walnuts, quartered
1 cup orange juice	Grated zest of 1 lemon	½ cup sugar

1. Combine the figs, orange juice, sugar, and lemon zest in a small saucepan over medium heat. Bring to a boil, then reduce the heat to low and simmer, covered, for 10 minutes. Drain well, and let the figs cool.

2. Cut a slit in the stem end of each fig. Fill the slit with some of the walnuts, allowing one piece to protrude from the opening. Roll the figs in the sugar and serve.

Yield: 20 candied figs, 10 to 12 servings

Ajweh Helou

WALNUT-STUFFED DATES

Here is a quick and easy snack, commonly made on Passover from the dates left over from making *haroset halebieh* (Aleppian Date Preserves). The meaty crunch of a walnut is always a pleasant textural contrast to the softness of dates.

1 pound Medjool dates, pitted	¼ cup sugar
1 cup whole walnuts	

Fill the hollow of each date with a walnut. Finish the dates by rolling in the sugar. These are best eaten fresh.

Yield: 30 stuffed dates

Haroset Halebieh

ALEPPIAN DATE PRESERVES

These traditional date preserves, which are eaten during the Passover *seder,* are a luscious memory for many Aleppian Jews the world over. The natural honey sweetness of the dates, combined with the walnuts, cinnamon, and wine, make a rich and earthy delight. Although these preserves are meant to symbolize the cement with which the enslaved Jews did bone-crushing work for the Egyptian Pharoahs, rest assured that you will not break a sweat making this recipe.

3 pounds pitted dates

½ cup sweet red wine

1 teaspoon ground cinnamon (optional)

1 cup chopped walnuts (optional)

1. Put the dates in a medium saucepan with enough water to cover them. Bring to a boil, lower the heat, and simmer, stirring frequently, until the dates are soft.

2. Pass the date mixture through a strainer or rotary grater. A food processor may also be used, mixing in 3 to 4 batches for 30 seconds at a time. Refrigerate.

3. Before serving, add the wine, cinnamon, and walnuts, if desired, and mix thoroughly.

Yield: 20 servings

❧ Nuts and Aleppian Jewish Cuisine ❧

Fistou Halabi — Pistachios

Pistachios have been on the gastronomic landscape for so long that archeologists have discovered remnants of pistachios in the ruins of villages dating back thousands of years.

The pistachios harvested from the hinterlands of Aleppo are renowned as some of the tastiest in the world. The generic Arabic name for pistachios was originally *fistou halabi,* meaning "Aleppian pistachios." Unfortunately, these Aleppian pistachios aren't available for export. However, pistachios from Central Asia and the Middle East are almost as good. Pistachios from California lack flavor, but remain popular because of their saturated green hue.

The flesh of the pistachio ranges from a pale to dark green color; its skin is papery and purple tinged. Due to their subtle flavor, pistachios are favored in a wide variety of dishes, from pastries (both sweet and savory) to ice creams and nougat. In Aleppo, guests at engagement parties and other happy affairs were often given a small bag of pistachios and *labas* (Candy-Coated Almonds, page 303) as a parting gift.

The pistachio is botanically related to the cashew, peach, and mango. Pistachio trees—capable of reaching thirty feet in height—take ten to fifteen years before they begin producing significant quantities of nuts. Often they bear a large crop one year and a small one the next. The trees grow in areas that typically experience long, hot summers and cool winters, such as Iran, Turkey, Syria, Afghanistan, Greece, Italy, and California.

The thin, edible skin of the pistachio can easily be removed from the nut meat by blanching it. Cover shelled pistachios with boiling water and let them stand for 4 to 6 minutes, then peel off the skins (see photo, page 267).

Loz — Almonds

Cultivated commercially in Spain and Portugal, the almond is widely used in the Levant. It is an important ingredient in sweet pastries and is often added to savory dishes. Almonds are toasted and used as a topping for rice. The nuts are sold fresh or as *labas* (Candy-Coated Almonds, page 303) in the Mediterranean markets. Very young, handpicked raw, unshelled almonds can be eaten with a light sprinkling of salt over their green skins. Almonds should be bought with their skins on, rather than blanched, because the peel acts as a protective coating that keeps them fresh. When blanching almonds, do so right before using them. Cover the almonds with boiling water and let them stand for 4 to 6 minutes. Drain and cool the nuts a bit before slipping off their skins.

Joz — Walnuts

This very versatile nut is used in both sweet and savory dishes. Walnuts are chopped and added to pastries and *bazargan* (Tangy Tamarind Bulgur Salad, page 44). They are used in a variation of *baklawa* (Pistachio *Filla* Wedges in Rose Water Syrup, page 251). Walnuts are not appreciated as much as pistachios, which are much more expensive, so walnuts should not be substituted in pastries made for honored guests. However, they can be used in everyday dishes. Walnuts should be purchased early in the season, sealed in tightly closed containers, and stored in the freezer or in a cool place.

❧ Roasted Nuts and Seeds ❧

Loz M'hammas — Roasted Almonds

1 pound raw almonds, blanched and peeled (see page 310)

1. Preheat the oven to 325°F.

2. Pour the almonds into a baking pan. Roast, stirring often, for 15 to 20 minutes, until firm. (Alternatively, the almonds can be roasted in a dry skillet over medium-low heat for 5 minutes.) Let the nuts cool. Store in an airtight container in a cool place or the freezer.

Bindaweh — Roasted Filberts

The filbert is a cousin of the hazelnut. Filberts, hazelnuts, and cobnuts all belong to the family of Corylaceae.

1 pound raw filberts
Kosher salt

1. Preheat the oven to 325°F.

2. Pour the filberts into a baking pan. Roast, stirring often, for 15 to 20 minutes until firm and lightly golden with a toasty smell. (Alternatively, filberts can be roasted in a dry skillet over medium-low heat for 5 minutes.) Let the nuts cool. Store in an airtight container in a cool place or in the freezer.

Bizr — Roasted Seeds

Roasted seeds are cracked and eaten in one quick motion by the expert Aleppian Jewish snacker. A table festooned with empty shells is usually evidence of a well-attended party or *sebbit* (festive Sabbath luncheon, page 334). The seeds are also eaten with a selection of fresh fruit after Sabbath meals. Roasted seeds are derived from a variety of fruits and vegetables: roasted squash seeds are known as *bizr er'eh,* watermelon seeds are called *bizr jab'as,* and the rest are known simply as *bizr.*

1 pound unshelled sunflower, watermelon, pumpkin, or squash seeds
1 to 2 tablespoons kosher salt

1. Preheat the oven to 325°F.

2. Rinse the seeds with water, pour them into a baking pan, and sprinkle liberally with salt. Roast the seeds in the oven, stirring often, for 20 to 25 minutes, or 30 to 35 minutes for larger seeds, such as pumpkin and watermelon. (Alternatively, the seeds can be roasted in a dry skillet over medium heat for 5 minutes.) Let the seeds cool. Store the seeds in an airtight container in a cool place or in the freezer.

Shrab al Loz شراب اللوز

SWEET ALMOND MILK

This drink is always served at the Aleppian Jewish engagement party called the Meeting of the Family (see page 362). Traditionally served on silver trays, sweet almond milk is passed around to guests entering the home. Symbolic of fertility, the intoxicating fragrance of this drink is unmistakably romantic and a special treat. The almond paste can be stored in the refrigerator for up to 2 weeks or in the freezer for several months. This is convenient because it takes time to prepare and can be done in advance for special occasions.

2 cups almonds, blanched and peeled (see page 310)	3 cups sugar
	2 teaspoons rose water

1. To make the almond paste, grind the almonds in a food processor with 1 teaspoon of water to obtain a pasty consistency. Process for about 1 minute, or until the paste holds together when squeezed between your fingers.

2. Transfer the almond paste to a medium bowl and add the sugar and 1 cup water. Stir the rose water into the almond mixture. Separate the mixture into 3 to 4 batches. In a blender, blend each batch on a high-speed setting for 3 minutes, or until the mixture is smooth and creamy.

3. Pour the almond mixture into jars and refrigerate. When ready to serve, mix 2 parts water to 1 part prepared almond mixture. Serve chilled over crushed ice in tall glasses.

Yield: 4 to 6 servings

Sahlab

FLORAL DRINK

Sahlab is a starch found in the ground bulb of the orchid *Orchis mascula.* The starch acts as a thickening agent and imparts a unique flavor to the hot milk-based beverage of the same name. The drink was a very popular tonic in seventeenth-century England and was said to cure gastrointestinal ailments.

Some *sahlab* mixes include other thickening agents, such as cornstarch. Pure *sahlab,* which can be recognized by its bitter taste when sampled raw, is very expensive and difficult to find today, though it is still available in the Middle East. Consult a Middle Eastern grocer for high-quality *sahlab* from a reputable producer.

4 cups whole milk

2 tablespoons powdered *sahlab*

3 tablespoons sugar

1 teaspoon rose water
or orange blossom water

2 tablespoons pistachios, shelled, blanched, peeled, and finely chopped (see page 310)

¼ teaspoon ground cinnamon

1. Combine 1 cup of the milk and the *sahlab* in a medium mixing bowl.

2. Bring the remaining 3 cups milk to a boil in a medium saucepan over medium-high heat. Pour the *sahlab* mixture into the boiling milk. Reduce the heat to low and simmer, stirring vigorously to prevent lumps, for about 10 minutes, or until the mixture thickens. Stir in the sugar and the rose water. Pour the *sahlab* into cups and top with chopped pistachios and a sprinkle of cinnamon.

Yield: 4 to 6 servings

Ayran

YOGURT DRINK

Originating just over the Syrian border in Turkey, *ayran* is very popular in Aleppo. Similar to the Indian *lassi,* it is a refreshing summertime drink that helps one beat the Levant's dreadful, furnacelike heat. *Ayran* is widely available for purchase, though it is often prepared at home, too. A touch of fresh or dried mint adds a nice soothing dimension to this beverage.

1½ cups plain yogurt

1 cup ice cubes

½ teaspoon dried mint or rose water
(optional)

In a large pitcher, mix the yogurt with 4 cups water. Add the ice and stir to thoroughly cool the mixture. Add the dried mint or rose water, if desired. Pour into individual glasses.

Yield: 4 to 6 servings

Shrab al Temerhindi

TAMARIND DRINK

In the markets of old Aleppo, *shrab al temerhindi* was served from a leather pouch and sold by the glass. Before the age of sodas, only natural drinks were available, and this was one of the most popular. It was a refreshing thirst-quencher, like lemonade here in the United States.

6 tablespoons *ou^c* (tamarind concentrate, page 41), homemade or store-bought

¼ cup sugar

1½ cups ice cubes

Combine the *ou^c*, 4 cups water, the sugar, and ice cubes in a large pitcher. Stir well and serve in tall glasses.

Yield: 4 to 6 servings

'Ahweh
(Arabic Coffee, page 318)

'Ahweh

ARABIC COFFEE

In the culture of Aleppian Jews, sitting and enjoying a cup of coffee holds as much ritual significance as high tea in England. A steaming rich cup of coffee is the hallmark of the vaunted Aleppian hospitality. Coffee is brewed in a long-handled copper pot shaped like an urn. The handle helps keep one's hands far from the high heat required to brew the coffee. The pot is called a *bri'eh* in Arabic and a *raquieh* in Armenian.

Arabic coffee is prepared in three ways: *helou* or *sukkar ziada* is the sweetest, *mazbout* is medium-sweet, and *murra* is unsweetened. You may add cloves or cardamom for flavor. Turkish and Armenian coffee are brewed in a similar fashion.

1 heaping teaspoon Turkish coffee (should be already pulverized)	1 teaspoon sugar, or to taste	Whole cloves or cracked cardamom pods to taste (optional)

ჲ Reading the Grounds: An Old Superstition ჩ

After drinking coffee, many Aleppians like to turn the cup upside down over the saucer to drain any remaining coffee and then turn it right side up to examine the patterns formed by the grounds settled at the bottom of the cup. Based on the shape of the patterns, the fortune of the drinker will be read. For example, wide spaces predict a long trip. Smaller spaces indicate a short trip. Small bloblike deposits foretell trouble. Larger ones predict that the drinker will come into money.

1. Fill a Turkish coffee pot with ½ cup water per serving and bring to a fierce boil. Remove the pot from the heat and add the coffee, sugar, and cloves or cardamom, if desired. Mix well. Return the pot to the heat. Bring to a boil (be careful not to let it boil over), then remove from the heat.

2. To serve, pour the coffee into demitasse cups. Some foam will be left in the pot. Top each cup with a small amount of the foam. The coffee grounds will settle to the bottom of the cups. Therefore, you should avoid stirring the coffee.

✑ *Note* ✑

Rakweh, the long-handled pot used to brew *'ahweh*, can be found in various sizes from very small (1 to 2 cups) to very large (10 to 12 cups). They are made from copper (traditional), brass, enamel, or stainless steel.

Yield: 2 to 4 cups

Chai شاي

TEA

Tea is the most popular beverage in the Middle East. In addition to being served as a beverage, it is often prescribed for many upper respiratory illnesses or problems with digestion. Tea made from the flower of the chamomile is said to relieve an upset stomach and intestinal gas. Tea leaves placed on a mild burn can be soothing.

4 teaspoons loose black tea leaves	4 or 5 cloves, or 1 cinnamon stick (optional)	Sugar, honey, lemon, or orange slices for serving (optional)

Shanoud and Regine Tawil, 1923

Warm a teapot by rinsing it with a small amount of boiling water. Drain the water. Add the tea and cloves, if desired, to the pot. Pour 4 cups of boiling water over the tea leaves. Let them steep for 3 to 5 minutes. If desired, serve with sugar, honey, lemon, or orange slices.

Yield: 4 cups

Chai a'Shab

HERBAL INFUSIONS

Herbal infusions are believed to have beneficial properties for minor ailments such as infant colic, upset stomach, nervous tension, and sleeplessness. They are very popular in the afternoon—alone or with a sweet—when coffee is not desired. In Aleppo, one of the most common infusions was a pretty blend of dried herbs called *z'hoorat,* which consisted of *khatmiyah* (similar to hibiscus), *shoshat al-darrah* (corn silk), *qoss'ayn* (an herb similar to wild thyme), *baboonj* (chamomile), and *ward* (roses).

2 tablespoons dried chamomile flowers, or an herbal combination

3 teaspoons sugar

Pour 3 cups of boiling water in a teapot. Add the chamomile and the sugar. Steep the infusion for 3 to 5 minutes. Serve in small tea glasses.

Yield: 4 to 6 cups

Chai b'Nana

MINT TEA

It is customary to pour this mint infusion from very high over the glass (never a cup) to create large bubbles. The glass is never filled completely. In old Aleppo, a shopkeeper would offer a customer a glass of tea, accompanied by the warm greeting *"ahlan!"*

In the summer, many Aleppian households have herb gardens with fresh mint, which is wonderful to have on hand to prepare the tea. When it is not in season, use dried mint.

1 tablespoon black tea	3 teaspoons sugar	4 sprigs fresh mint, or 1 tablespoon dried mint

Combine the tea, sugar, and mint in a teapot. Add 3 cups boiling water and steep for 5 minutes. Allow the leaves to settle, and serve in small tea glasses.

Yield: 4 to 6 cups

'Ahweh Beida

WHITE COFFEE

This hot drink made of boiled floral water was enjoyed by Aleppians at night as a noncaffeinated alternative to coffee. "White coffee" refers to any spice, herb, or aromatic (such as fenugreek) infused in hot water.

1 or 2 drops rose water
  or orange blossom water

Sugar to taste (optional)

Pour boiling water into a small coffee cup. Add a few drops of your floral water of choice. Sweeten with sugar, if you desire.

Yield: 1 cup

Vikki Levy holding a sanayiat Eliyahu NaNabi (ritual tray used to collect charity at circumcision ceremony), 1980 (courtesy of Sephardic Community Center Archives)

A SYRIAN GUIDEBOOK
TO
HOLIDAYS
AND
LIFE-CYCLE
EVENTS

The Sabbath table

Shabbat

שבת

THE SABBATH

Late Friday afternoon in a Jewish neighborhood reflects the storm before the calm of Shabbat, the Jewish day of rest: women double-parked on the avenue doing last-minute shopping, their children at home helping with the Shabbat preparations, men rushing home from work to shower and shave before evening synagogue services.

The lighting of twin candles just before sundown divides the frenzied week from the tranquillity and holiness of Shabbat. Traditionally, Aleppian Jewish men participate in the Sabbath preparations by placing wax candles in candlesticks or cotton wicks in oil for their wives to light later on. The act of lighting candles to usher in the sacred days of the calendar is one of the three principal obligations (*mitzvot*) of a Jewish woman. This is an auspicious time for a woman to pray privately for her family's needs and bless her children. Many women set aside money for charity beforehand. By the stroke of the eighteenth minute before sunset, the woman of the house lights the candles, work is prohibited, and all is quiet in the Jewish home. The kitchen activity ceases, the men are off to synagogue, the din of everyday home life—blaring music, shrill telephones, wheezing computers, and clacking keyboards—is silenced.

In ages past, the mystics in the community had a custom of going out into the fields to greet Shabbat. As they went, they would say *"likrat Shabbat lechu v'nelcha"* ("To greet Shabbat, let us go toward it"). They believed that Shabbat must be sought and embraced in order to reach the source of the blessing (*mekor ha'bracha*).

Jewish law prohibits thirty-nine kinds of labor on Shabbat. Significantly, the kindling of any kind of fire (or electricity) is forbidden, which restricts cooking. The rabbis have also prohibited travel, buying and selling, and other weekday tasks such as writing and sewing that would interfere with the spirit of Shabbat. All hot food is prepared ahead of time, which explains the madness of a Friday afternoon in an Aleppian Jewish household. However, prepared food, except soups and other liquid-based dishes, can be warmed by indirect heat; this usually entails the use of an aluminum sheet between pots and the burners, which are turned on before the Sabbath and left on for the duration. Preparations for Friday night dinner can start as early as Wednesday for certain labor-intensive dishes, but by Friday morning virtually every Aleppian Jewish kitchen is working up a full head of steam—and a very fragrant steam at that.

Food has an interesting analogy to the Shabbat objective of rest. Shabbat is understood as *me'eyn olam ha'ba*, a small dose of the peaceful life in the next world. The phrase refers to the concept that just as sleep represents one-sixtieth of the state of death, and a dream one-sixtieth of prophecy, so too, Shabbat is one-sixtieth of the next world, in which toiling will no longer be necessary. The proportion of one-sixtieth actually comes from the Jewish dietary laws, which assert that certain food mixtures may be deemed kosher if no more than one-sixtieth of the whole is unkosher. The beautiful metaphor comparing Shabbat to the slightest taste of the next world has a deep and spiritual resonance.

Friday Night Dinner סעודת ערב שבת

By the time all the food has been warmed and the men have returned from synagogue, the calm of the Sabbath begins to yield to hearty appetites that have been neglected all day. The glow of candlelight reflected in gleaming glass and the appearance of fine china on a white tablecloth are elegant departures from the modest, informal weekday table settings. Families often gather in extended form, married children bringing their spouses and young ones to their parents' home.

The man of the house ushers in the meal by chanting the songs *Shalom Aleichem* ("Peace Be Unto You") and *Eshet Hayil* ("The Woman of Valor," Proverbs 31:10–31), which is an ode to the woman of the house that lauds her qualities, efforts, and sacrifices. The Sabbath is then sanctified by the *kiddush* (or *'adus* in Arabic), a blessing chanted by the host over wine that welcomes the holy day of rest. Nearby is the bread that is covered with an embroidered cloth. The coverage is required to respect the bread, which on weekdays is blessed first. Here, the bread defers to wine, which is necessary to sanctify the meal. A blessing is said over the wine, and the host drinks from the cup. He then passes the wine to his wife, who takes a sip and passes it along to the rest of the guests in order of seniority. As the wine is passed, the guests greet one another with the expression *"Shabbat Shalom."* Children are blessed after kissing a hand of their grandparents and parents.

Then everyone washes each hand three times with a special vessel (a container that holds three ounces and

Tossing the bread at the Sabbath dinner

has no cracks) and says a ritual blessing. Upon returning to the table, the host or his eldest son uncovers the twin loaves of bread, which represent the double portion of *manna*, the miracle subsistence food that G-d provided the Israelites every Friday during their forty-year trek through the wilderness of Paran after their exodus from Egypt. Traditionally, Aleppians had Syrian flatbread on the Sabbath table; some even allotted twelve loaves to commemorate the twelve loaves of shewbread (*lehem hapanim* in Hebrew) displayed at the Jewish Temple. However, many contemporary Aleppian Jews break bread with *challah*, having been seduced by the pillowy richness of this Ashkenazic creation.

The host recites a blessing over the bread, tears off a piece from a loaf, dips it in salt three times, and eats it straightaway. One should hold the bread with all ten fingers when reciting the blessing to symbolize the ten *mitzvot* related to the production of bread. The ten fingers also symbolize the ten categories of work (as defined with regard to Shabbat), from ploughing through to baking. For this reason also there are ten words in the blessing over bread, and ten words in the verse "Everyone's eyes [are turned in] hope to You, and You give them their food in its time" (Psalms 145:15). Aleppian Jews avoid cutting the bread with a knife because the table symbolizes the altar of the Jewish Temple, where steel was forbidden. Also, knives are considered tools of warfare that have no place on the sacred Shabbat table. The use of salt harks back to the procedures of the Jewish Temple, which required the priests to sprinkle salt over the sacrifices before offering them. The Aleppian Jewish custom is to toss a piece of bread first to his wife and then to each guest, in order of seniority, no matter how far across the table the guests are sitting. This ritual is meant to distinguish this portion of mealtime bread from the bread that is passed by hand to mourners (see page 366). Tossing is intended to ward off tragedy and the hand-passed bread that attends it. Some also say that tossing makes clear that the bread comes from the hand of G-d and not from the host.

The meal itself is a much-anticipated event, featuring several courses of the most regal selections from the Aleppian repertoire. A roasted whole chicken or cut of beef (or both) is standard, along with one or two *mehshi* dishes (stuffed vegetables), perhaps two or three vegetable dishes, and *kibbeh hamdah* (Lemon-Mint Broth with Mixed Vegetables and Syrian Meatballs, page 97) or *keftes* (Tamarind-Stewed Meatballs, page 162), all of which are served with a heaping platter of rice. The menu combinations are truly endless, guaranteeing that everyone will leave the table with a full belly.

Lighting the candles for the Sabbath

Eshet Hayil

❧ The Woman of Valor ❧

A woman of valor who can find?
For her price is far above rubies.

אשת-חיל מי ימצא
ורחוק מפנינים מכרה

The heart of her husband safely trusts in her,
And he has no lack of gain.

בטח בה לב בעלה
ושלל לא יחסר

She does him good
And not evil all the days of her life.

גמלתהו טוב
ולא-רע כל ימי חייה

She seeks wool and flax,
And works willingly with her hands.

דרשה צמר ופשתים
ותעש בחפץ כפיה

She is like the merchant-ships;
She brings her food from afar.

היתה כאניות סוחר
ממרחק תביא לחמה

She rises also while it is yet night,
And gives food to her household,
and a portion to her maidens.

ותקם בעוד לילה
ותתן טרף לביתה
וחק לנערותיה

She considers a field, and buys it;
With the fruit of her hands she plants a vineyard.

זממה שדה ותקחהו
מפרי כפיה נטעה כרם

She girds her loins with strength,
And makes strong her arms.

חגרה בעז מתניה
ותאמץ זרועותיה

She perceives that her merchandise is good;
Her lamp goes not out by night.

טעמה כי טוב סחרה
לא-יכבה בלילה נרה

She lays her hands to the distaff,
And her hands hold the spindle.

ידיה שלחה בכישור
וכפיה תמכו פלך

She stretches out her hand to the poor;
Yea, she reaches forth her hands to the needy.

כפה פשרה לעני
וידה שלחה לאביון

She is not afraid of the snow for her household;	לא תירא-לביתה משלג
For all her household are clothed with scarlet.	כי כל-ביתה לבש שני
She makes for herself coverlets;	מרבדים עשתה-לה
Her clothing is fine linen and purple.	שש וארגמן לבושה
Her husband is known in the gates,	נדע בשערים בעלה
When he sits among the elders of the land.	בשבתו עם-זקני-ארץ
She makes linen garments and sells them;	סדין עשתה ותמכור
And delivers girdles unto the merchant.	וחגור נתנה לכנעני
Strength and dignity are her clothing;	עוז-והדר לבושה
And she laughs at the time to come.	ותשחק ליום אחרן
She opens her mouth with wisdom;	פיה פתחה בחכמה
And the law of kindness is on her tongue.	ותורת-חסד על-לשונה
She looks well to the ways of her household,	צופיה הליכות ביתה
And eats not the bread of idleness.	ולחם עצלות לא תאכל
Her children rise up, and call her blessed;	קמו בניה ויאשרוה
Her husband also praises her:	בעלה ויהללה
"Many daughters have done valiantly,	רבות בנות עשו חיל
but you exceed them all."	ואת עלית על-כלנה
Grace is deceitful, and beauty is vain;	שקר החן והבל היפי
But a woman that fears G-d, she shall be praised.	אשה יראת ה' היא תתהלל
Give her of the fruit of her hands;	תנו לה מפרי ידיה
And let her works praise her in the gates.	ויהללוה בשערים מעשיה.

❧ *Imbid* — Syrian Red Wine ❧

When Jews lived in Aleppo, there was no commercial sacramental wine available. This was mostly because of the Muslim prohibition against alcohol and the strict Jewish laws governing kosher wine production. To solve this problem, Aleppian Jews would purchase red grapes and make their own homemade cellar wine.

While the end result didn't put the great châteaux of Bordeaux out of business, Aleppian wine adequately served the lofty purpose of fulfilling the obligation to sanctify the Sabbath properly. Old-timers who grew up in Aleppo have jokingly observed that Aleppian wine was so high in alcohol content that when the time came for the Passover *seder,* which requires each participant to drink four cups of the wine, the men would be hard-pressed to finish the *seder* meal sober.

Wine has a revered place in Judaism because it is a symbol of the sacrificial lamb brought to the Jewish Temple in service of G-d. Given the exacting devotion of Aleppian Jews to Jewish law, it isn't surprising to hear of the great pains undertaken by Aleppian men to make their own wine so they could have a supply on hand to meet the important obligation of sanctifying the Sabbath.

After the meal, a family member may give a short discourse on the weekly Torah portion, then the family says *birkat ha'mazon*, the postprandial blessing, to thank G-d for His bounty. Then the family usually lingers around the table and chats over fruit and nuts. Cuts of fresh melon are a perennial favorite, along with *bizr* (roasted pumpkin and sunflower seeds, page 311). Some households serve cakes, but few guests have room for such heavy, flour-laden desserts. This is when the holy day of rest begins to work its spell over the sleep-deprived and overworked, who are known to doze off on a sofa amid the lulling buzz of conversation. Once fatigue sets in among the guests (or their toddlers), this usually signals the end of the visit as family members bid one another farewell and retire for the night.

The next morning is fairly relaxed for the woman of the house as the men and children head off to the synagogue (*k'nees* in Arabic) for prayer services (though many women attend as well). In synagogue the *hazzan* (cantor) leads the prayer service, the *ba'al koreh* (Torah reader) chants the weekly Torah portion in the melodic Aleppian tune, and the rabbi of the congregation usually offers a speech.

At some synagogues, after the services, congregants gather around a modest table of cakes and snacks as the rabbi says *kiddush* (the Sabbath pre-meal blessing). If a congregant is celebrating a life-cycle event that week, he will likely cater a large Shabbat lunch in the synagogue or at his home. On most Saturdays, men and children return home for a Shabbat lunch. A typical Shabbat lunch in an Aleppian Jewish home consists of a few *maza* dishes and a single hot dish that has been kept warm from Friday afternoon (technically classified as a *hameen*). Eating an additional hot dish that was not served at the previous night's dinner is an important ancient practice of the Aleppian community derived from oral Jewish lore. They do this to distinguish themselves from the Sadducees, a Jewish sect dating from the first century BCE who only ate cold dishes on the Sabbath because they limited their religious doctrine to the written law.

After the *sebbit* (festive Shabbat lunch, page 334) or the regular Shabbat lunch, there are usually a few hours left in the afternoon. Some nap, some take an afternoon stroll to visit friends and family, while others take up religious study or seek out a lecture given by one of many rabbis. These are the blissful hours that reveal Shabbat for what it is—a holy day of rest and spiritual rejuvenation, a welcome departure from the nonstop buzzing pace of the big cities where most Aleppian Jews live.

When the sun begins its descent into darkness, services beckon. There are two prayer services: In the afternoon prayer (*mincha*), the *hazzan* leads the prayers and the *ba'al koreh* chants an excerpt of the following week's Torah portion. After this service, the congregation breaks for the final meal of the Shabbat, called *seuda shelishit* (Hebrew for "the third meal"). There is usually an array of modest salads and Syrian flatbread to choose from, along with a selection of cakes. It is a positive deed to eat bread and wheat-derived foods because they call for the praiseworthy pre- and postconsumption blessings. Near the end of this minor meal, the rabbi of the congregation customarily gives a weekly lecture on any of a variety of topics; it can relate to the weekly Torah portion, involve a lesson in ethics, or provide a discourse on the laws of the Shabbat or an upcoming holiday. Following the *seuda,* the congregation convenes for *arbit,* the evening prayer.

After the evening prayers and upon the sighting of three stars in the sky (or, in North America, about 50 minutes after sundown, if it's cloudy), the *havdala* ceremony takes place. It marks the close of Shabbat and is a counterpoint to the Friday evening candle lighting

that marked the beginning. In this ceremony, the *hazzan* or the rabbi lights a braided candle with multiple wicks. He recites a blessing over wine, after which the congregants customarily smile at one another or emit a small chuckle as an omen for a good week to come. The rabbi then makes a blessing over a fragrance known as *besamim,* which for Aleppian Jews is usually *Ma Wared* (rose water), *Mazaher* (orange blossom water), or a bundle of herbs. It is said that the fragrance of *besamim* helps some of the sanctity of the Shabbat to remain through the coming week. A young child sprinkles the rose water from an ornate, bulbous, Turkish-inspired silver dispenser into the hands of the congregants. They bring their hands to their noses, inhale deeply, and collectively sigh with pleasure induced by the floral scent, which is meant to awaken the soul. The rabbi

Rose water dispenser for havdala *blessing*

then says a blessing over the flame as the congregants bend the fingers of their right hand over their thumb and hold them up to the light in front of them, which symbolizes the light created by Adam following the first day of rest. The rabbi closes the *havdala* with a blessing that officially separates Shabbat from the week, then drinks most of the wine and extinguishes the candle with the remaining wine. Traditionally, congregants dab drops of the wine on their eyes, foreheads, the backs of their necks, or in their pockets as a good omen. Then they return home to recite the *havdala* service for their wives and families.

Following the evening prayers, families have another meal that includes bread. This is called *seuda revi'it* ("the fourth meal") and is designed to escort the queenly spirit of Shabbat back to the heavens. It is said that the food eaten at this final meal nourishes the *luz*, which is the upper cervical vertebra that remains after a body fully decomposes. It is believed that, upon the coming of the Messiah, souls will reinhabit the bodies of the deceased, which will come to life, springing from the *luz*.

The *Sebbit*

While the typical Shabbat lunch consists of a few *maza* dishes and a selection of one or two hot dishes, the *sebbit* features a far more comprehensive menu, not to mention a jubilant and festive ambience. Part of the reason for this array of food is to help the body meet the high level of exultation that the soul experiences on this special Shabbat. *Sebbits* usually mark a happy life-cycle event such as the birth of a child, a bar mitzvah, or an impending wedding; some synagogues sponsor an annual or semiannual *sebbit* for the congregation itself.

Men and women are seated separately at *sebbits*. The men usually arrive en masse from synagogue. Each finds his place amid a cramped seating arrangement in a living room converted into a dining hall with long tables that seat at least fifty and usually over one hundred. The guests begin to eat and drink after the rabbi or host says *kiddush*. A wide selection of *maza* is usually available—*hummus* (Chickpea-Sesame Spread, page 27), *tehineh* (Sesame Spread, page 26), *bazargan* (Tangy Tamarind Bulgur Salad, page 44), *mehalallat* (Assorted Vegetables Pickled in Brine, page 68), *laham b'ajeen* (Miniature Tamarind Minced Meat Pies, page 50), *kibbeh nabelsieh* (Golden Ground Meat–Filled Bulgur Shells, page 53), *kuaisat* (Pistachio-Filled Ground Meat Shells, page 60). *Arak* (anise-flavored spirit), whiskey, and beer are the men's beverages of choice to accompany the *maza* items and hot entrées, all of which are passed around the table and heartily enjoyed. As appetites are sated, laughter and the spirit of celebration fill the air. Soon, the vocalists among the crowd belt out the first bars of a favorite *pizmon*, one of dozens of religiously themed, poetic songs inspired by Arabic melodies that the Aleppian Jewish community members have sung for generations. The others will join in chorus, loudly echoing the singer's tune and punctuating the song with rhythmic bangs on the table. This parade of song can go on for hours, or at least until the singers are exhausted, the *arak* bottles are empty, and the tables are covered with the empty shells of pumpkin seeds, a common *sebbit* snack.

On the women's side, a festive mood reigns, albeit at a lower volume. Women from young to old greet the hostess with a kiss on the cheek and wish her a *mabruk* (Arabic for "congratulations") on the joyous event that gave rise to the *sebbit*. All are wearing their finest clothes. They sit around circular tables, catching up with one another, and sampling the food—perhaps noting whether the *laham b'ajeen* has enough ou^c or whether the *tabbouleh* is perfectly lemony. The scene is warm and cordial, an opportunity for family and friends to gather over a delicious meal and enjoy one another's company.

Arak
(Syrian Anisette)

Shabbat Dinner

Khubz 'Adi—Ordinary Syrian Flatbread, page 18

Salata Arabi—Basic Syrian Salad with Lemon-Cumin Dressing, page 30

Salata Banadoura—Fresh Tomato Salad with Allspice-Lemon Dressing, page 34

Platter of sliced fennel, radishes, scallions, romaine leaves

Riz Halabieh—Classic Aleppian Rice, page 116

Kibbeh Hamdah—Lemon-Mint Broth with Mixed Vegetables and Syrian Meatballs, page 97

Fawleh b'Lahmeh—Tender Flanken with String Beans, page 159

Mehshi Banadoura—Tomatoes Stuffed with Ground Meat and Rice, page 141

Djaj Mishwi—Friday Night Roast Chicken with Potatoes, page 189

Rubuh'—Succulent Roast Veal Stuffed with Spiced Ground Meat and Rice, page 168

Platter of fruit—grapes, fresh figs, assorted berries, fresh plums and apricots, and sliced melons

Shabbat Lunch

❖

Khubz 'Adi—Ordinary Syrian Flatbread, page 18

Mehalallat—Assorted Vegetables Pickled in Brine, page 68

Zeitoon—Assorted Syrian Olives, page 73

Tehineh—Sesame Spread, page 26

Salata Arabi—Basic Syrian Salad with Lemon-Cumin Dressing, page 30

Shawki b'Zeit—Artichokes in Olive Oil and Lemon Marinade, page 40

Salatit Banjan—Smoky Eggplant Salad with Garlic and Parsley, page 33

Laham b'Ajeen—Miniature Tamarind Minced Meat Pies, page 50

Lahmeh fil Makleh—Aleppian Beef Stew, page 172
　OR
Djaj wa Rishta—Roast Chicken with Crispy Spaghetti, page 192

Platter of fruit—grapes, fresh figs, assorted berries, fresh plums and apricots, and sliced melons

Selection of pastries (optional)

*Platter for Rosh Hashanah
(The New Year Festival)*

Eìèd

عطل

THE HOLIDAYS

Rosh Hashanah ראש השנה
The New Year Festival

Rosh Hashanah literally means "the beginning of the year." In Hebrew it is called *Yom Ha Din,* "the day of judgment," when the whole world stands before G-d to be judged. This holiday is both a joyous celebration of the Jewish month of Tishrei and the start of the solemn *aseret yemei t'shuva,* the ten High Holy Days during which Jews engage in profound introspection and entreat G-d to inscribe their names in the Book of Life for the coming year. Aleppian Jews cultivate this spirit of repentance during the preceding month of Elul by reciting *selihot* (early morning prayers of forgiveness) daily and attending *hatarat nedarim* services, which are led by a panel of three rabbis, who annul the congregants' unfulfilled vows and promises so that they have a "clean record" before Rosh Hashanah.

THE NEW YEAR MEAL

The foods of the New Year holiday symbolize a wish for a sweet year. Aleppian Jews eat several symbolic foods during the Rosh Hashanah dinner, including sugar-dipped apples, *helou s'farjal* (Candied Quince, page 290), dates, pomegranates, and lamb's head. Anything sour, bitter, or overly spicy is avoided.

At the outset of the meal, after the blessing over wine, bread is blessed, torn, and then dipped in salt and then in sugar. A food that is customarily *not* eaten is nuts, for two reasons. First, pragmatically speaking, according to tradition, nuts cause the production of excess phlegm in the nasal and throat area, which can hinder the ability to recite prayers (the main focus of the holiday). The other reason is that according to *gematria,* a numerological system based on the Hebrew alphabet, the numerical value of the word "nut" in Hebrew (*egoz*) is equal to the numerical value of the Hebrew word for sin (*het*).

SYMBOLIC FOODS FOR THE NEW YEAR FEAST

Most of the following foods are eaten before the evening feast of Rosh Hashanah because of linguistic similarities between the names of these foods and various words that correspond to the wishes of the Jewish people for the coming year. Special blessings are recited before each of these items is eaten. The full meal follows after this ceremony.

DATES: The Hebrew word for "date," *tamar,* is similar to the Hebrew word for "to cease," *tam.* The hope here is that G-d will ensure that our enemies will cease harassing us.

APPLES: The primary symbol for a sweet year in all Jewish communities is an apple dipped in something sweet. Aleppian Jews dip their apples in sugar.

LEEKS: The Arabic and Hebrew words for "leek," *kerrateh* and *karti,* respectively, resemble the Hebrew word *karet,* which means "to cut off." Leek symbolizes the idea that we are asking G-d to cut off evildoers from harming the Jewish nation. Aleppian Jews make *ejjeh b'kerrateh* (Leek Fritter, page 222) to commemorate this concept.

SWISS CHARD: The Arabic word *silleq* is similar to the Hebrew word *salek,* which means "to remove" or "throw out." Again, Aleppian Jews eat Swiss chard in the hope that G-d will remove the community's enemies from its midst. The Aleppian Jewish dish of choice for this item is *silleq b'lahmeh* (Swiss Chard Stewed with Meat, page 89).

TRUMPET GOURD: In Hebrew this vegetable is called *kara,* which is closely akin to the Hebrew *karaa',* which means "to rip or tear." A blessing is made, asking G-d to tear up any oppressive decrees that prevail in any place that Jews dwell. Aleppian Jews prepare the gourd as a candied sweet, sometimes colored green, and usually flavored with rose water. The recipe for this sweet appears on page 296.

BLACK-EYED PEAS (*LUBIEH*): The Hebrew word for these beans is *rubiah,* which is similar to the word for "to increase"—*rab.* The black-eyed peas, therefore, symbolize increasing one's merits. The traditional dish served for this symbolic food is *lubieh b'lahmeh* (Black-eyed Peas with Veal, page 83).

POMEGRANATE (*RIMON*): This wonderful fruit inspires us to ask G-d to grant us merit and goodwill as bountiful as the fruit's numerous juicy, ruby-hued seeds, which symbolize Judaism's 613 commandments.

LAMB'S HEAD: Aleppian Jews traditionally eat from the meat of the lamb's head to symbolize that they will be leaders at the head rather than followers at the tail.

The meat is also a reminder of the ram that Abraham sacrificed instead of his son Isaac, whom he bound to an altar on G-d's command. Today, many Aleppians place a cooked, whole sheep's head on the table. *Muhah* (Brains in Olive Oil and Lemon, page 180) and *lissan w'zbeeb* (Spiced Tongue with Raisin Sauce, page 181) are the traditional dishes to symbolize the lamb's head.

NEW FRUIT: Following the rite of eating each of the symbolic foods, Aleppian Jews indulge in a fruit that just comes into season. Thanks to the ease of contemporary air transport, there is a bounty of exotic fruits available in major cities, so the fruit chosen for this honor is simply a matter of preference. Among some recommended exotic fruits are cherimoya, starfruit, prickly pear, rambutan, mangosteen, jackfruit, and dragon fruit. Alternatively, Helou Kusa Sha'riyya (Candied Spaghetti Squash, page 295) may be used.

ꙮ Blowing the *Shofar* ꙮ

The *shofar* is a ram's horn that is blown 101 times during the Rosh Hashanah morning prayers, signifying a time of judgment. (If Rosh Hashanah falls on Shabbat, the *shofar* is not blown at all.) The use of the *shofar* harks back to the command in Leviticus 25 to "transmit a blast on the horn" during times of importance. Historically, the *shofar* announced war or signaled the coming of peace or the commencement of a high holiday. On Rosh Hashanah the *shofar* serves as an alarm to awaken restive souls to repent: "Awaken you sleepers from your sleep and you who slumber, arise and remember your creator" (Maimonides, Laws of Repentance 3:2). To stay focused on the objective of repentance and introspection, it is a custom of the Aleppian Jewish community to look away from the *shofar* when it is being sounded.

Syrian communities treat their *shofars* as a precious inheritance. It is a beautiful and moving experience to hear a *shofar* that has been passed down over the ages from rabbi to rabbi. To follow the same traditions and hear the same heart-rending blasts as those heard by one's ancestors generations upon generations ago is at once humbling and exalting in a way that truly makes one feel connected to a lineage.

Rosh Hashanah Dinner

❖

Khubz 'Adi—Ordinary Syrian Flatbread, page 18

Riz wa Sha'riyya—Rice with Vermicelli, page 117

Djaj w'Sfiha—Roast Chicken with Stuffed Baby Eggplant, page 190

Kibbeh bi'Kizabrath—Cilantro-Tomato Soup with Syrian Meatballs, page 99

Medias Shawki—Artichoke Halves Stuffed with Ground Meat and Rice, page 153

Rubuh'—Succulent Roast Veal Stuffed with Spiced Ground Meat and Rice, page 168

Platter of fruit—grapes, fresh figs, assorted berries, fresh plums and apricots, and sliced melons

Selection of pastries (optional)

Rosh Hodesh ראש חודש
The New Moon

Rosh Hodesh is the first day of each new month. It is considered a minor holiday for women as a reward for their historical righteousness in not contributing ornaments and jewelry to make the Golden Calf. In the Hebrew Bible, the Golden Calf was an idol constructed by certain impatient Israelites who lost faith in Moses when he ascended Mount Sinai, where he eventually received the Ten Commandments after the passage of forty days. It is a custom for women to wear special clothes and to refrain from some everyday chores. Ideally, a special meal is served in honor of Rosh Hodesh.

Lulav *and* etrog *(palm frond and citron) for the holiday of Sukkot (The Festival of Booths)*

Sukkot סוכות
The Festival of Booths

Shemini Atzeret שמיני עצרת
The Festival of Assembly

Simhat Torah שמחת תורה
The Festival of the Torah

On the heels of the solemn Yom Kippur, there follow Sukkot, Shemini Atzeret, and Simhat Torah, a joyous eight-day trio of holidays that begin on the 15th of Tishrei and represent one of the purest and happiest celebrations in the Jewish calendar. This period is commonly referred to in Jewish prayer and literature as *zeman simchateinu*, "the season of our rejoicing."

The *sukkah* is where everything takes place during this festival: eating, singing, learning, and sometimes even sleeping. It is essentially an outdoor structure with a roof made of natural plant materials (such as bamboo or tree branches), symbolizing the tentlike dwellings that protected the Jews during their forty-year passage in the desert following their exodus from Egypt. Each night before starting the evening meal, Jews prepare themselves to connect to that particular spiritual channel created by their seven forefathers—Abraham, Isaac, Jacob, Moses, Aaron, Joseph, and David, collectively known as the *ushpizin*—welcoming one of them as an honorary *sukkah* guest.

Jews also celebrate Sukkot with the daily ritual of waving the *lulav* and *etrog*, which is done during the morning *Hallel* prayer to express praise to G-d. The *lulav* is a palm frond that is flanked by *hadasim* (myrtle leaves) and *aravot* (willows). The *etrog* is a citron, which is a bumpy and deeply aromatic citrus fruit.

The *lulav*-waving ritual of Aleppian Jews is complex and is based on the Kabbalah. The *lulav* holder begins by waving it southward to and from the chest three times. He then turns, repeating this motion while facing north, then east (with a slight variation), and then west, all the while slowly chanting the designated section of the *Hallel* prayer in a low tone. Following the waving ceremony, *hoshannot* (songs of praise) are recited. During this ceremony the Torah is brought out and congregants encircle it, holding *lulav* and *etrog*.

The last day of Sukkot is known as Hoshanna Rabba. The Kabbalah provides that it is on this day that G-d dispatches the decrees He sealed on Yom Kippur (The Day of Atonement). In the morning of Hoshanna Rabba there is a great ceremony of *lulav* waving, circling the prayer room seven times and beating the *aravot* willow branches on the floor. The falling leaves from the willow branch symbolize the desire for beneficial rain. Men stay up all night studying the Torah in order to ensure a good verdict for the coming year.

At the close of Sukkot, Aleppian Jews gather their *etrogs* to make tart, fragrant *helou etrog* (Citron Preserves, page 297), which is given to pregnant women to wish them an easy birth and healthy baby. Traditionally, this preserve also makes an appearance on the tree festival Tu b'Shvat (the new year festival for trees). Aleppian Jews also have a custom of saving their *lulavs* to ward off bad dreams. Following the Jewish custom of using one precept to fulfill another, the *lulav* is kept in the home until the eve of Passover, when it is used as kindling during the ceremonial burning of the *hametz* (leavened food).

The last day of Sukkot is joined with and immediately followed by the holidays of Shemini Atzeret and Simhat Torah. Shemini Atzeret celebrates the Jewish people's relationship with G-d. A key aspect of this day is the fervent request for rain, whereby the congregation pleads with G-d to grant enough to ensure a bounty of crops for the coming year.

Simhat Torah commemorates the transition between the final weekly Torah reading in the Book of Deuteronomy and the first reading in the Book of Genesis. For children, it is one of the most anticipated dates in the Jewish calendar. The congregation sings and dances with its Torah scrolls. Bags of candy containing *simsemiyeh* (Sesame Candy, page 305) and *labas* (Candy-Coated Almonds, page 303) are given to all the children at the close of the morning services. Every man in the congregation is encouraged to receive the honor of an *aliyah,* which is an invitation for a member or guest of a congregation to read from a portion of the designated Torah reading. There is also the custom of gathering the young boys of the congregation under one prayer shawl (*tallit*) for a collective *aliyah.*

There are no special dishes for this holiday. A typical holiday lunch is prepared and enjoyed by the adults, but kids must be pried from their lollipops, chocolate bars, and other confections in order to eat a proper meal—that is, if they haven't yet succumbed to the obligatory Simhat Torah tummy ache.

Sukkot Dinner

Khubz Simsom—Sesame Flatbread, page 21

Fūl Medammas—Warm Fava Beans, page 48

Salatit Batata—Lemony Allspice-Cumin Potato Salad, page 37

Riz b'Spanekh—Rice with Spinach, page 120

Farrju Mashwi—Grilled Chicken, page 196

Kibbeh b'Garaz—Sweet Cherry–Stuffed Beef Slices, page 166

Yebra—Grape Leaves Stuffed with Ground Meat and Rice, with Apricot-Tamarind Sauce, page 150

Baklawa—Pistachio *Filla* Wedges in Rose Water Syrup, page 251

Kra'bij—Marshmallow-Dipped Nut-Stuffed Pastry, page 269

Platter of fruit—grapes, fresh figs, assorted berries, fresh plums, apricots, and sliced melons

Selection of pastries

Lighting the menorah for Hanukkah (The Festival of Lights)

Passover seder *in Aleppo, Syria, circa 1937 (courtesy of Sephardic Community Center Archives)*

Hanukkah חנוכה
The Festival of Lights

Hanukkah commemorates the miraculous tale of the independent corps of Jewish fighters called the Maccabees. On the 25th of Kislev in 165 BCE, this small group of brave men, led by Judah of the Hasmonean family of Temple priests, rose from the town of Modi'in to defeat Antiochus IV and his Greek Seleucid armies. The Maccabees triumphantly reclaimed the Jewish Temple in Jerusalem and the land of Judea. The root of the word *Hanukkah* means "dedication," which refers to the rededication of the Jewish Temple to G-d and the Jewish nation after its prolonged desecration by the Seleucids.

Before the Maccabees' victory, Antiochus had ordered a campaign of mass Hellenization. Greek culture and thought were forced upon the Jewish inhabitants of Judea. He banned the celebration of Jewish festivals throughout Judea and even erected a statue of Zeus in the Jewish Temple. Gymnasia were set up instead of schools of Jewish learning. Men were forced to eat pork, and swine was sacrificed on the altar of the Jewish Temple. It was truly a miracle that the family of Maccabees was able to vanquish the great forces of Antiochus.

The precise miracle that led to the age-old custom of lighting an eight-branched candelabra (*menorah* in Hebrew) had to do with the scarcity of pure olive oil in Jerusalem when the Temple was recaptured by the Maccabees. A large *menorah* was kept lit at all times in the Temple. Once his men retook the holy grounds of the Temple, Judah immediately sought to light the *menorah*. However, the supply of olive oil at the Temple and throughout Jerusalem was contaminated by unclean Greek hands and was not acceptable for sacramental use. Judah's men found only a single sealed jug of oil, barely enough for one day of burning. Because it would take eight days to press new oil, the priests despaired that there would not be enough to keep the flames of the *menorah* burning. Twenty-four hours later, when the priests expected the *menorah* lights to be extinguished, they discovered that it was still lit. This miracle lasted a total of eight days, and then pure oil was added to the *menorah* to keep it burning perpetually.

Seeing the *menorah* gloriously aglow and under Jewish control once again was a triumph for the Jewish people in ancient times. To fulfill the requirement of publicizing that wondrous miracle, Jews light *menorahs* and place them outside their door front, or in a place inside their homes visible from outside, so that the burning lights are conspicuously on view. The *menorahs* are kept to the left of the front doorways because on the right is the *mezuzah* (a case attached to the doorposts of a house, containing a scroll inscribed with sacred passages). A person who enters the doorway will thereby be surrounded by *mitzvot* (religious obligations).

Aleppian Jewish women have a custom of refraining from doing any chores during the time that the *menorah* is lit. Also, because oil is the miraculous component of this holiday, Jews eat dishes that are fried in oil. Aleppian Jews partake of *ejjeh batata* (Potato Fritters, page 220), the wonderfully decadent *'ataiyef* (Stuffed Syrian Pancakes, page 258), and *zalabieh* (Fried Pastry Balls with Sugar Syrup Glaze, page 250). Cheese is traditionally eaten in honor of Judith, the heroine who tempted the Seleucid general Holofernes with cheese and wine. Holofernes heartily accepted Judith's offerings and fell asleep after becoming quite sated. Judith then killed him in his sleep. The deceased general's troops fled the battle camp upon hearing of Holofernes's death, bringing a Jewish victory in Jerusalem one step closer.

Those in the Aleppian Jewish community who originated from Spain have an especially unique Hanukkah custom. When lighting the *menorah,* they light an extra candle. The custom originates from the time that followed the 1492 Edict of Expulsion (see page 3). Jews from Spain journeyed east to the lands of the Ottoman Empire in the hope of finding tolerant lands. After safely arriving in Aleppo, having survived the tribulations of oppression and expulsion, these Spanish Jews lit an extra candle in recognition of the miracle of their safe arrival in Aleppo and the tolerance and brotherhood they found there.

Tu b'Shvat ט"ו בשבת
The New Year Festival for Trees

Celebrated on the 15th of Shevat, usually in January or February, this festival honors the new year for trees and the tithing of fruit. In the Land of Israel, this date marked the beginning of the period in which trees bore fruit after the winter season.

Today, this is a joyous festival during which it is customary to eat the seven species of fruit and grain mentioned in the Old Testament (wheat, barley, grapes, figs, pomegranates, olives, and dates) and other produce of the Holy Land. The seven species, along with an assortment of nuts, dried fruits, and pastries, are spread out on a large table. Children happily gather treats in cloth bags.

Purim פורים
The Festival of Lots

Purim celebrates the miracle that happened on the 13th of Adar in 356 BCE in the ancient city of Shushan, which is located in modern-day Iran near the southwestern town of Dezful. It was there that Esther, a clandestine Jewess in King Ahasveros's royal harem, arose to foil the decree of the king's evil minister Haman to destroy the Jews in the kingdom. Haman drew lots (*purim* in Hebrew) and selected the 13th of Adar as the date on which his decree of annihilation would take effect. To help her people avert a tragic end, Esther, at her own great risk, revealed her true identity to the king while he was making merry at a wine banquet. She asked him to issue a counterdecree. Ahasveros, enamored of Esther's purity, complied and issued an order protecting the Jews of his kingdom and permitting them to defend themselves against anyone seeking to do them harm. The Jewish people averted disaster, and their fortune was reversed. What was first anticipated to be a somber day of mourning and destruction turned into a joyous and momentous festival.

Purim is primarily observed by fulfilling four positive commandments: Jews are required to hear the reading of the Book of Esther (*megillah*) on the eve and on the morning of the festival, give charity to at least two poor people (*matanot l'evyonim* in Hebrew), send special parcels called *mishloah manot* to friends and family, and eat a sumptuous feast. Each *mishloah manot* must include at least two ready-to-eat foods; giving more than that is praiseworthy. Aleppian Jews arrange numerous baskets filled with candies, chocolates, fruits, nuts, and wine. Sweets that make a great addition to the *mishloah* are *simsemiyeh* (Sesame Candy, page 305), *halweh* (Sesame Sweetmeat, page 304), *baklawa* (Pistachio *Filla* Wedges in Rose Water Syrup, page 251), *graybeh* (Sweet Bracelet-Shaped Butter Cookies, page 267), *eras b'ajweh* (Date-Filled Crescents, page 268), and *assabih b'loz* (Nut-Filled *Filla* Fingers, page 261). The daylight hours of Purim are spent transporting one's festively costumed children to deliver these parcels.

The afternoon of Purim is dedicated to an elaborate feast, which usually includes numerous meat dishes and copious amounts of wine. The consumption of wine is encouraged on this festival because it was while under the intoxicating sway of wine that Ahasveros assented to Esther's bold request to help the Jews of his kingdom. Esther also called for a wine banquet as a ruse to summon Haman to the king's court to expose his treachery. There is a saying that on Purim one should drink until one can no longer distinguish between the righteousness of Mordechai (Esther's encouraging uncle) and the wickedness of Haman. Whether you choose to drink this much is up to you—but what better way to do so than with a fabulous meal of rich Aleppian dishes such as *laham b'ajeen* (Miniature Tamarind Minced Meat Pies, page 50), *kuaisat* (Pistachio-Filled Ground Meat Shells, page 60), *kibbeh b'garaz* (Sweet-Cherry–Stuffed Beef Slices, page 166), *yebra* (Grape Leaves Stuffed with Ground Meat and Rice, with Apricot-Tamarind Sauce, page 150), *rubuh'* (Succulent Roast Veal Stuffed with Spiced Ground Meat and Rice, page 168), and whatever else your festive heart desires.

SAMPLE MENU

The Purim Feast

Khubz Za'atar—*Za'atar* Flatbread, page 20

'Arnabeet Meqli—Fried Cauliflower Florets, page 95

Riz w'Zafran—Saffron Rice, page 121

Bamia b'Mishmosh—Okra with Prunes and Apricots in Tamarind Sauce, page 87

Shish Tawuq—Chicken, Pepper, and Tomato Kabobs, page 197

Kibbeh bil Sanieh—Baked Bulgur–Ground Meat Pie, page 171

Mehshi Basal—Caramelized Onions Stuffed with Ground Meat and Rice, page 147

Kra'bij—Marshmallow-Dipped Nut-Stuffed Pastry, page 269

Ma'amoul—Nut-Stuffed Pastry, page 272

Assabih b'Loz—Nut-Filled *Filla* Fingers, page 261

The Aleppian Ke'arah
(Seder Plate, page 350)

Pesach פסח
The Holiday of Our Freedom

"In the merit of the righteous women our forefathers were redeemed from Egypt"
—Babylonian Talmud, Sotah 116

A month after the feasting and gift-giving of Purim, Aleppian Jews celebrate Passover to commemorate G-d's many miracles in the course of redeeming the Jews from bondage in Egypt. This holiday has the broadest impact on food, mainly due to the prohibition against wheat products (*hametz*), which commemorates the unleavened flatbread (*matzah*) the Jews had to bake as they hurriedly fled from Egypt. Aleppian Jewish recipes, to some extent, do not undergo as profound an alteration on Pesach as do those of other Jewish communities because many of them do not require *hametz* (any product made of wheat, barley, spelt, rye, or oats that has been allowed to become leavened). For example, Syrian Jews have a custom of eating their beloved rice, which is not considered *hametz*, as well as various forms of *kitniyot* (a legal category that includes corn, peas, and legumes).

While the holiday of Passover is observed for eight days (or seven days in Israel) beginning on the 15th of Nisan (usually falling in March or April), the preparations for this holiday begin weeks earlier. In lectures on Jewish law, rabbis instruct Aleppian Jewish men about the holiday's stringent legal obligations. Women painstakingly examine rice three times to ensure that no wheat kernels are interspersed among the grains. Every corner of the household is cleaned, especially the kitchen. Pots, pans, and silverware must be cleansed of *hametz*, either through exposure to direct white-hot heat or by immersion in boiling water. Many families keep special cookware and silverware for Passover to avoid this chore.

The ceremony of *bedikat hametz* ("the search for *hametz*") entails a final, thorough search of one's property for any trace of leavened products. Before the search, ten pieces of bread are hidden by family members of the searchers, including the head of the household. The traditional tools of the search are a candle to light one's way, a knife to access stray crumbs of *hametz*, and a bowl to hold the *hametz*. At the end of the search, the ten pieces of *hametz* are set aside for burning the next morning.

During the morning of the eve of Passover, the Fast of the First Born (*ta'anit bekhorot*) is honored by Aleppian Jews. Every eldest child in his or her family attends morning prayers, after which the congregation's learning group organizes a ceremony (*siyum*) in honor of their completion of an entire book of the Talmud. Attendance at this ceremony permits the firstborn to cease fasting. At the ceremony, the final verses of the selected book are read and discussed. The learning group's leader declares the book completed and then makes a blessing over wine. The firstborn observing the ceremony must then bless and eat a piece of cake to fully relieve himself of the obligation of fasting.

After the morning prayer services, the head of the household undertakes the act of burning the remaining *hametz*. This is called *bi'ur hametz* ("the burning of the *hametz*"). The practice recommended by sages is to use the dried *lulav* (palm frond) and other plant matter that had been left to dry after Sukkot (The Festival of Booths). This is an exciting moment for children, who take pride in gathering twigs for kindling to help their fathers burn the *hametz*. The man of the house then says a blessing on the ceremony that renders any *hametz* inadvertently remaining in one's possession like the dust of the earth.

In Aleppo, during Passover, street vendors sold fresh *matzah* piled high on carts. The *matzahs* were round and as large as twenty-four inches in diameter. This *matzah* qualified as *matzah shemura* (literally, "supervised *matzah*"), which is made from grain that has been under constant supervision from harvesting until baking to ensure that the wheat is not adulterated with additional moisture. During the daytime hours before the first Passover *seder*, one is prohibited from eating *matzah*.

THE *SEDER*—TELLING THE STORY OF PASSOVER

A requirement of the Passover holiday is to tell our families, especially the young ones, about the exodus from Egypt, the touchstone moment in all of Jewish history. This is done by reciting the *Haggadah* (Hebrew for "narrative"), which contains many insights into the story of Passover. The reading is done during the *seder*, which literally means "order," an allusion to its precise, fourteen-phase structure.

It is incumbent on everyone to honor the occasion by dressing in one's finest. The evening's meal is a feast of the most sumptuous dishes. The table settings substitute the usual modesty and simplicity with an ornate tablecloth and shimmering finery. Pillows or plush chairs are provided so that everyone can lean comfortably, enjoying the meal as a king would; after all, Passover is a celebration of freedom and a time for the highest exultation.

The centerpiece of the *seder* is the ke'arah (Hebrew for "platter"), which holds the symbolic foods of the holiday (see the Aleppian *Ke'arah*, page 350): the *matzah*, bitter herbs, lamb shank, egg, celery, endive, and *haroset halebieh* (Aleppian Date Preserves, page 309).

❧ The Aleppian *Ke'arah* (*Seder* Plate) ❧

The Jews of Aleppo set up the Passover *seder* platter to represent the Ten *Sefirot,* a kabbalistic reference to different traits of G-d. This tradition was established by the Ari (Rabbi Isaac Luria, 1534–1572) who was the founder of a seminal branch of Kabbalah (mystical Judaism) in the Galilean town of Safed.

Matzah: Three large pieces of *matzah* are placed in the center of the platter.

Egg: It is darkened to look burnt and is a symbol of mourning for the Jewish Temple in Jerusalem, which was destroyed.

Zeroa: This is a roasted lamb shank to remind us of the Passover sacrifice offered at the Temple in Jerusalem. Jewish law requires that it not be broiled or grilled. The *zeroa* recipe on page 179 is the traditional Aleppian version.

Karpas: Usually a few ribs of celery. The leaves should be bundled to resemble the hyssop plant that was used by the Jews in Egypt on the first *seder* night to wipe the blood of the sacrificial lamb on their doorposts as a sign of their devotion to G-d (Exodus 12:22).

Maror: These bitter greens serve as a reminder of the bitterness of the Jews' slavery in Egypt. Aleppian Jews use romaine lettuce.

Hazeret: This is an analogue to the bitter greens. Aleppian Jews usually use endive or escarole.

Haroset halebieh **(Aleppian Date Preserves, page 309):** This is a sweet paste that Aleppian Jews make primarily from dates. It symbolizes the cement that the enslaved Jews were forced to use to build massive structures ordered by the Egyptian pharaohs.

The first phase of the *seder* is the blessing over wine. It is the first of four cups of wine blessed and consumed during the evening. The minimum amount per glass is 3½ ounces. Red wine is preferred for Passover because it signifies the miracle by which G-d turned the water of the Nile River into blood.

Phase two involves rinsing one's hands without a blessing, which is required before dipping any foods into liquid. Phase three is *karpas,* during which celery is dipped into saltwater. The saltwater symbolizes the tears shed by the Jews while in bondage.

The fourth phase is *yahatz.* According to kabbalistic tradition, the middle of three *matzahs* on the ceremonial platter is broken into two, one part in the shape of a *daled*

(the fourth letter of the Hebrew alphabet) and the other, larger part in the shape of a *vav* (the sixth Hebrew letter). When combined they equal ten, corresponding to the Ten *Sefirot* (the core concept of kabbalistic metaphysics). The *vav* is set aside as the *afikoman* (a special piece of *matzah* to be saved until after the meal) and is wrapped, symbolizing the lamb that was sacrificed in the Jewish Temple on Passover.

It is an Aleppian Jewish custom to then take turns holding the *afikoman* over one's shoulder while reciting in Hebrew, *"Mish-aro-tam zeru-rot be-simlo-tam al shikh-mam u'bnai Yisrael a'su k'dbar Moshe"* ("Their kneading troughs being bound up in their clothes upon their shoulders, and the children of Israel did according to the word of Moses") (Exodus 12:34–35). Then the following dialogue is spoken:

Guests (in unison, in Arabic): *Where do you come from?* (*"minwen jai'yeh?"*)

Seder participant: *Egypt!*

Guests: *Where are you going?* (*"la'wen ra'yekh?"*)

Seder participant: *Jerusalem!*

Guests: *What are your provisions?* (*"ishu zawatak?"*)

Seder participant: *Matzah and maror* (*bitter greens*).

This interesting colloquy, which suggests a nosy border official interrogating a wayward Jew leaving Egypt, is meant to allow the *seder* participants to relate to the Exodus as if it were they themselves who fled Egypt, which is how the sages of old recommended the *seder* be conducted. The *afikoman* is then hidden by one of the participants. The purpose is to keep the children awake, alert, and attentive throughout the ceremony. The children who later find the hidden *afikoman* receive a reward.

The fifth and lengthiest phase then begins: *maggid* ("the telling"). The essential story is told in this part of the *seder*, beginning with the Four Questions as recited by the youngest participant. The general question is: "Why is this night different from all other nights?" The specific questions are

> "Why on all other nights we do not dip our vegetables even once, but tonight we dip twice?
>
> "Why on all other nights we eat bread or matzah, but tonight we eat only matzah?
>
> "Why on all other nights we eat many vegetables, but tonight we eat maror?
>
> "Why on all other nights we eat and drink either sitting up or reclining, but tonight we all recline?"

The group responds by chanting the answer, beginning with "We were slaves to Pharaoh in Egypt . . ."

Toward the end of this phase, each of the Ten Plagues is recited. For each plague, it is customary to pour some wine into a pot, which is held by unmarried girl. She looks to the side to avoid the plagues, just as the plagues avoided the Jews in Egypt. The girl then leaves the room and disposes of the wine. Soon after this rite, a second cup of wine is drunk.

The sixth and seventh phases are the ritual rinsing of the hands—this time with a blessing—and the blessing and consumption of *matzah*. *Maror*, the bitter green, is eaten for the eighth phase. Aleppian Jews favor endive or romaine lettuce dipped in *haroset halebieh* (Aleppian Date

Preserves, page 309). The ninth phase is done in honor of the great Jewish sage Hillel, who devised a sandwich called *korekh*, made of romaine lettuce and *haroset* between two pieces of *matzah*. Hillel ate the whole thing in one go. During the time of the Jewish Temple, the three obligations of *pesach* (sacrificial lamb), *matzah*, and *maror* had to be eaten together at one time rather than one after the other. Today, only *matzah* and *maror* are eaten together. This phase is followed by the ceremonial partaking of egg and lamb shank, designated for Passover in commemoration of the sacrifices at the Jewish Temple.

For the tenth and most anticipated phase, food is brought to the table and the feast begins. A traditional Aleppian Jewish Passover meal consists of rice, a few vegetable dishes, a couple of *mehshi* (stuffed vegetable dishes), *keftes* (Tamarind-Stewed Meatballs, page 162), *djaj mishwi* (Friday Night Roast Chicken with Potatoes, page 189), and *rubuh'* (Succulent Roast Veal Stuffed with Spiced Ground Meat and Rice, page 168).

Haggadah from Aleppo, Syria, circa 1890s (courtesy of Albert J. Shehebar)

The eleventh phase requires the children to search the house for the *afikoman,* which was hidden earlier in the *seder.* After it is found, the *afikoman* is the final food consumed for the night.

Some Aleppian Jews save a small fragment of *afikoman* for a pregnant woman to eat when she later delivers her child. Childless couples also take care to eat the *afikoman.* These customs are attributable to the numerical value for the words *afikoman* and *ken yirbeh* ("they will multiply" in Hebrew). During the Jews' period of bondage in Egypt, Pharaoh was alarmed by the increasing Jewish population and concerned that they might align with an enemy and pose a risk to his kingdom. In Exodus 1:10 he said,

"Lest they multiply" (*pen yirbeh*) and later ordered that all Jewish firstborn male infants be killed. Sages have commented that G-d, upon hearing Pharaoh, retorted, "They shall multiply" (*ken yirbeh*).

The twelfth phase is the postmeal blessing, after which the third cup of wine is drunk.

During the last two phases, the *seder* participants recite praises and songs thanking G-d for the miracles of Passover and expressing the hope that by next year's *seder* the Messiah will arrive and G-d will bring them to a rebuilt Jerusalem. The final cup of wine is drunk during this part of the *seder.* By this time, the revelry and songs of the *seder* have carried it well past midnight in Aleppian Jewish households.

Rabbis from Aleppo, Syria (courtesy of Rabbi Ephriam Levy, Jerusalem)

Shavuot שבועות
The Festival of the First Fruits and the Giving of the Torah

Shavuot commemorates two Jewish events of significance. Celebrated on the 6th of Sivan, Shavuot represents the anniversary of G-d's communication of the Torah to Moses at Mount Sinai for transmission to the Jews for all time—an awe-inspiring, unparalled moment in the annals of Jewish history. Shavuot also coincides with the seasonal spring harvest in the Land of Israel. Every year at this time, first fruits were brought to Jerusalem from all over the hinterlands for donation at the Temple.

On the first night of this festival, Aleppian Jews honor the gift of the Torah by staying up all night at synagogue and studying with fellow congregants. During the daytime prayers, it is customary to read the Book of Ruth and *Azaharot,* a liturgical poem covering the 613 precepts of Judaism, written by Solomon ibn Gabirol, the great poet and thinker of eleventh-century Spain.

Aleppian Jews customarily eat one dairy meal on each day of this two-day festival as a reminder of G-d's promise that the Jews would settle the Land of Israel, which the Torah describes as flowing with "milk and honey." The dairy meal is also a reminder that our ancestors had just received the Torah (and its dietary laws) and did not have both meat and dairy dishes available. *Calsonnes w'rishta* (Buttery Noodles with Cheese Ravioli, page 127), *sambousak* (Buttery Cheese-Filled Sesame Pastries, page 212), assorted *jibns* (frittatas), and *'ataiyef* (Stuffed Syrian Pancakes, page 258) regularly appear on the Aleppian Shavuot table. However, in keeping with the requirement of eating meat on holidays and Shabbat, Aleppian Jews make an effort to eat one meat meal during each day of this holiday as well.

The Shavuot Lunch

✣

Khubz Za'atar—*Za'atar* Flatbread, page 20

Laban—Yogurt, page 241

Imwarrah b'Jibn—Cheese-Filled *Filla* Triangles, page 216

Hummus—Chickpea-Sesame Spread, page 27

Tabbouleh—Crunchy Tomato, Parsley, and Bulgur Salad with Cumin, page 31

Mehshi b'Leban—Rice-Stuffed Zucchini with Butter Sauce, page 234

Burghol b'Jibn—Bulgur with Cheese, page 130

Samak Mehshi b'Snobar—Whole Stuffed Fish with Pine Nuts, page 204

Riz ib Haleb—Aleppian Rice Pudding, page 284

Assabih b'Sutlaj—Custard-Filled Fingers in *Filla*, page 260

Grapes and sliced melon

Exterior of a home, Jamaliya neighborhood, Aleppo, Syria, circa 1900 (courtesy of Sephardic Community Center Archives)

FAST DAYS

There are six fast days in the Jewish calendar. Because the prohibition against eating is the essence of these solemn days, they are discussed apart from the holidays. However, the two 25-hour fasts, Yom Kippur and Tisha b'Ab, are worth discussing briefly here because there are certain customs associated with the pre- and post-fast meals. The other four minor fasts last from sunrise to sunset. There are no unique food-related customs associated with them and thus they are summarized below under a single heading.

Yom Kippur יום כיפור
The Day of Atonement

Yom Kippur, which falls on the 10th of Tishrei, is the holiest day in the Jewish calendar. Known as the Day of Atonement, it is the only fast day that arises from a biblical prescription; the five other fasts have been designated by the sages of the past to commemorate tragic events in Jewish history. On Yom Kippur, each Jew is penitent, completely devoted to accounting for his or her sins and pleading with G-d to judge him or her kindly as He decides the fate of the Jewish nation for the coming year. On this day, Jews deprive themselves of the pleasurable activities of eating, drinking, donning leather shoes, applying cosmetics, and indulging in spousal cohabitation in order to focus their concentration on prayer and repentance.

Jews far and wide follow the custom of *kaparot*, whereby they purchase chickens for slaughtering the night before Yom Kippur. The concept behind *kaparot* is to offer the chicken as a substitute for the fate one deserves for one's own sins of the past year. Jews perform this rite as a way of asking G-d to be merciful and accept the chickens' lives instead of their own. Many older Aleppian Jews have memories of the chickens being kept all night in closets or bathrooms in the *haushes* (courtyards) of old Aleppo. The slaughtered chickens are then given to the poor or prepared for the pre-fast meal, which is considered a holiday meal and is usually eaten with bread, demonstrating optimism for a good year.

The Pre-fast Meal on the Eve of Yom Kippur

Platter of romaine lettuce hearts and cut celery ribs

Riz w'Djaj—Rice with Chicken, page 194

Bizeh b'Jurah—Green Peas and Rice with Coriander and Meat, page 118

Beida bi'Lemouneh—Velvety Lemon Sauce, page 198

Keftes—Tamarind-Stewed Meatballs, page 162

Mehshi Kusa—Zucchini or Yellow Squash Stuffed with Ground Meat and Rice, page 143

Watermelon, grapes, sliced cantaloupe, and honeydew

Break-the-Fast Meal Following Yom Kippur

Chai b'Nana—Mint Tea, page 332

'Ahweh—Arabic Coffee, page 318

Ka'ak—Savory Anise-Seed Rings, page 22

Sambousak—Buttery Cheese-Filled Sesame Pastries, page 212

Salata Banadoura—Fresh Tomato Salad with Allspice-Lemon Dressing, page 34

Fūl Medammas—Warm Fava Beans, page 48

Kusa b'Jibn—Zucchini-Cheese Frittata, page 227

Calsonnes w'Rishta—Buttery Noodles with Cheese Ravioli, page 127

Samak Meqli—Fried Fish, page 201

Graybeh—Sweet Bracelet-Shaped Butter Cookies, page 267

Eras b'Ajweh—Date-Filled Crescents, page 268

Platter of grapes

The Pre-fast Meal on Tisha b'Ab

✦

Khubz 'Adi—Ordinary Syrian Flatbread, page 18

Mujedrah—Rice with Brown Lentils and Frizzled Caramelized Onions, page 125, or

Shurbat Addes—Thick and Hearty Red Lentil Soup with Garlic and Coriander, page 106

Romaine lettuce leaves

Tisha b'Ab תשעה באב (the Ninth of Ab)

This fast day falls in mid-July or August. It represents the most tragic day of the Jewish calendar and is considered a day of collective mourning. Both the First and Second Temples of Jerusalem were destroyed on this day in history, in 586 BCE and 69 CE, respectively. The Edict of Expulsion that marked the end of the Jewish community in Spain became effective on this day in 1492 (see page 3).

Nine days before this fast, from the beginning of the month of Ab, Aleppian Jews eat dairy meals only. Except for the Sabbath meal and Rosh Hodesh (page 342), meat and wine are forbidden.

Seudat ha'mafseket, the meal that precedes the fast, is considered a humble, solemn exercise, which is a contrast to the pre–Yom Kippur meal. A simple cooked dish that customarily contains eggs or lentils or any round food, which is symbolic of the mourning period, reminds Jews of the cyclical nature of life. *Shurbat addes* (Thick and Hearty Red Lentil Soup with Garlic and Coriander, page 106) or *mujedrah* (Rice with Brown Lentils and Frizzled Caramelized Onions, page 125) typifies the kind of dish that's made for this meal.

Following the meal, prayer services are conducted into the night. Congregants sit on the floor in an act of collective mourning and dolefully read the Book of Lamentations (*Eicah*).

Minor Fast Days תעניות קטנות

THE FAST OF GEDALIA: Falls on the 3rd day of Tishrei, immediately after Rosh Hashanah. It commemorates the execution of Gedalia ben Ahikam, the governor of Jerusalem in 586 BCE (Jeremiah 41:2).

THE TENTH OF TEBET: Falls eight days after the end of Hanukkah, usually in late December or early January. It commemorates the first day of the siege of Jerusalem by Nebuchadnezzar of Babylonia in 586 BCE.

THE FAST OF ESTHER: Falls on the 13th of Adar, the day before Purim (page 347). The fast commemorates the private fast that Queen Esther undertook before the Jews of Persia were to be gathered and executed under Haman's edict.

THE SEVENTEENTH OF TAMUZ: Marks the date when Nebuchadnezzar breached the walls of Jerusalem. Three weeks later, on the 9th of Ab, 586 BCE, Jerusalem fell and the First Temple was destroyed. Usually this fast occurs in late June or July. During the three-week period that commences with this fast, Aleppian Jews do not participate in any kind of celebration and avoid risky activities, especially during the nine days preceding Tisha b'Ab.

Wedding portrait of Jack and Betty Shalom,
Aleppo, Syria, 1923 (courtesy of Sephardic
Community Center Archives)

LIFE-CYCLE EVENTS

Brit Milah ברית מילה
Circumcision of the Newborn Male

The birth of any child sparks an endless chain of phone calls in the Aleppian Jewish community. The announcement of a birth is truly a momentous time in Judaism, and the wonderful news is spread like wildfire. When the newborn is a boy, the rite of circumcision is performed on his eighth day. In Hebrew this ceremony is called a *brit milah*, signifying the special covenant, or *brit*, that G-d forged with the Jewish people several millennia ago.

Aleppian Jews gather the night before the *brit milah* to conduct a ceremony called *shadd al'asseh*. It includes a reading from the Zohar, the primary Jewish mystical text. *Shadd al'asseh* literally means "the pulling of the pods," a reference to the myrtle branches used for rituals. According to kabbalistic teachings, myrtle branches protect the newborn male child from the clutches of Satan, who wants to hinder him from entering the covenant of the Jewish people. This gathering is essentially a study session attended by at least ten men close to the boy's family. Once the session is over, the men sing *pizmonim* (liturgical songs) and enjoy an array of small delicacies and sweets, including *sambousak* (Buttery Cheese-Filled Sesame Pastries, page 212), *ma'amoul* (Nut-Stuffed Pastry, page 279), and *al mazieh* (Pudding with Rose Water and Nuts, page 276).

The next morning, following prayers, the *brit milah* takes place in the family's home or the synagogue. The ritual surgeon, called a *mohel*, performs the circumcision. A special *parokhet* (ornate slipcover) embroidered with the name of Elijah the Prophet is draped over a chair, which is left empty during the ceremony. The chair is set aside for Elijah because he is an eternal witness of the Jewish people, casting an aura of positive energy over the occasion.

Observing the rite is an honor, and the observers are affording them great merit in the eyes of G-d. A beautiful three-tiered tray called *sanaiyat Eliyahu HaNabi* ("the tray of Elijah the Prophet") is passed around. It is adorned with stunning flowers, and lit candles surround the edge of each tier. Upon seeing the tray, guests place cash and coins on it as a good omen. After the circumcision, the tray and all its contents are auctioned off to the highest bidder, who may bid up to several hundred dollars for it. The winner may then choose to donate all of the tray money to charity or use it as a kind of sacred seed money, or *mammon shel berakha* ("blessed money"), to fund a new business or contribute toward a down payment on a house.

The rite of the *brit* begins with the boy's entrance into the room, traditionally in the arms of one of his grandmothers. The crowd parts to make way for her, and she hands the baby off to the *sandak* (derived from *syndikos*, Greek for "caretaker"), usually one of the boy's grandfathers, who sits on a chair and places the child on his knees. The *mohel* and the boy's father each recite a blessing before the child is circumcised. Upon completion of the rite, the baby is calmed with a dab of sweet red wine soaked in a gauze pad, and the rabbi makes a final blessing over the ceremony. As is usually done during happy events, a blessing is then made on a heady fragrance such as rose water to stimulate the soul's participation in the positive occasion. At this point the baby is named.

The infant is then taken into the arms of his other grandmother and brought to a quiet place to recuperate. The guests gather around the *sandak*, who is considered a conduit for special blessings on this day, and request a personal blessing from him.

During the rite, the mother is not present in the same room. However, she is in attendance at the special meal that follows. Traditionally, she appears dressed in a long white gown. Some of the wine blessed by the *mohel* is given to her as a special honor.

The meal after the *brit* is a dairy breakfast that includes a large tray of soft white cheeses, baskets of bread, finger food such as *sambousak* (Buttery Cheese-Filled Sesame Pastries, page 212), *spanekh b'jibn* (Spinach-Cheese Frittata, page 224), *imwarrah b'jibn* (Cheese-Filled *Filla* Triangles, page 216), and *kusa b'jibn* (Zucchini-Cheese Frittata, page 227). Even those who are in a rush to get to work take the time to say a blessing over a piece of Syrian flatbread filled with *jibneh shelal* (Twisted White String Cheese with Nigella Seeds, page 236).

The Birth of a Girl הולדת בת

On the Sabbath following the birth of a girl, her father is honored by his congregation with a call to the Torah, which called an *aliyah*. Following the *aliyah*, the father states the name of his infant daughter. After prayers, the girl's family usually hosts a *sebbit* (festive Sabbath luncheon, page 334) to celebrate the birth.

Pidyon Ha Ben פדיון הבן
Rite of the Firstborn Male Child

The *pidyon ha ben* takes place on the evening of the thirty-first day in the life of a firstborn male. This obligation applies only if both parents are not descended from the tribe of Levi. In this ceremony the boy's parents give five silver coins to redeem him from a *kohen* (a member of the priestly class from the tribe of Levi, descended from Aaron). This ancient rite derives from the time when the Jewish nation was preparing to return to the Land of Israel after the long exile in Egypt. They were commanded to "bring to G-d every male that initiates the womb [i.e., the firstborn]" (Exodus 13:12). Up until then, according to the Jewish system of sacrifice rituals, firstborn males were dedicated to G-d as priests. After the Exodus, the priesthood shifted to the tribe of Levi, which was then headed by Aaron. From that point on, this rite served to redeem firstborn males from their original dedication to G-d.

THE CEREMONY

The child's father, mother, and the *kohen* sit at a table. Traditionally, the boy's mother dresses for the occasion in her bridal gown, though that custom has waned in recent years. She begins the rite by declaring that the boy is her firstborn and that it was a natural delivery and he must be redeemed. The *kohen* then states that the boy is indeed a firstborn child and G-d requires that he be redeemed in exchange for five silver coins.

The *kohen* then asks the father if he wishes to redeem his son. The father responds in the affirmative. The father then gives the coins to the *kohen* and recites the blessing

Brit milah *(circumcision ceremony), circa 1970 (courtesy of Sephardic Community Center Archives)*

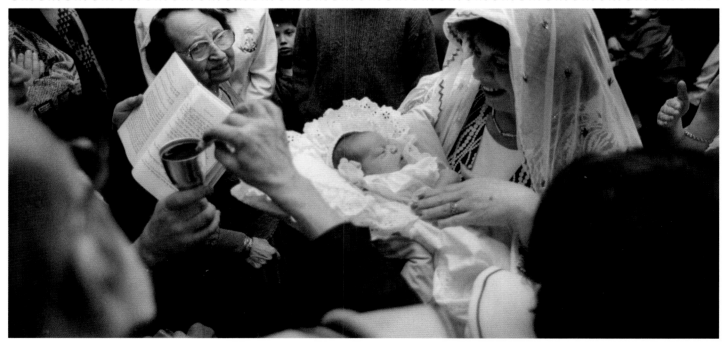

for the rite. After receiving the coins, the *kohen* confirms the receipt of the coins and the redemption of the boy. The *kohen* concludes with an encouraging blessing, hoping that the boy acquires a thorough education in the Torah and marries while his parents are still living. The *kohen* then holds his hand upon the boy's head and recites the special priestly blessing and a blessing over wine to sanctify the rite. The *kohen* drinks from the wine, and then passes it to the parents. The coins, which are believed to be a source of good fortune, are auctioned off. Afterward, the guests then sing celebratory *pizmonim* (liturgical songs) as they move into the room where the meal is being served.

Bar Mitzvah בר מצווה
The Rite of Reaching Manhood

The first turning point in a boy's life is his *bar mitzvah*, signifying the passage from boyhood into manhood. When a boy reaches the age of thirteen, he is no longer a minor and is thus fully obligated to observe the laws of Judaism.

This momentous transition is marked by calling the boy up to the Torah (an *aliyah*). After many weeks of practicing for this moment, the boy ascends to read a portion of Torah before the congregation. This reading is performed anytime the Torah is read, which includes Monday, Thursday, the Sabbath, Rosh Hodesh (the first of the month), the middle days of Passover and Sukkot, and during Hanukkah.

Weekday *bar mitzvah* readings are usually followed by a breakfast in honor of the newly minted man. Often, the *bar mitzvah* honoree gives a speech on a topic in Jewish law or ethics relating to the weekly Torah portion. The thrust of the speech is the young man's recognition that he is now responsible for his deeds and realizes they impact not only him and his family but the entire Jewish nation. The boy also expresses gratitude to his parents, extended family, and teachers. When the boy reads the Torah on the Sabbath, a *sebbit* (festive Sabbath luncheon) is usually held afterward. Most families hold a weekday reading for family and friends and a Sabbath reading for fellow members of their synagogue.

Another major part of turning thirteen is the obligation to don *tefillin*, the phylacteries that are worn by a Jewish man during weekday morning prayers. The binding of the *tefillin* is a lifelong obligation binding the boy to G-d. *Tefillin* consist of two small leather boxes through which thin, long strips of black leather are woven. The *tefillin* are worn on the head and the weaker arm. They contain portions of the Torah handwritten on small pieces of parchment by expert scribes. Aleppian Jews take the purchase of *tefillin* seriously and order the highest quality

David Hedaya at his bar mitzvah, *1950 (courtesy of Sephardic Community Center Archives)*

made by the finest craftsmen and scribes in Israel. When the boy reads his Torah portion on a weekday, he dons *tefillin* for the first time, which is a moment of great pride, promise, and hope for his father and other male relatives.

The bar mitzvah: *father and son*

Torah cases

Aleppian Jewish Marriage Festivities
חגיגות נישואים יהודיות בחאלב

In the Aleppian Jewish community, the acceptance of a man's proposal of marriage by his beloved triggers a cascade of events unrivaled in the Jewish life-cycle. Beginning with the night of the proposal and concluding with seven nights of banquets after the wedding ceremony, these are among the most festive occasions in Aleppian Jewish culture.

THE MEETING OF THE FAMILY

Formally known as the *kinyan* (Hebrew for the formal execution of an agreement), this event takes place at the home of the bride-to-be's family after the couple's engagement is announced. This rather small gathering attended by the relatives of the engaged couple is their first chance to meet and welcome one another into their respective families. The minute a guest sees any of the parents of the engaged couple, he or she says, *"Mabruk!"* (Arabic for "congratulations"). The celebrating parent responds with *"Abalek,"* an expression that means "wishing you the same good fortune for your children." If the guest does not have any unmarried children, the proper response is *"abal il zghy'reen,"* meaning "May the same happen for your grandchildren."

The girl's family usually prepares an array of dishes and sweets for the event, such as several *maza* salads, *kibbeh nabelsieh* (Golden Ground Meat–Filled Bulgur Shells, page 53), *laham b'ajeen* (Miniature Tamarind Minced Meat Pies, page 50), *ka'ak bi'loz* (Almond Cookie Wreaths, page 263), and a few *helous* (candied fruits). *Shrab al loz* (Sweet Almond Milk, page 312) is served, too.

It is customary for the couple's relatives to send over a large bouquet of white flowers in honor of the occasion. These flowers beautify the house and elevate the occasion. To enliven the atmosphere in which the guests fete the newlyweds-to-be, the family hires a group of musicians to play a *nobeh,* which is a concert of Arabic music.

THE *SWANEE* AND THE *MIKVEH*

A special reception takes place to honor the day that the bride goes to the *mikveh* (Jewish ritual bath) for the mandatory ablutions preceding a Jewish woman's wedding. The *mikveh* also serves as an introduction to the laws of family purity and is one of three *mitzvot* that a married woman must fulfill (the others are separating a piece of her bread dough and lighting Sabbath candles).

The bride-to-be is accompanied to the *mikveh* by her close female relatives and friends. After emerging from the bath, she is greeted with a round of ululations (*zaghloot* in Arabic), which are a common expression of joy sounded by women in the Arab world on happy occasions. A tray of sweets and *'ahweh* (Arabic Coffee, page 318) are sometimes served.

Before the *mikveh* ceremony, a more formal reception, called a *swanee,* is attended by a wider circle of women close to the couple's families. The word *swanee* is derived from the Arabic word for "trays" or "platters," and is a reference to the trays of gifts purchased by the young woman's fiancé and brought to the reception by his mother. One of the significant gifts is a purse that holds a silver coin that is used to pay for the *mikveh.* Other bridal gifts include lingerie, fine soaps, perfume, pearls, and other finery. At the *swanee* the trays of gifts are set upon a long table to be presented to the bride. This elegant display is the centerpiece of the event. A large array of sweets and pastries are served along with *shrab al loz* (Sweet Almond Milk, page 312), a highly regarded symbol of fertility among Aleppian Jews.

In the days of old Aleppo, the event was known as the *hamman al aroos* (Arabic for "the bride's bath"). It was a lavish party held in a bathhouse early in the evening. Women would take over the baths and sing, dance, and ululate, festooning the bride-to-be with *labas* (Candy-Coated Almonds, page 303), sweets, and jewelry as well as a small sachet of *beyloun b'ward,* a rose-scented clay that was used to cleanse one's hair in the days before liquid shampoo.

HONORING THE GROOM
ALIYAH AND THE *SEBBIT*

On the Sabbath before the wedding, the groom attends his synagogue in the company of his father, future father-in-law, and close friends. The young man is called to the Torah for an *aliyah* on this occasion. At that moment, the *me'saader* (synagogue ritual manager) proclaims *"Arus!"* and the congregation spontaneously begins to sing the appropriate *pizmon* in honor of the groom. After he steps down from the Torah, children distribute rose water to the congregants so that they can bless the fragrance in his honor. Often, a few men from each of the couple's families are then called to Torah. After prayers, the groom's family hosts a *sebbit* (festive Sabbath luncheon) for family and often the entire congregation.

Antique brush set (gift for bride given at the traditional swanee, *page 362)*

Sam Haber and Nizha (Dweck), Aleppo, Syria, 1890 (courtesy of Sephardic Community Center Archives)

S. R.

Mʳ & Mᵐᵉ Jacob Hazan

Mʳ Helfon Chalom

ont l'honneur de vous faire part du

mariage de leurs enfants

Mᵉˡˡᵉ Sophie

avec

Mʳ Raphaël

et vous prient de vouloir bien assister à la Bénédiction
Nuptiale qui leur sera donnée le Jeudi 1ᵉʳ Octobre 1925
à 4 h. p. m. à la maison de Mʳ Jacob Hazan à Djémilié

Alep, le 17 Septembre 1925

Abdo and Gitta Sultan signing the ketubah *(Jewish marriage contract), 1946*
(courtesy of Sephardic Community Center Archives)

Wedding invitation, Aleppo, Syria, 1925
(courtesy of Renee Hazan)

THE WEDDING
ERES

On the day of the wedding and throughout the following week, the bride and groom are likened to a queen and king. In fact, these titles can be applied to them throughout their marriage, as long as husband and wife treat each other as such. The wedding day is customarily spent in prayer, with repentance for past sins and hopeful entreaties to G-d for a bright future as the couple embark upon their new life together.

The wedding of one's child is one of the most anticipated and joyous moments in the lives of Aleppian Jewish parents. The first order of business at the wedding is the execution of the *ketubah* (Jewish marriage contract). The fathers of the bride and groom finalize the terms of the marriage with the mediation of a rabbi. The bride and groom both sign, as do two witnesses. The groom is then asked by the rabbi to produce a white handkerchief. He then asks the groom, "Do you accept upon yourself all the obligations to your bride as you indicated by your signature in the *ketubah* before two witnesses and in the amount of $55.18?" The groom answers in the affirmative, officially closing the contract, as it were.

After the *ketubah* is executed, the couple's marriage must be consecrated by a rabbi. The guests, numbering anywhere from four hundred to one thousand, stream into the main hall of a synagogue or large banquet room. With all eyes focused on the couple, the groom escorts his bride under a canopy called the *chuppah,* where the rabbi and members of the immediate family are standing in wait. Blessings are made over wine to satisfy the needs of the body and the fragrant herbs or rose water to enliven the soul. The third blessing is the long wedding blessing. The couple then sips from the wine. Usually, rabbis familiar with each family say a few words about the special characteristics of the bride and groom and wish them *bayit ne'eman*, a home that is devoted to Torah and *mitzvot*.

Jews have a ceremony in which the groom presents a silver coin, not as a gift but as an act of acquisition. The coin is inspected by the rabbi, and then the groom recites the words *harei aat me'kudeshet li be'kaspat hadein k'dat Moshe ve Yisrael*, meaning "Behold, you are sanctified to me with the silver of this coin according to laws of Moses and Israel." He then hands the silver coin to his bride, and the witnesses joyously proclaim *"Mekudeshet!"* ("She's married!").

A *tallit* (prayer shawl) is held over the bride and groom by their fathers. Seven special wedding blessings are recited by rabbis and distinguished relatives. The bride and groom then partake of wine, and the sacred priestly blessing of the *kohanim* is said by those standing under the *chuppah.* In commemoration of the Second Temple of Jerusalem that was destroyed in 69 CE, the groom closes the ceremony by declaring in Hebrew, "If I forget you, O Jerusalem, let my right hand forget her cunning" (Psalm 137:5), and exultantly stomps on a glass.

The guests break into song and applause, and the newlyweds are accompanied by their jubilant friends to a bridal suite. The bride and groom retire to their suite for a short time, while their guests begin the lavish wedding meal, which often lasts all night and into the wee hours of the morning.

It is common for Aleppian Jews to hold weddings in the month of Elul (typically August or September). The month is an acronym for the phrase *ani le'dodi ve'dodi li* (Song of Songs 6:3), which means, "I am my beloved's and my beloved is mine." Some say that another reason for the popularity of an Elul wedding is that the *chuppah* ceremony confers complete forgiveness to the married couple, which is the best state of being for the High Holy Days of Rosh Hashanah and Yom Kippur that soon follow the end of Elul.

Aleppian Jewish brides sometimes observe an old custom called *kepse.* This custom provides that a woman should not attend the wedding of a friend if it falls within forty days of her own wedding. It is believed that such attendance may cause a delay in the impending pregnancies of the bride and her friend. A related custom dictates that Aleppian Jewish women should not attend the weddings of their friends until forty days after they give birth to a child.

SHEVA BERAKHOT

After the wedding, many newlyweds observe *Sheva Berakhot,* seven days of rejoicing (literally, "seven blessings"). Each night, the bride and groom are guests of honor in the home of a family member or a close friend. A large menu is prepared for the guests. *Pizmonim* of many musical styles are sung in honor of the new couple, and at least one of the guests gives a speech, interweaving Jewish ethical concepts with special praise for the wonderful couple.

Hanukkat HaBayit חנוכת הבית
Dedicating a New Home

A tremendous milestone in the life of any family is moving into a new home. Because home is the site of so many important customs and holiday feasts, Aleppian Jews regard the dedication of a new home with great reverence.

Generally, Judaism prescribes that the owner of a new home nail a *mezuzah* (a case enclosing a sacred parchment) on each doorpost in the house within thirty days of moving in. The homeowner recites blessings that seek the removal of evil spirits and the introduction of holiness into the home.

In addition, Aleppian Jews keep certain symbolic items in their new homes and places of business. Among the items used for this custom are the following:

A HOLY BOOK: For example, a *siddur* (prayer book), the Five Books of Moses, or the Book of Psalms. These items recognize that the foundation of a Jewish home and of one's business activities should be built and sustained on the holy teachings of the Torah.

NIGELLA SEEDS (*HEB AL BEREKEH*): The name of these seeds, which are used in *jibneh shelal* (Twisted White String Cheese with Nigella Seeds, page 236), is similar to the word *beraka*, or "blessing." They symbolize abundance and good fortune.

OLIVE OIL: A sign of purity and light. The olive is a symbol of domestic stability because it lasts a long time and is an omen for a long life.

Rabbis from Aleppo, Syria (courtesy of Rabbi Ephriam Levy, Jerusalem)

YEAST: A symbol of fertility; it is an omen that a couple will be blessed with many children who will continue in the right path and perform good deeds.

SALT: This mineral is prized for its enduring qualities and is an omen for a long life. Salt is said to be a necessary part of every meal because it takes the place of the sacred blood offered during the sacrifices performed at the Jewish Temple. The Talmud likens salt to the Torah because, just as the world cannot exist without salt, the world cannot endure without the Torah.

Aleppian Jews prefer to move into their home on a Tuesday or a Thursday. The Book of Genesis describes these days as "good," and Tuesday doubly so. On Wednesday, the moonlight is thought to be at its weakest, which is not a desirable sign.

When a home is ready for dedication, a small portion of it is left unfinished as a somber reminder that the Jewish Temple, the spiritual home of the Jewish people, is no longer standing. Also, it is customary to hang a print of the text of Psalm 67 formed into the shape of a *menorah*, the seven-branched candelabra that stood in the Jewish Temple; this is a reminder that a home should be a light unto its community, just as the light of the *menorah* in the Jewish Temple illuminated the world.

Kaparot, which is a ritual of Yom Kippur (page 354), is also practiced in honor of a new home. This mystical and ancient custom is performed by sponsoring the slaughtering of a chicken as a substitute punishment for the sins one committed during the year. The *kaparot* ritual is performed on the lawn of the new home. A live chicken is swung over the sponsor's head and a prayer is recited. The chicken is then slaughtered.

The Rites of Mourning טקסי אבלות

The Syrian community maintains its own sacred burial society known as *hevra rodfeh zedek*. This group of volunteers takes care of all the arrangements relating to the preparation of the deceased, the funeral service, and the burial, as well as arrangements for the house of mourning, where the family of the deceased will sit for seven days and receive those who want to offer condolences.

Jewish law mandates a prompt burial. Therefore, the funeral takes place during the first morning after death. At the funeral, rabbis and relatives of the deceased eulogize the departed. The funeral is a time of deep sadness for all involved, and it is an important obligation among Aleppian Jews to attend and comfort the mourners.

As soon as members of the deceased's family return to the house of mourning, the rabbi enacts *kriah*, tearing the mourner's shirt. The mourner then recites the blessing *barukh dayan ha'emet* ("blessed is the True Judge"). A meal of condolence (*seudat havra'ah*) then follows. Peeled hard-boiled eggs and Syrian flatbread are handed to the mourners. A large candle is then lit and left to burn until it extinguishes itself, usually a week later.

Food plays an important role during the somber seven-day mourning period known as *shibah* (Hebrew for "seven"). The meals, at which family and friends of the deceased assemble, feature symbolic round foods such as hard-boiled eggs, chickpeas, olives, and *ka'ak* (Savory Anise-Seed Rings, page 22). Round foods help remind the mourners that life is cyclical and death is a phase in G-d's plan for each individual. Food is plentiful at mourning houses for more than reasons of comfort: it encourages visitors to recite blessings over the food, which elevate the soul of the deceased, aiding it to reach the World to Come.

In the mourning house, the mourners sit on the floor on thin pillows. Mirrors are covered and the mourners are prohibited from performing any rites of vanity and beautification, such as bathing, shaving, wearing makeup, and donning leather shoes. Males in mourning cannot shave for an entire month.

The mourners' businesses are closed during the mourning week. Throughout the week, some study the *Zohar* (the primary Jewish mystical text), and the *Sefer Tehillim* (the Book of Psalms) is read by visitors to elevate the soul of the deceased.

Among Aleppian Jews, there is a unique custom barring a visitor from paying two visits to the mourners. Thus, if someone makes a second visit but cannot return at a later date for a third one, he exits the house and reenters for a few moments for a third visit. This custom stems from the kabbalistic notion that any action done in pairs or even numbers may cause metaphysical damage to one's soul. The rationale behind this concept is that G-d is one and all-powerful, and anything that doesn't reduce back to the number one represents heresy and a disbelief in G-d's omnipotence and oneness. Though scholars posit that this principle doesn't apply to the performance of good deeds, one can surmise that the Aleppian custom is an extracautious, compassionate measure designed to avoid bringing any additional and undue misfortune on the house of an already beleaguered mourner. As visitors exit the mourning house, they say to the mourners, in Hebrew, "May you be comforted from heaven."

On the Sabbath of the mourning week, the male mourners change into Shabbat clothes and attend their synagogue. During prayers they sit in the back row, far from their usual seats. It is customary for other congregants to sit beside the mourners to comfort them.

After the mourning period, the deceased is further eulogized in a ceremony called the *arayat*. It usually takes place seven days, thirty days, and eleven months after the death of the deceased. The ceremony begins with a reading from the *Sefer Tehillim* by rabbis and members of the family and is followed by a series of eulogies by family members in which the good character and contributions of the departed are expressed through fondly recalled anecdotes. Following the speeches, a reception is held for all the attendees. Fruit, nuts, *ka'ak* (Savory Anise-Seed Rings, page 22), an array of pastries such as *sambousak* (Buttery Cheese-Filled Sesame Pastries, page 212) and *spanekh b'jibn* (Spinach-Cheese Frittata, page 224), and sweets such as *baklawa* (Pistachio *Filla* Wedges in Rose Water Syrup, page 251) and *kanafe* (Ricotta-Filled Shredded Wheat Pastry, page 255) are served so guests can bless the food and further elevate the soul of the deceased.

For eleven months following the death of a loved one, male mourners recite the *kaddish* (prayers of praise) during the three daily prayers. During this eleven-month period and for part of the twelfth month, the mourners do not attend joyous occasions or other forms of entertainment. On the anniversary of the death of the deceased, the mourner lights a memorial candle. Male mourners recite the *kaddish* on this day and, on the previous Sabbath, were called to the Torah in memory of the departed.

CLOSING NOTE

The delightful cuisine of Aleppian Jews is just one example of our community's deep passion and love of life. While we adore holding celebrations and attending festivities, we also accept the difficulties that life brings, knowing that we have the support of our families and fellow community members to get us through these hardships. This outlook is the bedrock of the Aleppian Jewish community, informed by our strict observance of the traditional ways of Judaism and the high value we place on charity and good deeds, an ethic passed down over the centuries and developed by the vaunted scholars and rabbis of Aleppo who preceded us.

We Aleppian Jews also embrace the structure of the Jewish holidays that give our lives shape and significance. Our precisely timed life-cycle experiences and our enduring and unique customs are what make the Aleppian Jewish community so special and spiritual. In this book, I have aimed to celebrate the full expression of this community's soul, which is a blessing to experience and a joy to share.

المصطلحات
CULINARY GLOSSARY

Acidulated water—Lemon juice combined with water, used to prevent discoloring of fruits and vegetables such as artichokes.

Aleppo pepper—A chile pepper of moderate heat (10,000 Scoville units) grown in northern Syria. Usually sold as a powder (see page 44).

Allspice—Redolent of nutmeg, clove, juniper berries, black pepper, and cinnamon, allspice is derived from a single source: the dried berries of a myrtle tree grown in the Caribbean (*Pimenta dioica*). Known in Arabic as *bahar*.

Alya—(Arabic) Fat from the fat-tailed species of lamb common to the Levant. Used as a cooking fat in non-kosher Syrian recipes.

Asal b'tehnieh—(Arabic) Breakfast dish of honey with *tehineh* (sesame paste).

Baboonge—Arabic term for chamomile. Used in infusions.

Bulgur—Cracked wheat, produced by parboiling, drying, and cracking hard wheat kernels. Sold in coarse, medium, and fine grades.

Cardamom—Native to South Asia, this spice is composed of the seeds of the herb *Elettaria cardamomum*. A member of the ginger family, notable for its spicy warm flavor that also has trace notes of eucalyptus, it is the third most expensive spice after saffron and vanilla. In Arabic cookery, it is used to flavor coffee.

Cheesecloth—A light, fine-mesh gauze used to strain liquids or wring moisture from a solid.

Cilantro—Also known as coriander, an herb related to parsley and indigeous to southern Europe and the Mediterranean.

Citron—Indigenous to northeast India, an exceptionally fragrant citrus fruit, mainly composed of inedible rind and rather dry inner flesh. Loosely resembles a lemon but is larger and bumpy, with a small rounded stem (*pitom* in Hebrew). Used ritually during the festival of Sukkot; known as *etrog* in Hebrew.

Coriander seed—A strong, assertive spice whose aroma resembles cumin, it is often ground with garlic into a paste in Aleppian Jewish recipes.

Cumin—A pungent spice with a nutty flavor and aroma. In Syrian cookery, it is often combined with lemon juice to dress salads.

Curd cheese—Soft cheese made from unfermented curds.

Dried eggplant skin—A product found primarily in the Middle East and Turkey, which is plumped and then stuffed (see *s'fiha,* Stuffed Baby Eggplant with Ground Meat and Rice, page 138).

Endoring—The practice developed by Turkish and Arab court cooks of dying foods for lavish presentation. Red, green, and gold are common endoring hues.

Filbert—Common name for the cultivated species of hazelnut, the hard-shelled fruit of the hazel tree, and a member of the *Corylus* genus.

Filla (**also known as phyllo and filo**)—*Filla* is an extremely thin and delicate puff pastry dough that was invented in Istanbul by Ottoman-era bakers.

Flanken—A Yiddish butcher's term, referring to part of the chuck cut taken from the short ribs of beef.

Grape leaves—The leaves of a grapevine, clipped and brined, and usually stuffed with rice or *hashu* in recipes such as *yebra* (Grape Leaves Stuffed with Ground Meat and Rice, with Apricot-Tamarind Sauce, see page 150). Available brined in jars in Middle Eastern and gourmet grocers.

Hashu—Spiced meat and rice mixture used in many Aleppian Jewish meat dishes, especially stuffed vegetable recipes (*mehshi*).

Kanafe—Unprocessed shredded wheat used most notably in a cheese-filled pastry of the same name (see page 255).

Khatmiyah—(Arabic) A flower similar to hibiscus; used in infusions.

Laban tasa—Literally, "fresh yogurt" in Arabic, an expression called out by local dairy merchants in old Aleppo.

Mahlab—Pulverized pit of the St. Lucie's or black sour cherry; used primarily to lend an herbal note to *ka'ak* (Savory Anise-Seed Rings, see page 22) and other Middle Eastern bakery goods.

Marjoram—An herb with numerous species and subspecies, it generally has pale green leaves and a delicate, sweet flavor. Most often compared to oregano.

Mastic—Clear, aromatic resin from the plant *Pistacia lentiscus,* which is grown throughout the Mediterranean. Used as a jelling agent in Middle Eastern sweets.

Ma'vdeh—(Arabic) A squash corer; used to hollow out vegetables for *mehshi* recipes.

Mehshi—Arabic cookery term for stuffed vegetable or meat recipes.

Nasib—Literally, "fate" or "destiny" (Arabic). Refers to finding one's soul mate as well as the perfect job or house.

Nigella seed—Indigenous to the Levant, the roughly shaped seeds of the plant *Nigella sativa* are jet black with a matte finish. The pungent flavor is used in baked goods such as *ka'ak* (Savory Anise-Seed Rings, see page 22). Also misleadingly known as black onion or caraway seeds.

Okra—Commonly grown in tropical climes, this horn-shaped vegetable is extremely popular in the Eastern Mediterranean and Middle East, where it is much smaller and more flavorful than varieties grown in the West. Its most recognizable characteristic is the glutinous substance that fills the inner cavity. Soaking okra in acidulated water before cooking will lessen its glutinous texture.

Orange blossom water—(*Mazaher* in Arabic) Liquid flavoring agent distilled from the fragrant blossoms of Seville oranges.

Ou—Tamarind concentrate. Redolent of apricots and dates, it imparts a tangy-sour flavor to stews and sauces.

Pine nut—The fruit of the stone pine (*Pinus pinea*), the sweet, rich meat of these costly nuts is toasted and used to flavor Aleppian Jewish rice dishes. A cheaper variety is grown in China but not recommended.

Pistachio—Indigenous to Eastern Mediterranean, the Levant, and Central Asia, the fruit of the tree *Pistacia vera* is adored in the Middle East. The variety native to Aleppo is highly regarded and the source of the Arabic appellation for the nut, *fistou halabi.* Appears in many Aleppian Jewish sweets and adorns rice dishes.

Pomegranate—The bulbous red fruit of the small evergreen tree, native to Persia. Its interior is composed of a yellowish membrane that surrounds numerous rubylike seeds, which yield a tart and refreshing juice.

Quince—A yellow-skinned fruit that looks and tastes like a cross between an apple and a pear. Turns an attractive red-orange when cooked into a preserve or sweetmeat.

Qoss'ayn—(Arabic) An herb similar to wild thyme; used in infusions.

Rose water—(*Ma Wared* in Arabic) A liquid flavoring distilled from rose petals. It is used to flavor Middle Eastern sweets.

Saffron—The world's most expensive spice, it is composed of the threadlike red stigmas of the *Crocus sativus* plant. In Middle Eastern cuisines, it is used in minuscule quantities to impart a pleasant floral aroma and golden hue to rice dishes.

Samna—(Arabic) Clarified butter.

continued

Semolina—Native to the Mediterranean and known in Arabic as *smead,* it is a flour derived from hard durum wheat. Retains a granular texture during cooking and is used as a thickener in Aleppian Jewish sweets.

Shoshat al-darrah—(Arabic) Corn silk; used in infusions.

Sumac—Grown throughout the Middle East, composed of the ground dried berries of the sumac shrub (*Rhus coriaria*). Purple and sour, it is used to season fish and in *za'atar* spice blends.

Sweetbreads—The thymus glands of a veal, calf, or lamb. Often delicately fried. Kosher varieties are expensive and difficult to obtain.

Swiss chard—Leafy green with large, crinkled leaves and thick stems, both of which are edible. One of the symbolic foods eaten during the festival of Rosh Hashanah.

Taa'—(Arabic) Cattle intestines ; used as a natural sausage casing.

Tahini—Sesame seed paste. Main ingredient in *tehineh* (Sesame Spread, page 26).

Tamarind—Known in Arabic as *tamr hindi* (literally, "Indian date"), the fruit contained in the hearty pod of the *Tamarindus indica* tree, which is native to tropical Africa. Principal component of *ou^c* (page 41).

Trumpet gourd—Long and tubular in appearance, the vegetable is edible only while young. As it matures and dries out, its shell becomes extremely hard.

Ward—(Arabic) Rose ; in Syria, dried rose petals are used in infusions.

Za'atar—Arabic name for the hyssop plant. It generally refers to a spice blend composed of hyssop or thyme, toasted sesame seeds, sumac, salt, and marjoram. Used with oil to flavor Ordinary Syrian Flatbread (*khubz 'adi,* see page 18) and in salad, poultry, and fish dishes.

Zibbeh—(Arabic) Butter .

المصطلحات

GLOSSARY OF FOREIGN WORDS AND EXPRESSIONS

Abal'ak—"May your children be blessed with the same fortune" (Arabic); said in response to *Mabruk* ("Congratulations") by the host of marriage-related festivities to a person who has at least one unmarried child.

Abal'ak il zghy'reen—"May the same fortune be bestowed upon your grandchildren" (Arabic); said in response to *Mabruk* ("Congratulations") by the host of marriage-related festivities to a person whose children are married and has unmarried grandchildren.

Adi zaman al-batinjan—Egyptian saying used when someone contradicts himself; literally, "It's eggplant time" (Arabic). Harks back to an age when the eggplant was regarded with suspicion.

Afikoman—(Hebrew) A portion of unleavened bread (*matzah*) eaten after the Passover *seder* meal.

Af'wen—"You're welcome" (Arabic); said in response to *Shuk'ren,* or "Thank you."

Ahlan wa sahlan—An Arabic greeting expressing warmth and hospitality. Often truncated to *"ahlan."*

Al-jazira al-hadra—Literally, the "green island" (Arabic). Name given to the Iberian peninsula by Arab conquerors in 711 CE.

Ani le'dodi ve'dodi li—"I am my beloved's and my beloved is mine" (Hebrew; Song of Songs 6:3).

Aram Soba—(Hebrew) The biblical name for Aleppo; still used in Jewish communal circles to refer to Aleppian Jewish traditions and customs.

Aravot—(Hebrew) Willows used during the festival of Sukkot in combination with the *lulav* (palm frond), *etrog* (citron),

and *hadasim* (myrtle) in a daily ritual called *hoshannot.*

Assabih—(Arabic) Literally, "fingers"; descriptive term for certain finger-shaped sweets.

Barukh dayan ha'emet—"Blessed is the True Judge" (Hebrew); saying recited during the traditional seven-day mourning period.

Beyloun b'ward—(Arabic) A rose-scented clay.

Conversos—(Spanish) Jews who converted to Christianity in response to the Spanish Inquisition.

Cuscusu—Literally, "minced into small pieces" (Arabic); source of the word *couscous.*

Daled—The fourth letter of the Hebrew alphabet. It is an Aleppian Jewish custom to break a portion of *matzah* into the shape of a *daled* and a *vav* and use one for the *afikoman.*

Dara'bukkah—(Arabic) Lap drum.

Fadal'u—(Arabic) "Welcome."

Franj (or *Francos*)—(Arabic) Name given to a group of Jews who arrived in Aleppo from Italy in the sixteenth century and lived in the city as citizens under French protection.

Furn—(Arabic) Communal ovens commonly used in nineteenth-century Aleppo.

Genizah—(Hebrew) A repository for worn-out sacred books and writings.

Hadasim—(Hebrew) Myrtle leaves used in *hoshannot* ritual during the festival of Sukkot (see entry for *aravot*).

continued

Haggadah—Literally, the "narrative" (Hebrew); the title of the book from which Passover *seder* participants recite passages concerning the Israelites' exodus from Egyptian bondage.

Hakhnasat orkhim—Literally, "receiving guests" (Hebrew); refers to the Jewish precept encouraging hospitality.

Haleb—Arabic name for Aleppo; means "milk" or "he milked," referring to the ancient legend of Abraham's passage through the city, during which he fed the poor with the milk from his goats on the city's slopes.

Hametz—(Hebrew) Term encompassing all leavened foods that are forbidden during Passover.

Hamman il-aroos—Literally, the "bride's bath" (Arabic); a pre-wedding ritual among Aleppian Jews.

Harei aat me'kudeshet li be'kaspat hadein k'dat Moshe ve Yisrael—Hebrew phrase meaning, "Behold, you are sanctified to me with the silver of this coin according to laws of Moses and Israel." Said by the groom to his bride during the Jewish wedding ceremony.

Haush—(Arabic) Structure traditionally found in old Aleppo, with multiple residential dwellings surrounding an inner courtyard.

Hefle—(Arabic) Party.

Hevra rodfeh zedek—(Hebrew) Sacred burial society of the Aleppian Jewish community.

Insh'allah—"May it be G-d's will" (Arabic).

Juderia—(Spanish) Jewish enclaves in pre-Inquisition Spain.

Kaddish—A prayer of praise said several times during each of the three daily prayers; mourners are obligated to say a specific *kaddish* during each prayer.

Kaparot—Repentance ceremony involving the slaughtering of chickens as a sacrifice in place of oneself; derived from the Hebrew word for "to forgive."

Karet—(Hebrew) Literally, "to banish"; a religious term describing excommunication, one of the strictest forms of punishment in Temple-era Judaism.

Karpas—The rite of the Passover *seder* during which celery is dipped into saltwater to symbolize the tears of the Israelites who labored as slaves in Egypt.

Ke'arah—Literally, "platter" (Hebrew); refers to the traditional platter used during the Passover *seder* that displays the customary foods of the meal.

Kemaya—(Arabic) An amulet containing sacred Jewish writings. The amulet is worn as a pendant and is thought to provide protection, bring about success, and reinforce the wearer's commitment to his or her faith. A scribe writes the enclosed text with pure thoughts and during predetermined beneficient times prescribed by the Kabbalah.

Ken yirbeh—"They shall multiply" (Hebrew), from Exodus 1:12.

Ketubah—(Hebrew) Jewish marriage contract.

Khan—(Arabic) Storehouse attached to a public market.

Kiddushin—(Hebrew) The Jewish marriage ceremony.

Kinyan—(Hebrew) The formal execution of an agreement.

Kuaiseh—Literally, "beautiful" (Arabic).

Likrat Shabbat lechu v'nelcha—"To greet Shabbat, let us go toward it" (Hebrew).

Mabruk—"Congratulations" (Arabic).

Mammon shel berakha—Literally, "blessed money" (Hebrew); refers to monies collected for charity during a life-cycle event.

Maqamat—The system of classical Arabic melodies.

Marranos—(Spanish) Derogatory term used following the commencement of the Spanish Inquisition; for Jews who were outwardly Christian but practiced Judaism in secret.

Maza haza—"What's this?" (Arabic).

Me'saader—(Hebrew) Organizer of synagogue rituals.

Mekudeshet—Literally, "she's consecrated" (Hebrew); celebratory exclamation said upon the completion of a wedding ceremony.

Mezuzah—(Hebrew) A case enclosing a sacred parchment bolted to the right side of each doorpost in a Jewish home or business.

Mohel—(Hebrew) Ritual surgeon who performs the circumcision rite called the *brit milah*.

Mukhabarat—(Arabic) Syria's secret police.

Must'arabia—Literally, "would-be Arabs" (Arabic); refers to Jews who were native to the Arab lands.

Nay—(Arabic) Flute.

Nobeh—(Arabic) A performance of classical Arabic music.

Parokhet—(Hebrew) Ornate slipcover used in the Jewish Temple to separate the Holy of Holies from the rest of the Temple sanctuary; also refers to a curtain that drapes the ark in which a *Sefer Torah* is kept in a synagogue.

Qanun—(Arabic) Zither, a stringed musical instrument.

Sanaiyat Eliyahu HaNabi—(Hebrew) The tray of Elijah the Prophet; used during a *brit milah* (circumcision rite) to collect money for charity.

Sandak—(Hebrew) The person who holds an infant boy as he is ritually circumcised; derived from *syndikos* (Greek for "caretaker").

Sayyid al-khudar—Literally, "lord of the vegetables" (Arabic); colloquial for eggplant.

Sefer Torah—(Hebrew) A parchment scroll inscribed with the text of the Five Books of Moses from which a portion is read every Monday, Thursday, and Sabbath during the morning prayer. Aleppian Jews enclose these scrolls in fanciful wood or metal cases.

Sefirot—(Hebrew) Kabbalistic concept referring to the ten emanations that comprise the qualities of G-d comprehensible to mankind.

Seuda revi'it—Literally, the "fourth meal" (Hebrew); the meal that follows the *havdala* ceremony that formally ends the Sabbath.

Seudat ha'mafseket—(Hebrew) Meal that precedes a fast; generally, refers to the meals before the 25-hour fasts of Yom Kippur and Tisha b'Ab.

Seudat havra'ah—(Hebrew) Meal eaten to commence Judaism's seven-day mourning period (*shibah*).

Shebeh—(Arabic) A cloth-enclosed stone, usually worn as a pendant.

Shekhinah—(Hebrew) G-d's divine presence.

Shibah—Literally, "seven" (Hebrew); the name for Judaism's traditional seven-day mourning period.

Shohet—(Hebrew) A slaughterer trained under Jewish law.

Shuk'ren—"Thank you" (Arabic); precedes *Af'wen*, or "You're welcome."

Sifrah daimeh—Arabic adage, meaning "May your table always be plentiful."

Souq—(Arabic) Public market.

Suffeh—Aleppian Jewish term for a high level of domestic orderliness.

Tambour—Clay oven with a rounded interior cavity used to make *khubz 'adi* (Ordinary Syrian Flatbread, page 18) and other Middle Eastern breads.

Tehillim—(Hebrew) The Book of Psalms.

Temekeh—(Arabic) A tight-lidded tin crisper used to store *ka'ak* (Savory Anise-Seed Rings, page 22).

T'mazza—(Arabic) To savor in little bites.

'Ud—(Arabic) Lute, a stringed musical instrument.

Vav—The sixth letter of the Hebrew alphabet. A portion of the *afikoman* eaten after the Passover *seder* meal is broken to resemble this character (see entries for *afikoman* and *daled*).

Yad Hashem—Literally, "the hand of G-d" (Hebrew); used to describe unexplainable events.

Zeman Simchateinu—Literally, "the time of our rejoicing" (Hebrew).

Zwarh bala azimeh—(Arabic) Unexpected guests.

BIBLIOGRAPHY

المراجع

Abadi, Jennifer Felicia. *A Fistful of Lentils: Syrian-Jewish Recipes from Grandma Fritzie's Kitchen.* Boston: Harvard Common Press, 2002.

Al-Baghdadi (A. J. Arberry, trans.). "Kitab al-Tabikh." In *Medieval Arab Cookery: Papers by Maxime Rodinson and Charles Perry with a Reprint of the Baghdad Cookery Book.* Devon, England: Prospect Books, 2000.

Benjamin of Tudela (Marcus Nathan Adler, trans.). *The Itinerary of Benjamin of Tudela.* Malibu, Calif.: J. Simon, 1983.

Braudel, Fernand. *The Mediterranean and the Mediterranean World in the Age of Philip I.* Berkeley, Calif.: University of California Press, 1996.

Burns, Ross. *Monuments of Syria.* London: I. B. Tauris, 1999.

Catton, Sam. *Men of Faith and Vision: A Personal Recollection.* Brooklyn, N.Y.: Simcha Graphic Associates, 2001.

Chabbott, Linda, and Abraham Chabbott. *The Rose of the Valley: A Compilation of the Laws of Family Purity According to the Sephardic Custom.* Brooklyn, N.Y.: Sephardic Legacy Press, 1996.

Congregation Shaare Rahamim. *Halachot and History of Shabuot with Azharot.* Brooklyn, N.Y.: Congregation Shaare Rahamim.

———. *The Shaare Rahamim Hanukah Booklet.* Brooklyn, N.Y.: Congregation Shaare Rahamim.

———. 2002. *The Shaare Rahamim Haggadah.* Brooklyn, N.Y.: Congregation Shaare Rahamim.

Davidson, Alan (ed.). *The Oxford Companion to Food.* Oxford, England: Oxford University Press, 1999.

Davis, (Rabbi) Avrohom. *The Metsudah Tehillim.* Brooklyn, N.Y.: 1983.

Dayan, Rae. *For the Love of Cooking.* Southfield, Mich.: Targum Press, 2000.

Dobrinsky, (Rabbi) Herbert C. *A Treasury of Sephardic Laws and Customs.* New York: Yeshiva University Press, 1986.

Dolader, Miguel-Angel Motis. "Mediterranean Jewish Diet and Traditions in the Middle Ages." In *Food: A Culinary History* (Flandrin, Jean-Louis, ed.): 224–46. New York: Penguin, 2000.

Feuer, (Rabbi) Avrohom Chaim. *Tehillim Treasury.* Brooklyn, N.Y.: Mesorah Publications, Ltd., 1993.

Friedman, Saul S. *Without Future: The Plight of Syrian Jewry.* New York: Praeger, 1989.

Ganzfried, (Rabbi) Solomon (Hyman E. Goldin, LL.B., trans). *Code of Jewish Law: A Compilation of Jewish Laws and Customs.* New York: Hebrew Publishing Company, 1927.

Gitliz, David M., and Linda Kay Davidson. *A Drizzle of Honey: The Lives and Recipes of Spain's Secret Jews.* New York: St. Martin's Press, 1999.

Glezer, Maggie. *A Blessing of Bread: The Many Rich Traditions of Jewish Bread Baking Around the World.* New York: Artisan, 2004.

Goitein, S. D. *Jews and Arabs: Their Contacts Through the Ages.* New York: Schocken, 1974.

———. *A Mediterranean Society: The Jewish Communities of the Arab World as Portrayed in the Documents of the Cairo Geniza.* Berkeley, Calif.: University of California Press, 1967–1973.

Goldstein, Joyce. *Sephardic Flavors: Jewish Cooking of the Mediterranean.* San Francisco: Chronicle Books, 2000.

Hai, Ben Ish. *Entering the Orchard.* Jerusalem: Feldheim Publishers, 2004.

———. *Walking in His Ways.* Jerusalem: Feldheim Publishers, 2005.

Helou, Annisa. *Lebanese Cuisine.* New York: St. Martin's Griffin, 1998.

Heschel, Abraham Joshua (Joachim Neugroschel, trans.). *Maimonides: A Biography.* New York: Farrar Straus Giroux, 1982.

Israel Museum. *Treasures of the Aleppo Community.* Jerusalem: Israel Museum, 1988.

Khayat, Marie Karam, and Margaret Clark Keatinge. *Food from the Arab World.* Beirut: Khayats, 1959.

Khoury, Philip S. *Syria and the French Mandate: The Politics of Arab Nationalism, 1920–1945.* Princeton, N.J.: Princeton University Press, 1987.

Kiple, Kenneth F., and Kriemhild Coneè Ornelas (eds.). *The Cambridge World History of Food.* Cambridge, England: Cambridge University Press, 2000.

Kitov, Eliyahu (Nachman Bulman, trans.). *The Book of Our Heritage: The Jewish Year and Its Days of Significance.* Jerusalem: Feldheim Publishers, (1968): 1.–3.

Luzzatto, Moshe Chayim. *Mesillat Yesharim: The Path of the Just.* Translated by Shraga Silverstein. Jerusalem and New York: Feldheim Publishers, 1996.

MacFarquhar, Neil. "Beneath Desert Sands, an Eden of Truffles." *New York Times,* April 14, 2004: F4.

Mann, Vivian B., Tjomas F. Glick, and Jerrilyn D. Dodds (eds.). *Convivencia: Jews, Muslims, and Christians in Medieval Spain.* New York: G. Braziller/Jewish Museum, 1992.

Marcus, Abraham. *The Middle East on the Eve of Modernity: Aleppo in the Eighteenth-Century.* New York: Columbia University Press, 1989.

Marks, Gil. *Olive Trees and Honey: A Treasury of Vegetarian Recipes from Jewish Communities Around the World.* Hoboken, N.J.: Wiley, 2005.

———. *The World of Jewish Cooking.* New York: Fireside Simon & Schuster, 1996.

Meyerson, Mark D. *A Jewish Renaissance in Fifteenth-Century Spain.* Princeton, N.J.: Princeton University Press, 2004.

Miller, (Rabbi) Yisroel. *Guardian of Eden.* Jerusalem and Spring Valley, N.Y.: Feldheim Publishers, 1984.

Mizrahi, Max. *Syrian Cooking in America.* Staten Island, N.Y.: Mearer Associates, Inc., 1995.

Montagu, Lady Mary Wortley. "To the Abbé Conti, May 17, 1717." In *The Norton Book of Travel,* (Paul Fussell, ed.): 142–47. New York: Norton, 1987.

Nasser, Joëlle, and Michelle Nasser. *The Cooking of Eveline Nasser: A Love Story in 72 Recipes.* São Paulo: Dados Internacionais de Catalogação na Publicação, 2000.

Nathan, Joan. "The Legacy of Egyptian Rose, In Time for Passover." *New York Times,* March 20, 2002: F5.

———. "Rosh Hashanah Means Sugar, Spice for Syrians." *Milwaukee Journal-Sentinel,* September 4, 2002. www.jsonline.com/story/index.aspx?id=71324.

Neuman, Abraham A. *Jews in Spain.* Philadelphia: Jewish Publication Society, 1942.

Perry, Charles (trans.). *A Baghdad Cookery Book: The Book of Dishes (Kitab al-Tabikh).* Devon, England: Prospect Books, 2005.

Perry, Charles. "Kitab Al-Tibakhah: A Fifteenth Century Cookbook." *Petits Propos Culinaire* 21 (1985): 17.

———. "The Oldest Mediterranean Noodle: A Cautionary Tale." *Petits Propos Culinaire* 9 (1981): 42.

Pinchasi, Shemuel. *Chaim Va'Chessed: Laws and Customs for the House of Mourning.* Jerusalem: Machon Imrei Shefer, 5761.

Roden, Claudia. *The New Book of Middle Eastern Food.* New York: Knopf, 2000.

——. *The Book of Jewish Food: An Odyssey from Samarkand to New York.* New York: Knopf, 1996.

——. "Early Arab Cooking and Cookery Manuscripts." *Petits Propos Culinaire* 6 (1980): 16.

——. "Tabbouleh! Tabbouleh! Tabbouleh!" *Petits Propos Culinaire* 2 (1979): 61.

Rodinson, Maxime (Barbara Yeomans, trans.). "Recherches sur les documents Arabes relatifs a la cuisine." In *Medieval Arab Cookery: Papers by Maxime Rodinson & Charles Perry with a Reprint of the Baghdad Cookery Book.* Devon, England: Prospect Books, 2000.

—— (Barbara Inskip, trans.). "Ma'muniya East and West." *Petits Propos Culinaire* 33 (1989): 15.

Rosenberger, Bernard. "Arab Cuisine and Its Contribution to European Culture." In *Food: A Culinary History* (Flandrin, Jean-Louis, ed.): 207–23. New York: Penguin, 2000.

Sabato, Haim (Philip Simpson, trans). *Aleppo Tales.* New Milford, Conn.: Toby Press, 2004.

Sasson, Grace. *Kosher Syrian Cooking.* RGD Publishing, place unknown, 1970.

Scherman, (Rabbi) Nosson, and (Rabbi) Meir Zlotowitz. *Woman to Woman: Practical Advice and Classic Stories on Life's Goals and Aspirations.* Brooklyn, N.Y.: Mesorah Publications, Ltd., 1996.

The Sephardic Heritage Foundation (Rabbi Shimon H. Alouf and Sam Catton, eds.). *The Kiddush Book for Sabbath and Holidays.* Brooklyn, N.Y.: Sephardic Heritage Foundation, 1989.

The Sephardic Women's Organization of the Jersey Shore (Poopa Dweck, ed.). *Deal Delights.* Deal, N.J.: The Sephardic Women's Organization of the Jersey Shore, 1976.

Sternberg, (Rabbi) Robert. *The Sephardic Kitchen: The Healthful Food and Rich Culture of the Mediterranean Jews.* New York: HarperCollins, 1996.

Stillman, Norman A. *The Jews of Arab Lands: A History and Source Book.* Philadelphia: Jewish Publication Society, 1975.

Sutton, (Rabbi) David. *Aleppo: City of Scholars.* Brooklyn, N.Y.: ArtScroll, 2005.

Sutton, Joseph A. D. *Aleppo Chronicles: The Story of the Unique Sephardeem of the Ancient Near East, In Their Own Words.* New York: Thayer-Jacoby, 1988.

——. *Magic Carpet: Aleppo-in-Flatbush: The Story of a Unique Ethnic Jewish Community.* New York: Thayer-Jacoby, 1979.

Tapper, Richard, and Sami Zubaida (eds.). *A Taste of Thyme: Culinary Cultures of the Middle East.* London: I. B. Tauris, 2001.

Tatz, (Rabbi) Akiva. *Living Inspired.* Southfield, Mich.: Targum Press, 1993.

Twena, Pamela Grau. *The Sephardic Table: The Vibrant Cooking of the Mediterranean Jews—A Personal Collection of Recipes from the Middle East, North Africa and India.* Boston: Houghton Mifflin Company, 1998.

Uvezian, Sonia. *Recipes and Remembrances from an Eastern Mediterranean Kitchen: A Culinary Journey Through Syria, Lebanon and Jordan.* Northbrook, Ill.: Siamanto Press, 2004.

Waines, David (ed.). *In a Caliph's Kitchen.* London: Riad El-Rayyes, 1989.

Wolfert, Paula. *Mediterranean Grains and Greens: A Book of Savory, Sun-Drenched Recipes.* New York: HarperCollins, 1998.

——. *The Cooking of the Eastern Mediterranean: 300 Healthy, Vibrant, and Inspired Recipes.* New York: HarperTrade, 1994.

Wright, Clifford A. *Mediterranean Vegetables: A Cook's ABC of Vegetables and Their Preparation.* Boston: Harvard Common Press, 2001.

——. *Mediterranean Feast: The Story of the Birth of the Celebrated Cuisines of the Mediterranean from the Merchants of Venice to the Barbary Corsairs.* New York: Morrow Cookbooks, 1999.

Zenner, Walter P. *A Global Community: The Jews from Aleppo, Syria.* Detroit: Wayne State University Press, 2000.

INDEX

B

continued

continued